HUE

Vietnam's Last
Imperial Capital

By the same author

ABOUT THE AUTHOR

Carol Howland is an experienced travel writer, a former feature writer for a national magazine and a contributor to more than a dozen British newspapers. Following a mid-career foray into stockbroking, she edited two finance magazines. But early in her career, she wrote and revised guidebooks and more recently, returned to travel writing. Enthralled by the country, she has published four books exploring Vietnam's cultural heritage. She now lives in France.

'Carol Howland has written four travel books, that had they been written and read by the intelligentsia of America before the Vietnam War, would have made the US pause and take stock of the state of affairs in this small, now well-known country.

'The author's meticulous research into the customs, traditions and cultural history of Vietnam are a mind opening revelation to the uninitiated traveller. She explores the exotic venues of an historically turbulent culture that is vibrantly alive and growing in spite of today's conflicts among the powerful nations of the world.

'Reading her series of books on Vietnam, *Dragons on the Roof, Hanoi of a Thousand Years, Hoi An – Vietnam's Historic Port, and Hue – Vietnam's Last Imperial Capital,* is a deeply rewarding experience. Without even mentioning the Vietnam War, she leads the reader on a journey through the cities and countryside of this beautiful Asian country and the mysterious mindset of the proud, persistent and independent people of Vietnam. Her descriptions of the ancient civilizations in the early years and how the country developed through Taoism, Confucianism, Hinduism, Buddhism, and Catholicism leave the reader with an astounding wealth of information to synthesize in order to appreciate the varieties of experience one can expect when visiting this country.

'From the tale of the two Vietnamese Trung sisters who repulsed the An Chinese in 40 AD through the expulsion of Kublai Khan, the Japanese in WWII, the French Colonialists, and infamously, the US, to the beautiful flower gardens, architecture, cuisine of the rich and poor, to the type of jewellery worn in the imperial court of Hue, she writes in great detail of the marvels of manners and grace still apparent in the Vietnamese people.

'First published in Hanoi by Vietnam's publisher of foreign language books, her books celebrate Vietnamese culture, a remarkable series of books that elucidate the many faces of Vietnam. Her wit, insights and thoroughness permeate the writing and bring joy, excitement and expectation to the would be traveller and historian. Read them, go to Vietnam, and follow her suggestions to have a really rewarding experience in Vietnam!'

Ken Embers, Vietnam representative for Globalism; Director of English Programs and Projects for Vietnam Children's Libraries International; Captain, helicopter pilot, Vietnam 1968-69.

'Like a military reporter, Carol Howland embeds herself with her subject. However, her strategy is less military than empathy and Howland has not only the gift of insight but the gift of friendship: she leaves her subjects like a long lost pal, a priceless asset in this big hearted but still endlessly enigmatic country.'

Peter Howick, Columnist, *The Evening Herald,* Dublin

HUE

Vietnam's Last
Imperial Capitol

CAROL HOWLAND

MYNAH BIRD BOOKS

Published by Mynah Bird Books 2018
1 Regents Court, 10 Balcombe Road
Branksome Park, Poole, Dorset BH13 6DY

First published 2015 by The Gioi Publishers
46 Tran Hung Dao Street, Hanoi, Vietnam

ISBN – 13: 978-1-999843632
ISBN – 10: 1999843630

To the kind people of Hue,

to Professor Buu I, who answered

countless questions, and to those

scholars from whose works I have

so heavily drawn.

CONTENTS

9

INTRODUCTION

THIEN MU PAGODA

Speak gently to reach the soul
– Vietnamese proverb

In the slanting, late afternoon sun, all is still. Only the waters of the Perfume river are moving, shimmering, rippling, meandering silently. Turning from the steps leading up to the pagoda, clusters of flamboyant blossoms explode amongst the lace of pale green leaves, forming a canopy for the brightly painted dragon boats lining the river bank. It might be a scene from a slightly too colourful Hue watercolour on silk, painted for a tourist. Only it is real, one of those quiet moments that stops time.

It was here, eighteen years ago, just up river from Hue, standing on the steps of Thien Mu pagoda, that I first fell under the gentle spell of Hue. From somewhere unknown sprang a premonition that this was not the last time that I would gaze out over the Perfume river. An idea, no more than a wandering, stray thought surfaced – why not find a spot somewhere nearby, overlooking this peaceful river and stay here for a while, why not stay here maybe for a year?

Turning to climb the steps to the pagoda, my footsteps were hesitant. Why was I having such a powerful, emotional reaction to a country I scarcely knew? Even years later, there is no facile explanation. Yes, returning to South East Asia had been a bit like returning to a second, half-forgotten home. Cambodia had been home to my family during the early years of the Vietnam War, but because we were advised not to drive to Saigon, we never went. So Vietnam became the forbidden fruit on the far side of the Truong Son Mountains. Having finally arrived, having returned to a place I had yearned to visit in my youth, I yearned to stay a while longer.

Up seven tiers of steps, four indigo and yellow obelisks mark the entry to the pagoda. The spirituality of Thien Mu is almost palpable. Probably more than any other, Thien Mu, Hue's oldest pagoda, reflects the Buddhist heart of Hue people.

11

It was built, more or less, by divine decree. Touring this area, Lord Nguyen Hoang, who had led the Nguyen clan south in their momentous migration from Hanoi in 1558, was told a legend – that a mysterious, old lady had appeared and prophesied that a great lord would pass by here and build a pagoda on Ha Khe hill. Having heard the providential legend, Lord Nguyen Hoang could do no more than comply. His first modest pagoda built in 1601 was named after the mysterious 'celestial lady', Thien Mu.

This was at a time when Lord Nguyen Hoang still found himself the very uneasy governor over the not so recently conquered southern territories, Dang Trong, where the defeated Cham people had ruled central and southern Vietnam for a millennium. Having come from the North, the Nguyens were Confucians, a philosophy more than a religion, based on a strict structure of respect for authority: uppermost respect for the king, a wife for her husband, children for their parents, younger brothers and sisters for their elder brother. But Confucianism, Nguyen Hoang realized, was not a religion to appeal emotionally to a belligerent, conquered people.

So despite his own Confucianism, he decided to adopt and support Buddhism as a national religion in the hope that the human kindness and generosity of Buddhism would help to pacify an unfriendly, antagonistic, diverse people and build a unified nation, bringing peace and harmony to his troubled, mixed population.

Three generations later in 1665, the fourth Nguyen lord to rule this region renovated and enlarged Thien Mu. And in 1695, the devoutly Buddhist, sixth ruling Nguyen lord, Nguyen Phuc Chu, invited Thich Dai San, a Zen master and scholar from China, to preside over Thien Mu as abbot. Hue has long considered itself to be the centre of Buddhism in central and south Vietnam.

As time passed, the territories of Dang Trong evolved into a land of three religions: Confucianism, Buddhism and Taoism, with faint echoes here and there of the Cham's early goddess worship. Their later Hindu worship of Siva, celebrated in their brick temple towers, all but disappeared, at least in Hue.

In 1710, the same devout, sixth Nguyen governor, Nguyen Phuc Chu, greatly enlarged Thien Mu and commissioned a huge bronze bell, named Dai Hong Chung, considered to have been the earliest 'precious bell' of Central Vietnam. Standing higher than a man and weighing more than three tonnes, it was said to be audible from a distance of ten kilometres.

Unhappily, no more. I long to hear the old bell, but it stands silent under a protective tower. Now, playing hide-and-seek, children squeak gleefully as they squeeze into the narrow spaces between the bell and the walls of its tower, school children who might well have learnt to recite the famous poem:

The winds breeze through the bamboo trees;
It's time for the bell tolling from Thien Mu
and the cock waking up and crowing
from Thu Xuong-Nguyet Bieu today.

These days, the old bell has been replaced by a newer bell, weighing only about four hundred kilos (900 pounds), which tolls one hundred eight times, twice daily, reminding people of the one hundred eight miseries of life, encouraging them to practice meditation and to perform meritorious acts to free themselves from their sufferings. As well as having the old bell cast, the devout Nguyen lord also built the grand, triple-entrance gate beneath a central tower. Colourful, giant guardians leer from each side of the gate's openings.

By 1802, two centuries after Thien Mu was first built, the Nguyens had become emperors – rulers of all Vietnam. The Vietnamese usually refer to their rulers as kings, explaining that Vietnam never really had an empire; their rule only extended over the Chams in the South. But as their highly ritualized courts were modelled on the Confucian Chinese Qing dynasty court; as their kings exercised complete power over their subjects – a misdemeanour by a mandarin might mean literally, off with his head, or worse; as their kings and mandarins dressed in elaborately embroidered silk court robes, scroll-toed platform boots and wore extraordinary headgear, the Western mind tends to think of them as emperors.

Nearly half a century later in the 1840s, the fourth Nguyen emperor, Nguyen Thieu Tri, built Phuoc Duyen tower, twenty-one meters high (63 ft), now framed by two, gloriously blooming, frangipani trees, the first glimpse of the pagoda one sees on approach from the river. Still the tallest religious structure in all of Vietnam, Phuc Duyen tower has become an icon of Hue. It is said that each of its seven stories formerly held a golden Buddha.

In another tower, carved on a stele mounted on the back of a stone tortoise, symbol of longevity, one of Emperor Thieu Tri's poems records the Buddhist history of the pagoda. Once through Nguyen Phuc Chu's gate, the noise and scent of the present jerk one out of the past. From the wide, grassy lawns comes the smell of freshly-mown grass as a young monk swings a screeching strimmer from side to side. At the door of Dai Hung, the main hall of the pagoda, like believers, priests, mandarin, lords and emperors before me, I slide out of my sandals before stepping over the threshold – always a high threshold to cause worshippers to bow their heads in respect.

The scent of joss sticks wafts from within the shadowy hall, dominated by a laughing, shiny, roly-poly statue of Maitreya, Buddha of the Future – and Prosperity. These days he sits encased under glass as protection from those who cannot resist touching, one hand to his ear as though he were trying to hear through the glass. Three yellow-robed monks face the altar, one chanting prayers, one tapping a wooden *mo,* the third tapping a bronze gong. From somewhere unseen comes a high jingling. Behind the altar, three more Buddhas – of the past, present and future – loom benignly over the procedures.

Outside again, behind the pagoda, a grid of very old, potted bonsai trees stand to attention like grizzled mandarin in a paved courtyard, as they may have done for centuries.

Off to the left, an aged Austin banger peers rather incongruously out of an open garage – the vehicle that carried Buddhist monk, Thich Quang Duc, to Saigon in 1963. In protest at the persecution of Buddhist monks by Ngo Dinh Diem, then Catholic president of South Viet Nam, Thich Quang Duc doused himself with petrol, sat down in the lotus position and set himself alight – in self-immolation – a photo that electrified the world. Ironically, Ngo Dinh Diem had been born in Hue. His father was headmaster of Quoc Hoc High School (still functioning); his brother was a Catholic archbishop. So it was all a bit personal.

This old pagoda has seen troubled times, but also intensely spiritual times through the centuries.

A few steps further on, a young monk busily feeds a family of white rabbits, allowed to roam freely. Surrounded by pine trees at the far extremity of the grounds, a multi-storied stupa honours Hoa Thuong Thich Don Hau, chief abbot of the pagoda during its reconstruction after a storm in 1904.

Whether it was the captivating view from the steps of Thien Mu or the emotional realization of how much this pagoda has meant spiritually to the people of Hue, that stray thought all those years ago grew into a twinkling desire, a yearning, then into a pressing urge – if bureaucratic mountains could be scaled . . .

Bureaucratic mountains *were* scaled, enabling me to return to Vietnam, indeed for a year, and later, for numerous long stays over the years. During that first long stay in Vietnam, I did spend some time living on the bank of the Perfume river, but inevitably, curiosity about the rest of the country drew me elsewhere and the book to have been entitled *A Year on the Perfume River* evolved into *Dragons on the Roof.* Only now, am I finally seeking the heart of Hue.

Oddly, it had been a photograph that first tweaked my curiosity about Vietnam, a photo of the nine sacred urns in front of Hien Lam pavilion in the Citadel of Hue's Purple Forbidden City. Those immense bronze urns, head-high on their sturdy legs, looked so forbidding, so alien, so eternal, and to what purpose? Strange, how a photograph can niggle at the mind. That was long before the days of Google, and it was years before I actually laid eyes on them.

Vietnam is a country that seizes the soul, never quite to let go. Why? Initially, the warmth and beauty of the countryside: the jade sea and brooding peaks of Halong Bay; the dark, misty mountains; the tangled jungles and lushness of tropical flowers; the swaying palms and the green brocade of ripening rice paddies; the slim sampans on placid rivers. And the colours: the deep hues of the silks and the lacquer-ware in the shops, the patina of red lacquer and gilt in the imperial palaces. Add the spirituality of pagodas and a shivering cascade of traditional string music. Also, the depth, richness and sophistication of Vietnam's culture that stretches back for more than two thousand years. But far more than these, the proud and dignified people, sensitive and sentimental, poetic and mystical, draw one back. This is a very complicated and highly civilised nation with a long, turbulent history, a nation of open, generous and kindly people, moreover, people of immense talent, energy and above all, resilience. One can only admire them. All these call me back, again and again.

Yet even amongst the Vietnamese, the people of Hue are held in immensely high esteem, for their sophistication and distinctive style, for their refined cuisine, and for their development of the arts. Vietnamese architecture, sculpture, gardens, the performing arts, scholarly literature and poetry – all of these reached their apogee under the Nguyen dynasty. Hue's distinctive royal cuisine went far beyond mere cooking, culminating in an art form – presumably to please finicky Nguyen emperors.

15

While it may no longer be the capital of the nation, Hue remains the cultural and intellectual heart of the country. Hue's artists and writers have long been and continue to be inspired by its poetic gardens; by the elegance of its royal palaces and pagodas, temples and tombs; by its river and landscapes, and by the beauty and charm of Hue women. Hue people retain a certain reserve and politesse, a quiet air of aristocracy, the legacy of court life inherited from their still-remembered grandparents, leavened by the warmth and kindness of Buddhism.

From the beginning, the Nguyen lords set out to be different – different from the Le rulers in Hanoi. From very early on, they encouraged and fostered the arts, they built theatres and commissioned playwrights and musicians, they founded a school to train professional performers – even awarding them mandarin ranks and paying them government salaries.

As emperors, the Nguyens built grand palaces and beautiful residences surrounded by highly designed gardens. Nguyen emperors held poetry competitions amongst their mandarin, and the upper cornices of the palaces of Hue's Citadel are decorated with poems. Moreover, the Hue dialect is considered to be the most refined and gentle in all of Vietnam – *ca Hue* love songs can only be sung in the soft Hue dialect. It is even said that the Hue dialect is not suitable for news reading or discussing politics!

However, writing poetry is deeply embedded in the Vietnamese psyche. Long before Hue became the capital, one of the royal doctoral examinations to become a mandarin in Hanoi demanded that the candidate compose two genres of poems to strict form. Poetry writing reached a pinnacle during the Nguyen dynasty of Hue – the last imperial dynasty to rule Vietnam – which only ended in 1945, when the last Nguyen emperor, Bao Dai, abdicated to the Communists. So Vietnam's imperial – feudal – court reigned at least in name, right up to and within living, photographic memory. I was sure that there would still be people around who remembered it – and indeed, there were.

PART I

A BIT OF HISTORY

ROOTS – WHERE DID HUE PEOPLE COME FROM?

A nation is bound not by the real past,
but by the stories it tells itself,
by what it remembers, and what it forgets.
– French philosopher, Ernest Renan

That the people of Hue are distinctly different from other Vietnamese is in part due to their roots. Since prehistoric times, central Vietnam, midway along Vietnam's twelve hundred-mile (2,000 km) coastline, has been a melting pot of peoples. This ethnic melange is one of the reasons why Hue people are so singularly distinctive, linguistically and perhaps philosophically.

The area around Hue was where the prehistoric Dong Son culture of the North met the prehistoric Sa Huynh culture of the South. The northern Dong Son people left no architectural relics, only fine bronze jewellery and enormous, intricately decorated, bronze drums. To place them in historic context, the prehistoric Dong Son-Viet tribes living north of present-day Hanoi were defeated by the Chinese – in 179 BC. The Chinese established three administrative trading districts that extended deep into central Vietnam, their borders unknown. The Han dynasty succeeded the Qin in 111 BC. Chinese domination – and cultural influence – endured over the northern half of what is now Vietnam for a thousand years.

Happily for us, the Chinese kept detailed historical records, no doubt written from a Chinese point of view and in the case of generals, composed to enhance their military merit in the eyes of their rulers. Though archaeologists treat these Chinese records with a measure of scepticism, they do give some indication of what happened, how, when and where.

Having conquered Nan Yue, the three early trading districts, the later Han dynasty renamed their southernmost trading district, Rinan, which included part of central Vietnam occupied by the Sa

Huynh people. Rinan, which means South of the Sun, is thought to have included the coastal area south of the Ngang Pass (a bit more than halfway between Hanoi and Hue), although Rinan's borders remain unknown.

Incredibly, the bureaucratic Chinese conducted a census of Rinan in the year 2 AD, recording a population of 69,485 people from 15,460 households, according to British archaeologist Ian Glover.

In central and southern Vietnam, the Sa Huynh people, who lived along the river banks, were so-called because the huge burial jars of these seafaring, trading people were first discovered by archaeologists at a place called Sa Huynh (south of Hue, Danang and Hoi An). Like the Dong Son, they left no architectural legacy, but beautiful jewellery made of semi-precious stones, glass and gold, hidden away in their huge jars, buried along the banks of the rivers.

The Sa Huynh disappeared mysteriously, sometime towards the end of the first century AD, almost suddenly, without explanation widely accepted by historians and archaeologists to this day.

The Sa Huynh were replaced, followed, overcome, or subsumed by another seafaring people, who arrived and settled along these very same rivers in central and southern Vietnam, sometime around 200 BC, people who eventually became known as the Chams.

The Chinese first traded with the Sa Huynh people and later, with the Chams. According to Ian Glover, Chinese annuls tell us that their only trading partners in mainland South East Asia during the first millennium AD were the Chams.

Chinese records speak of ten kingdoms south of Rinan, their own southern-most trading territory. Cham kingdoms or city states, based on clans, extended from north of Hue to east of Ho Chi Minh City. The Chams built and carved brick temple tower complexes and sculpted statues dedicated to the worship of Siva. So yes, they were Hindu, but strangely, there were no Indian settlements along this eastern Vietnamese coast – 'because the Chinese were already there' asserts one archaeologist – only the influence of Hindu priests, who arrived either by sea on board traders' ships or overland from India via Burma, Thailand, Cambodia and Laos.

Archaeologists insist that there is absolutely no archaeological evidence to support the premise, but I cannot help but wonder, if those same Indian traders who delivered the Hindu priests to the Chams, might have seized, or bought the Sa Huynh people as slaves from the Chams, as the Indian trading post at Oc Eo near the

Cambodian border of Funan had been set up expressly for that purpose – to find produce to trade for gold in Java! Cham history remains an exciting, developing, on-going, unfolding detective story, still being unravelled by archaeologists with each new dig.

Hinduism overlaid and became amalgamated with the Cham people's worship of a mother goddess, Yang Po Ino Nagar, also known as Uma and Uroja (she had numerous names). Many of the Cham's finely carved, brick temple towers – some 7th-14th C, pre-dating Angkor – remain standing at Myson near Hoi An, where they were badly bombed during the Vietnam War, and further south, where they stand undamaged, apart from the weathering of centuries of a monsoon climate: at Qui Nhon, Nha Trang and Phan Thiet.

Both the earlier Sa Huynh and the Chams are thought to have come from somewhere in Indonesia or Malaysia – a tribe in Sarawak still speaks a language that can be understood by present-day Chams, those remaining, who now live concentrated around Phan Rang on the coast further south and in the Mekong Delta. Sa Huynh jewellery and the burial jars of these sea-faring traders have also been found in Paluwan in the Philippines.

In 192 AD, there was a rebellion against direct Chinese taxation in Xianglin, the southernmost part of Rinan, resulting in a newly formed, independent southern territory, including what is now Hue. It became known by a confusing number of names: Lam Ap (Forest City), a shortened version perhaps of Tuong Lam Ap (Elephant Forest City); the Chinese called it Linyi.

An early Chinese writer described the people of Lam Ap as both warlike and musical with 'deep eyes, a high straight nose and curly black hair' – so decidedly, un-Chinese.

However, the Chinese were not so easily dissuaded by the rebellion of their southernmost trading territory. In 446 the Song army marched south and sacked a walled city they called Khu Tuc and killed the Lam Ap general, Pham Phu Long, then marched south to Lam Ap, where they stormed the walled town and citadel.

Looting temples and treasury, the Song carried back to China an astonishing, estimated half a tonne of gold. Whether the gold was looted from Khu Tuc near Hue or from Lam Ap (Simhapura-Tra Kieu – upriver from Hoi An) further south, or both, and whether or not Linyi-Lam Ap was Champa, they were a rich prize. This was not a scattering of primitive huts. Ian Glover has written that the capital of Linyi, as described in the Chinese *Shuijingzhu,* 'was surrounded by

19

rectangular walls measuring two and a half miles (4 km) in perimeter, the packed earth walls rising seven metres high, topped by brick walls for another three metres with four gates and wooden palisades of up to five tiers high, oriented east-west, with a river flowing north, the principal gate facing east. The *Shujingzhu* also tells of fifty separate quarters, eight temples and pagodas, a brick or tiled palace and densely packed houses.'

According to Glover, this type of rectangular citadel enclosure matches that discovered at the site of Thanh Loi near Hue on the south bank of the Perfume (Huong) river – but also that of the citadel at Tra Kieu, upriver from Hoi An.

Champa – and there is much dispute amongst historians and archaeologists as to where it was and even if it actually existed as a political entity – according to Chinese sources, consisted of ten kingdoms, city states, each ruled by a clan, sometimes fighting amongst themselves, sometimes allied against aggressors. A sea-going, trading people, the Chams repeatedly nibbled aggressively at the southern Chinese trading territories, and later, continued their almost continuous territorial wars against the Viets after the founding of Die Viet in the north in 938.

Conversely, the Viets were constantly pushing further south in what they called their Nam Tien movement (Nam meaning south, Tien meaning running), as they had nowhere else to go: China to the north, the mountains and the Khmer to the west, the South China Sea (known as the East Sea in Vietnam for sensitive political reasons) to the east. As well as being deeply religious and building fine temples, the sea-faring Chams were, indeed, a war-like people, who whenever their Chinese trading partners ceased trading during political upheavals, turned to piracy.

As this central area fell within Linyi, Hue, Danang and Hoi An further south were liberated from the Chinese much earlier than the North. The Viets in the North remained under Chinese domination until 938 AD when they established a new, independent nation, Die Viet (Great Viet), which extended south to the Cham territories.

This highly contested border between Cham and Viet lands was in constant dispute. These were turbulent times. The Viet capital moved north in 1010 from Hoa Lu to a new capital, Thang Long, the earlier name for Hanoi. In 1044 the Viet king, Ly Thai Tong, sacked and destroyed the by then capital of Champa, Vijaya, present day Qui Nhon, a third of the way south from Hue to Saigon. To avenge this defeat, in 1068 the King of Vijaya invaded Thang Long. The Viets retaliated by again reconquering and reoccupying Vijaya. The Cham king, Rudravarman III (known to the Viets as Che Cu) was taken captive and eventually purchased his freedom for a ransom of three northern districts of his realm – north of Hue.

Enemies of the Chams seemed to come from all directions. In 1145, a Khmer army under the powerful king, Suryavarman II, builder of Angkor Wat, who already controlled much of Thailand, and who had ambitions to extend his kingdom to the east coast of the peninsula, attacked and occupied the Cham capital, Vijaya.

The Khmer were driven out eventually by the Chams, led by Jaya Harivarman I. Thirty years later in 1177, the Cham King, Jaya Indravarmadeva of Vijaya, retaliated by sacking Angkor in a surprise attack, rowing up the Mekong river.

The Khmer king, Jayavarman VII, builder of the Bayon and Angkor Thom, in turn defeated the Chams and imposed thirty years of Khmer rule over Vijaya – and recorded for posterity on the *bas reliefs* of the Bayon, the earlier surprise attack by the Chams, rowing up the Mekong river.

The tide began to turn decisively against the Chams in the thirteenth century when the Mongolian hordes of Kublai Khan – an army of 40,000 – descended out of the plains of China, invading Dai Viet in the North as well as Champa – three times – in 1257, 1284 and 1287. The Chams and the Viets, traditional enemies for centuries, allied to drive out the Mongols and became so close that in 1307, the head of the old Cham king turned to folly – or did it?

Jaya Simhavarman III (Che Man), builder of the still standing temples of Po Klaung Garai in Phan Rang (Panduranga), in his last lust, some sources say, rashly ceded his two northern provinces of O and Ly (Ri), which include what is now Hue, to the Viets – in exchange for the hand of a northern Viet princess, Tran Huyen. Other sources say that the provinces were ceded as a settlement after the Mongolian invasions. However, might it not have been the old Cham king's last-stand attempt to resolve the centuries-old dissension between the Chams and the Viets – a marriage of political union? In any case, soon after the wedding, the old king died. To the national outrage of the Chams, Viet warships invaded Champa to rescue the princess from the Cham tradition that a wife follow her husband in death. So the princess, Tran Huyen, returned to her homeland in the North, but the Cham territories were not returned to Champa.

21

These newly acquired territories remained intractable, partly due to the collapse of the Tran dynasty in the North around 1400, the weakness of the short-lived Ho dynasty, a painful reoccupation of the North by the Chinese Ming dynasty (1418-1428), and continuous further conflicts over these disputed territories between the Le dynasty of the North and Champa.

The Viets finally defeated the Chams, decisively, again at Vijaya (present-day Qui Nhon) in 1471. By then, the Viets had already started their long migrations south. However, these former Cham territories remained restless, belligerent, untamed frontier – a mediaeval Wild South, known in the North as Dang Trong. The Chams were still sore about their lost territories less than a century later when Nguyen Hoang arrived in as governor in 1558.

For many centuries, what is now Vietnam – the steep mountain valleys and coastal plains east of the mountainous spine of the Indo-Chinese peninsula – was almost constantly at war: the Viets with the Chinese or the Chams; the Chams with the Chinese, the Viets, the Khmer and even the Javanese.

Add into this mixture of the Dong Son and Sa Huynh peoples, and later the Chams, the matriarchal mountain tribes inland, who speak Mon-Khmer languages, with whom both the Sa Huynh and the Chams traded over the centuries. Overlay this mixture of Mon-Khmer, Austronesian-speaking peoples with the population of the much later arriving, Austro-Asiatic-speaking Viet people from the North (who call themselves Kinh), who started migrating southward to the Hue region.

In time, Central Vietnam became dominated by the more numerous, ambitious Kinh people from Dai Viet in the North, who ruled over the defeated, spiritual people of the South (Champa).

The North and the South of Vietnam, which included Central Vietnam, were divided ethnically, linguistically, politically and culturally, really one could say, until Nguyen Hoang began his efforts towards pacification, unification and nation building in the late sixteenth century and later, when the Nguyen established their dynasty in Hue, uniting the whole of the country politically for the first time in 1802. But that's to leap over nearly three hundred years of tumultuous history.

WHO WERE THESE NGUYEN?

It is by the trial of misfortune
that one recognises a faithful subject
– Vietnamese proverb

How and why Hue became the capital begins by unravelling a Machiavellian intrigue in the earlier imperial court of Thang Long (Hanoi). But for a few quirks of history, Hue might never have been, or conversely, might still be the capital of Vietnam. Hue is not the *ancient* capital as stated in numerous guidebooks – the nineteenth century is hardlyancient. Very likely, ancient is a corruption of the French word *ancien,* which means *former.* So to give it its proper distinction, Hue was the last imperial capital of Vietnam, ruled by the Nguyen dynasty from 1802 to 1945, though the French very forcefully took control in 1884. (See Historic Appendix).

Thereafter, the Nguyen court acted as little more than a puppet regime until the last emperor abdicated in 1945 to the Communists. Then, after Dien Bien Phu, following the Geneva talks of 1954, Vietnam was partitioned, Hue in the South until the fall of Saigon – 'liberation' and reunification in 1975.

Historically, court life in Thang Long (Hanoi) seems to have been a whispering tangle of intrigue, one faction against another, courtiers and clans vying with one another for favour – and power. In the sixteenth century capital, several generations of the Nguyen clan were active in royal court and military affairs under the Le dynasty, always in competition with another family, the Trinh.

The story goes that during the reign of Le Tang Tong (1533-1548), Nguyen Hoang (1525-1613) heard a rumour that his brother-in-law, Trinh Kiem, was plotting to have him assassinated. Hard on the deaths, possibly assassinations, in battle of both his father and brother, the assassination rumour seemed all too credible. To escape these court intrigues, Nguyen Hoang managed to get himself appointed governor of the new, formerly Cham, frontier southern region, Dang Trong. In 1558, he moved South with his extended family, his dead father's army and a good many artisans, to pacify

Dang Trong and ostensibly to fight the Mac, another family who were vying for power against the weak Le king. They settled in the former regions of O and Ly (Ri) provinces of Champa, which they renamed: Thuan Chau and Hoa Chau, *chau* meaning territory. The confusion between Ly and Ry is explained as a question of pronunciation.

These provinces had been first annexed by the Viets as early as 1069, but wars between the Viets and the Chams had continued incessantly until the Chams were decisively defeated in 1471. To build a harmoniously unified society from an aggressive, conquered nation composed of a diverse, mixed population, the Nguyen lords had their work cut out for them.

Nguyen Hoang first established his headquarters – and citadel fortresses – in 1558 at the villages of Ai Tu and Tra Bat in Quang Tri Province, just north of present-day Hue. The nine successive Nguyen lords – governors – threatened by the Trinh lords from the North and surrounded by remnants of the restless, warring Chams, nervously moved their headquarters to Phuoc Yen, a few miles north of what was to become Hue in 1626; to Kim Long, near Thien Mu pagoda in 1636; to Phu Xuan, present-day Hue in 1687; then to Bac Vong, a bit to the north-east in 1712; and finally, back to Phu Xuan in 1738 – at the south-east corner of today's Citadel – where it remained and became enveloped by Hue as the city grew.

The original Nguyen lord, Nguyen Hoang, quietly worked away as governor, ostensibly to develop Dang Trong, the southern region, gradually building up his own military power and establishing an administrative structure mirroring the royal court in Thang Long, on the face of it, still supporting the weak Le king in Hanoi. In 1570, he was appointed governor of an additional southern area, Quang Nam, which includes Danang and Hoi An. This gave him even more land and he busily settled more emigrants, who either volunteered or as often as not, were forced to move to the new territories.

Had the rumour of the assassination plot not reached Nguyen Hoang in the first place, he would never have moved South and most probably, the Nguyen would never have developed a sufficient power base from which to challenge Trinh power in Thang Long. Nor would there be a city called Hue.

The Nguyen were becoming ever more powerful in their southern fiefdom. They refused to pay tribute to the court in Thang Long after 1627 – tantamount to declaring themselves independent. They were almost constantly at war with the Trinh clan.

The animosity between the North and South goes back long, long before the Vietnam War.

A few generations later, following the death in 1765 of the Nguyen lord, Nguyen Phuc Khoat – also known as Vo Vuong, Marshal Prince, who had extended Nguyen territory into Laos and Cambodia – the Hue court fell under the control of a corrupt mandarin, Truong Phuc Loan, who incurred the wrath of the people by levying excessively heavy taxes.

From a family of merchants, three brothers from Tay Son (south of Hue near present day Qui Nhon) mounted a revolt (1773-1778), that became known as the Tay Son Rebellion. They quickly took Qui Nhon, a third of the way south to Ho Chi Minh City. Seizing the opportunity, the Trinh lords sent a large army south and captured the Nguyen lord's capital, Phu Xuan in 1774. The Nguyen had left their capital insufficiently defended, either off fighting the Mac, another competing clan, or as another source suggests, the Khmer, the Nguyen being intent upon expanding their territory to the west.

Chased south from Phu Xuan, the Nguyen court and clan took refuge in Gia Dinh (the earlier name for Saigon). From Phu Xuan, the Trinh army marched south where it was stopped by the Tay Son with whom they negotiated a tactical truce. The Trinh were allowed to withdraw, leaving a few troops in control of Phu Xuan; the lands further south remained under the control of the Tay Son.

In 1776, the Tay Son chased the Nguyen army and court further south of Gia Dinh (Saigon) to Vung Tau, where they assassinated the entire Nguyen clan – the method of toppling rulers in those days. The leader of the Tay Son brothers, Nguyen Hue, then returned to Phu Xuan and defeated first the Trinh army garrisoned there, then marched his army north where he defeated the powerful Trinh clan, power behind the Le throne, on their home turf. In Thang Long (Hanoi), the weak Le king remained at least nominally a vassal of China, so following the first engagement, he fled north to seek military assistance from the emperor of China, who obligingly – one need not wonder at his motives – ordered the viceroy of Canton to proceed south immediately at the head of an army of a 100,000 men.

The Tay Son, hearing of the Chinese advance, laid waste the towns and villages along their route, destroying the source of provisions for the advancing army. The Chinese were forced to fall back, long before they reached the frontier of Tonkin – at least, that is one version of the story, as recorded by a French naval captain, employed by the Nguyen court. In Hanoi, the story reads rather differently. Invaded by the Chinese, who thought they had detected a moment of weakness after the defeat of the Trinh, the battle culminated in the Tay Son army vanquishing the Chinese army in the Dong Da district of the capital, Thang Long. In the North, the Tay Son brothers have been deified as folk heroes, who unified half the country for the first time from Qui Nhon north to Hanoi, freeing the Viet people from the troublesome Nguyen.

In both versions, one of the three Tay Son brothers, Nguyen Hue, crowned himself Emperor Quang Trung in 1778 – the Vietnamese always changed their names when they became emperor – and married Princess Le Ngoc Han, a girl of sixteen and the favourite daughter of the weak, defeated, former Le king (Le Hien Tong). As emperor, Quang Trung ruled for only four years before his own death at forty in 1792 – some say he was poisoned. Despite the age gap and the obvious political advantage of marrying the daughter of the deposed ruler, the marriage must have been a happy one, for the young queen, a widow at twenty, expressed her grief at his death in a now famous poem.

Wind pours its cold into the room
Orchids wither on the veranda
Smoke covers the crypt of the deceased,
The shadow of the royal coach is gone.
Alone, I weep over my fate.
Heaven, why did you shatter our union?
How to tell my misery, my pain
Deep as the ocean, boundless as the sky,
I look to the East, sails glide in all directions,
I see only immensity of sky and water.
I look to the West,
Mountains and trees spread as far as the eye can see.
To the South, wild geese wander,
To the North, mist covers forests with a white shroud.
Though I search, the more this separation weighs upon me,
Will my affliction awaken echoes in that far beyond?
I see the moon through sorrow, its brilliance tarnished,
A fine dust veils its silvered glow.
I am ashamed to look at myself in the mirror,
My love shattered, alone, I wander on the deserted shore.

The flowers I look at return my grief.
Camellias cry tears of dew.
Watching the flitting bird, my heart is torn,
A turtle-dove flies solitary, seeking its companion.
Each landscape wears its own desolation,
Where are the joys of former days?
One moment only and the world collapsed,
So life goes, to whom can I complain,
Love and fidelity, as immense as heaven and earth,
My grief grows as my days endure.
To whom may I confide my torment and pain?
Let sun and moon bear witness!
                                        (tr Huu Ngoc)

Some, particularly in the North, think that if the liberal Emperor Quang Trung had lived to rule, say for twenty years, the country might have remained united with the capital – not in Hue – but at his family seat in Qui Nhon. Not surprisingly, a huge statue has been erected in Hanoi to commemorate the hero, Quang Trung, who first unified the country from Qui Nhon northward and who sought to liberate the people from the worst repression of Nguyen feudalism.

NGUYEN STRUGGLE TO POWER

He who sows the wind will reap a whirlwind
– Vietnamese proverb

The Nguyen rise to power from regional governors to rulers of Vietnam unfolds like a swashbuckling period drama of warring clans, clashing armies and fiery battles on land and sea that lasted throughout several centuries of civil wars.

When the Tay Son assassinated the Nguyen clan south of Gia Dinh (Saigon) in 1777, they did not quite annihilate the Nguyen. They missed one young 'prince', fifteen-year-old Nguyen Phuc Anh, who managed to escape to Ha Tien on the west coast of the Mekong delta near the Gulf of Siam (now the Gulf of Thailand).

People often ask, how did the French happen to be in Vietnam? It was a slow, creeping process of usurping power.

In Ha Tien, the escaped prince, Nguyen Phuc Anh, met a French missionary, Pierre Pigneau de Behaine (1741-1799) – a fateful meeting that was to affect his destiny and that of Vietnam. Pignaeu de Behaine, known as Adran, helped him to hide on the island of Pulo Wai (now Phu Quoc), off the coast at Ha Tien. Adran calculated that were he to support the restoration of this young Nguyen Anh to power, the spread of Catholicism would benefit in South East Asia.

As the sole remaining male survivor of the Nguyen clan, and no doubt concerned at its survival, Nguyen Anh hastened to marry his first wife, Tong Thi Lan, who bore him two sons. The first son died soon after birth; the second, Prince Nguyen Phuc Canh, was born in 1780. Nguyen Anh married a second (simultaneous) wife, Tran Thi Dang, soon after.

To those of us accustomed to daily military reportage in an era of instant communication and rapid deployment of troops, the pace of Asian warfare four centuries ago feels almost turgid. By 1780 Nguyen Anh had rallied enough of an army to capture Gia Dinh (Saigon) from the Tay Son, but only two years later in 1782, the Tay Son retook Gia Dinh and Nguyen Anh again was forced to flee to Pulo Wai (Phu Quoc) island.

He had been joined in the attack by a French adventurer named Manuel, who chose to blow up his ship and himself rather than surrender to the Tay Son.

The battles for Gia Dinh see-sawed back and forth, Nguyen Anh escaping to Phu Quoc, sometimes chased by the Tay Son from island to island, once to an island called variously Poulo Condor, or in Vietnamese, Con Lon (now Con Dao), where fortunately for Nguyen Anh, the Tay Son fleet was sunk in pursuit by a storm.

In 1783, Pigneau de Behaine travelled to Siam to seek military aid. He was joined in Bangkok by Nguyen Anh in 1784. The king of the new Chakri dynasty, Rama I, obliged by providing him with 20,000 men and 300 ships, which enabled him to take two provinces on the south coast of the Indo-China peninsula, bordering the Gulf of Siam. But in 1785, they were defeated once again in the Saigon river by the Tay Son, who held the well fortified city of Gia Dinh. Most of the Siamese troops were killed as well as Nguyen Anh's. Again, Nguyen Anh fled to Siam with his remaining troops and entourage where the king of Siam granted them refuge.

Meanwhile in Siam, relations with Rama I turned decidedly frosty when he discovered that Nguyen Anh had also sought military aid from the Portuguese, Rama I considering himself to be Nguyen Anh's protector.

Suddenly, the Siamese court seemed a less friendly place, hostile even. So in 1787, Nguyen Anh and his followers, some 1,500 people, decided to flee secretly under the cover of darkness, commandeering whatever Siamese and Malay vessels lay in the harbour – leaving only a thank you note for the King of Siam. They reached the island of Pulo Wai (Phu Quoc) safely, which Nguyen Anh then fortified as best he could against attack, threatened now he feared, by both the king of Siam and the Tay Son brothers.

At this point Nguyen Anh must have been feeling utterly desolate. Together, Pigneau de Behaine and Nguyen Anh drafted a document, requesting military aid from the French court of Louis XVI. In exchange, Nguyen Anh would cede to France the port of Hoi An and the island of Con Lon, (now Con Dao). Nguyen Anh granted Pigneau de Behaine the authority to negotiate on his behalf with the French king. Fearing for his family's safety on Pulo Wai, in an act of good faith he committed his four-year-old son, Nguyen Phuc Canh, to the care of the French missionary, earnestly entreating him in the event of any misfortune befalling himself, to act as a father and a friend to his young son, advising and assisting him, and instructing him never to lose sight of his lawful dominions of which his father had been deprived by violence and usurpation. Accepting the charge, Pigneau de Behaine and the little prince set sail for Pondicherry (India) and France in December of 1785.

Behaine spent a year in Pondicherry, lobbying unsuccessfully for military support, setting sail again and arriving in France in February 1787. Imagine the stir the tiny oriental prince must have created on being presented to the glittering French court in Versailles. He was painted by Mauperin and allowed to play with Louis-Joseph, the Dauphin of France, who at the time was about the same age.

Behaine had trouble raising enthusiasm for a French invasion of Vietnam in the financially-strapped French court. The French Revolution was less than two years away. Finally, through dogged persistence he managed to convince certain naval officers that 'France would be able to dominate the seas of China and of the archipelago.'

Not only did the king honour Pigneau de Behaine with the title, Bishop of Cochin China, he was also appointed Ambassador Extraordinary and Plenipotentiary to the Nguyen Court – yet to be established. Finally, the Treaty of Versailles, dated 28 November 1787, was drawn up and signed by Pigneau de Behaine on behalf of Nguyen Anh and by the French Foreign Minister Montmorin on behalf of King Louis XVI.

According to the treaty, France would send 1,200 infantrymen, 200 artillery troops, 250 African troops, and guns and ammunition to help Nguyen Anh regain power. In exchange Nguyen Anh would cede to France the port of Hoi An and Con Lon (Con Dao) Island, give France exclusive trading rights in Vietnam, send men to help France whenever necessary and donate a ship to France each year. After a year of tenacious negotiations in France and signing of the Treaty of Versailles, Pigneau de Behaine and the little prince set sail from France in December 1787, with only a two-ship escort – the *Dryade,* captained by Kersaint, and the *Pandour,* commanded by de Preville. They arrived in Pondicherry in May 1788, carrying their precious treaty, thinking the governor of Pondicherry would fulfil the French side of the treaty. What Pigneau de Behaine did not know was that the French Foreign Minister Montmorin had sent instructions leaving it to the discretion of the French envoy in Pondicherry to choose, when, or if at all, to comply with the terms of the treaty!

It was only in Pondicherry that the priest discovered the duplicity of the French king and angrily declared, 'I shall make the revolution in Cochin China alone.' He used what funds he had solicited in France to enlist French volunteers and collected more funds for the Nguyen cause from the Pondicherry merchants, who had long coveted trading rights in Hoi An.

This pretentious Treaty of Versailles, which the French king failed to honour, served later as the justification for France's official interference in Vietnam's affairs. It was presumed by the French that in exchange for the money collected privately from the Pondicherry merchants to mount an attack against the Tay Son, that France would be permitted to establish a trading post through which they would be allowed to trade freely – and even to build a garrison.

Eventually, the French envoy in Pondicherry grudgingly provided two ships: the *Meduse,* captained by Rosily, and a frigate. Pigneau de Behaine procured two more ships: renamed the *Dragon* and the *Phoenix,* captained by Jean-Baptiste Chaigneau and Philippe Vannier. Reciting the names of the handful of Frenchmen involved, brings their wildly foolhardy venture into sharp focus. Jean-Marie Dayat deserted from the *Pandour,* one of the original escorts, and was put in charge of supplies. Rosily deserted from the *Meduse* with twelve men and was charged with recruiting adventurers. The little party of four ships left Pondicherry 19 June 1789 and arrived at Vung Tau 24 July 1789.

Sources vary enormously as to the total of how many French personnel came to Vietnam to serve the Nguyen cause. One source says fourteen officers and eighty men; another says twelve officers and between one and four hundred men.

However few French were dedicated to the Nguyen cause, they were immensely effective.

Meanwhile, during the time that Pigneau de Behaine and the little prince were away, Nguyen Anh had once again captured Gia Dinh (Saigon) in 1788 and by 1790, controlled most of the Mekong delta. By 1792 the Frenchman, Olivier de Puymanel, had built a Vauban-style fortress at Gia Dinh, another at Dien Khanh and taught Nguyen Anh's army the use of artillery. He had also trained 600 men in European military techniques – another source says 50,000 men of Nguyen Anh's army. Jean-Marie Dayot and Jean-Baptiste Chaigneau trained the navy and by 1792, had built up a fleet of two European warships and fifteen frigates. Dayot and his brother made maps of the coastline. And of utmost importance, the French were put in charge of weapons procurement.

Dayot went to Manila and Macao to obtain arms in 1790. Puymanel made two trips to Macao in 1795 and 1796 to obtain weapons from the Portuguese and Barizy sailed to Malacca and Penang to exchange goods for arms. In 1795, Puymanel also travelled to Riau (Sumatra) to trade rice for armaments and in 1797 and 1798, to Madras (India) to negotiate payment for the *Armada* – Laurent Barizy's ship, which had been captured by the British (it was eventually returned).

An Englishman, John Barry (who later served as under-secretary of the English Navy for many years) recorded a description of the departure of the Nguyen fleet in 1792, numbering three sloops of war, each with a French officer and 300 men, 100 galleys loaded with troops, 40 war junks, 200 ships and 800 transport boats – the Nguyen fleet that forced the harbour of Qui Nhon in 1792.

In that same year, 1792, the Tay Son king, Quang Trung, died, of a sudden, inexplicable illness. Following his death, the succession fell to his young son, Quang Toan, who ruled nominally from 1792 until 1801, power at first vested in the hands of mandarin acting as regents. Quang Trung's brothers, Nguyen Lu and Nguyen Nhac, began to squabble militarily. Certain Tay Son generals, disillusioned with the rule of Quang Trung's successors, defected to the side of Nguyen Anh.

His army and navy now strong, Nguyen Anh defeated the Tay Son fleet and took Qui Nhon decisively on 5 June 1801. Only ten days later, 25 June 1801, he captured Phu Xuan (Hue), assassinating Quang Trung's son, Quang Toan, who by then had grown up and assumed the Tay Son command.

However, Nguyen Anh spared the life of Quang Toan's wife or intended (sources disagree), the princess Le Ngoc Binh, taking her as his third wife. As the princess Le Ngoc Binh was the sister of Le Ngoc Han, the wife of Quang Trung – also the daughter of the weak Le king, Le Hien Tong – the Vietnamese have a famous saying in regard to this peculiar turn of events, the daughter of a king, who married to two kings.

'What a strange thing destiny is,
The princess got married to two kings respectively!'

From Phu Xuan (Hue), Nguyen Anh marched north and seized Thang Long (Hanoi) on 20 July 1802, wreaking vengeance on his father's old enemies, the Trinh. In so doing, he proclaimed himself Emperor Gia Long – Gia from Gia Dinh in the South, Long from Thang Long in the North. The first of thirteen Nguyen emperors, he founded a new – and Vietnam's last – feudal dynasty, unifying the entire country for the first time from the Mekong delta to the Chinese border after three hundred years of intermittent internecine war. Naturally, he moved the capital to his family's traditional stronghold, Phu Xuan. The capital was renamed Hue as the Hoa of Thuan Hoa reflected an inauspicious Chinese name. In Thang Long, the old northern capital, he destroyed the grand palaces of the Trinh clan – his father's enemies. He also, eventually, demoted the old capital from being called Thang Long (Flying Dragon) to Hanoi (City by the River).

At last, the long struggle between the Trinh and the Nguyen was over, but the bitterness between North and South remained and remains still. Looking back to original sins, if there had been no rumour in the sixteenth century that a Trinh was about to assassinate his Nguyen brother-in-law, the South would never have become such a power base. If Nguyen Hue as Emperor Quang Trung had survived a longer reign, the northern part of the country might have remained unified. And if Nguyen Phuoc Anh, had not invited the military support of the French, but received aid from the Dutch or the Portuguese, how different the history of Vietnam might have been. To this day, it is because of this early collaboration with the French that many Vietnamese in the North blame the Nguyen dynasty for handing over the country to France. In the North, there is a sardonic saying: 'Gia Long carried home the snake that killed the chicken.'

33

THE FRENCH ADVANCE

New spirits fear old ones
– Vietnamese proverb

To follow the chronology of France's creeping advance into Vietnam is to thread our way through a labyrinthine path of approaches, snubs, attacks – and regicides – over a period of nearly a century. This was at a time when colonies were in vogue, following the early explorations of the Portuguese and Spanish in the fifteenth and sixteenth centuries. The Dutch, British, Italian and French rushed into global competition for trade and colonization. To pin down exactly how Vietnam fell under French domination is to work through a succession of strong resistance and fateful treaties. Had religion not been mixed into the endeavour, had trade remained the only objective, it is just possible that colonization in Vietnam might never have taken place.

Under the newly installed first Nguyen emperor, Gia Long (formerly Nguyen Anh), the Frenchmen who had aided him to gain power – Jean-Baptiste Chaigneau, Philippe Vannier, de Forsans and Despiau – were named military mandarin in his court. Each was honoured with a personal escort of fifty soldiers and exemption from kowtowing to the emperor at court. Chaigneau, Vannier and Barizy married into Vietnamese Catholic families. Under Gia Long, foreign ships traded at Hoi An, Danang (the French called it variously Tourane, Turon) and Saigon. French ships were granted privileged status and Catholic missionaries were free to preach and build churches. So the priest, Pigneau de Behaine, had been right in his surmise that if he were to aid the young Nguyen prince to regain power, this would help the spread of Catholicism in Vietnam. Ironically, he died in 1799, two years before his protégé, Nguyen Anh, gained power.

Had King Louis XVIII of France left well enough alone, history might have remained more peaceful. But in 1817, Louis XVIII sent a diplomatic mission to the Nguyen court, led by Baron Kergariou, demanding that Gia Long respect the Treaty of Versailles. Not surprisingly, Gia Long refused, replying that France had never honoured its side of the Treaty. Home in France on leave in 1819, Chaigneau was appointed French Consul to the Hue Court. However, by the time he returned to Hue in 1821, Gia Long had died (1820).

With Gia Long's death, the political climate swiftly changed. Gia Long's son, Prince Canh, the little prince who had gone to France, having grown up, had died, following the siege of Qui Nhon. Yet instead of allowing the succession to pass to Prince Canh's son, Gia Long had chosen his fourth son to succeed him, crowned Minh Mang – deliberately chosen for his strong-mindedness and aversion to foreigners. Although Gia Long had been aided considerably by the French, he had always remained wary of the threat posed by the French and their Catholicism to his rule based on Confucianism.

The Catholic missionaries preached monogamy – opposed to the Confucian system built on polygamy, which provided an ever-spreading network of loyal family relationship ties, permeating society from numerous royal wives and concubines. Furthermore, the Catholic missionaries declared ancestor worship nothing more than superstition – ancestor worship rooted in Confucianism, which held loyalty to the emperor, the son of heaven, above all other relationships. To denigrate ancestor worship was therefore to undermine the basis of the Nguyen ruler's sacred, royal authority. Responding to this change in attitude in the Hue court, Chaigneau and Vannier left Vietnam in 1824, taking their Vietnamese families with them to France. In 1825, a French diplomat, Hyacinthe de Bourgainville, was dispatched with a letter from the French king. It was returned on the spurious grounds that no one at court could read French – tantamount to an official snub.

In February 1825, Minh Mạng even went so far as to issue an imperial edict forbidding foreign missionaries to enter Vietnam and ordering Vietnamese Catholics to denounce their religion. He also ordered missionaries already in the country to relocate to the capital city – ostensibly to act as translators, in actuality to stop them from proselytizing. The following year, France appointed another member of the Chaigneau family, Eugene, to become French consul in Hue. But failing even to obtain an audience with the emperor after three years in Hue, he left in 1829. The Vietnamese court clearly wanted nothing further to do with the French.

The heroic general, Le Van Duyet, who had led the siege of Qui Nhon in Nguyen Anh's struggle to power, had been rewarded a fairly autonomous governorship in Gia Dinh (Saigon). Duyet and many high ranking mandarin had opposed the succession of Minh Mang, favouring Prince Canh's pro-Catholic son. Following Minh Mang's imperial edict, Duyet openly disobeyed, providing protection to Catholics and missionaries in Saigon. On Duyet's death, Minh Mang angrily ordered the desecration of his tomb – the ultimate dishonour – and executed sixteen of his relatives. Somehow, Le Van Khoi, Duyet's son, escaped. Inflamed, he promised to protect Catholicism and declared himself in favour of restoring the line of Prince Canh, tantamount to treason. In 1833, Father Nguyen Van Tam led 2,000 Vietnamese Catholic troops in revolt, seizing much of southern Vietnam. Gia Long had been right to be wary of the Catholics. It took three years of fighting for Minh Mang to suppress the revolt. Father Joseph Marchand was captured and executed (1835). Minh Mang issued further anti-Catholic edicts in 1836 and 1838 – and executed six more missionaries. Yet despite his aversion to Catholicism, having watched the defeat of China in the Opium War, Minh Mang did an abrupt volte-face and sent a delegation to Paris in 1840, offering free trade for France in exchange for military support, should Vietnam be attacked by a foreign country. Having been offered what the French had coveted for several centuries, the offer was shunned at the behest of the Paris Foreign Missions Society 'as a rebuke for an enemy of the religion.'

Following Minh Mang's death in 1841, his son and successor, Thieu Tri, shared his father's anti-Catholic sentiments, but took a slightly softer approach, agreeing to release five missionaries from prison. In 1843, jealous of the British success in China, France sent a fleet to Turon (Danang), ostensibly 'to support the British in China' – as well as to curb the persecution of Catholic missionaries.

Two years later, another French mission was ordered to Vietnam to seek the release of Bishop Dominique Lefèbvre, who had entered Vietnam illegally a second time, as missionaries were forbidden to enter Vietnam. Again in 1847, two French warships, the *Gloire* and the *Victorieuse* under the Captains Lapierre and Rigault de Genouilly, dropped anchor at Danang, seeking the release of two French missionaries, again the Bishop Dominique Lefèbvre, who had secretly and illegally re-entered Vietnam yet again, and another missionary named Duclos – as well as seeking the freedom of worship for Catholics in Vietnam. While waiting, the French detected what they what they considered to be suspicious activities and sank five Vietnamese ships, destroying any hope of negotiations, then sailed away. Emperor Thieu Tri was furious and ordered the capture and killing of all Christian missionaries in Vietnam. He even offered rewards to those who could capture a foreign missionary. But Thieu Tri, the poet emperor, was a sick man and died of his illness, aged thirty-seven, shortly after issuing the decree. This bombardment of Danang in 1847 was the first military skirmish between the French and the Vietnamese – disregarding the Catholic War in the South.

In September 1856, the French ship, the *Catinat* under Captain Le Lieur, dropped anchor in Danang and handed a letter from Napoleon III to the Vietnamese representative, saying that a French envoy would be arriving shortly. The Vietnamese representative opened the letter and left it on the beach – interpreted as a deliberate insult. The envoy announced by Napoleon III's letter, De Motigny, duly arrived in January 1857, requesting establishment of a consulate, a trading post in Danang, the opening of free trade – and free missionary activities in Vietnam. The Hue Court was deeply divided as to whether to negotiate with the French or to resist militarily. The Emperor Tu Duc, who had succeeded Thieu Tri in 1847, refused the French requests. Execution of yet another Spanish priest in the North in 1857 was perhaps the excuse the French had been waiting for. In 1858, France attacked Danang, but met strong Vietnamese resistance and moved off to the South.

In a stated mission to stop the persecution of Catholic missionaries and 'to secure the unimpeded propagation of the faith in Vietnam,' Napoleon III sent Charles Rigault de Genouilly in 1858 with a fleet of fourteen gunships, 3,000 men and 300 hundred Filipino troops provided by the Spanish. They attacked Danang in 1858 and occupied the city. Tellingly, he was accompanied by Bishop Pellerin, as adviser. From Danang the French fleet sailed south and took Saigon in 1859, possibly made easier by Saigon still feeling rankled over Minh Mang's viciousness in putting down the earlier Catholic insurrection. Rather unexpectedly, de Genouilly was rebuked for his actions and was replaced by Admiral Page – with instructions to obtain a treaty protecting the Catholic faith, but not to seek territorial gains.

Tu Duc's army of 10,000 attacked Saigon during 1860-1861, but French reinforcements – 70 ships and 3,500 soldiers, returning from fighting in China – defeated the Vietnamese forces in February, 1861. Tu Duc must have realized that his army clearly had no hope against the better armed French.

In the Treaty of Saigon of 1862, the Emperor Tu Duc was forced to cede to France the island of Poulo Condor (Con Dao), Gia Dinh (Saigon), and the provinces of Bien Hoa and Dinh Truong to the east of Saigon. French colonization had seriously begun. A year later, Tu Duc sent a diplomatic mission under Phan Thanh Gian to France in an attempt to recover the lost territories, to which Napoleon III at first agreed. But Napoleon's cabinet convinced him to cancel the agreement in 1864. In that same year, all territories under French control in the South were declared a French colony – Cochin China.

In 1867, the French defeat of the fierce resistance movements in the South resulted in French occupation of a further three provinces in the Mekong delta containing the cities: Vinh Long, Ha Tien and Chao Doc.

On 20 November 1873, with a small expeditionary force of fewer than two hundred men (one source says only one hundred men), Francis Garnier captured Hanoi's citadel. If a small expeditionary force could take Hanoi's citadel, Emperor Tu Duc realised that he had no chance against a full French army.

Tu Duc was forced to recognize French control over Cochin China in a second Treaty of Saigon on 15 March 1874, as well as opening the ports of Qui Nhon, Haiphong and Hanoi to the French. The French were given a land concession to install a Navy Cantonment along the Red river (Song Hong) in Hanoi, opening the river to international commerce from its mouth to the Chinese province of Yunnan – had the river been navigable as far as Yunnan. It wasn't. The treaty – barely – retained the independence of Annam (Central Vietnam). Despite strong and determined Vietnamese resistance movements, Tu Duc was simply out-gunned by the French.

One of the clauses of the treaty established a French diplomatic mission in Hue. The first French Chargé d'Affaires, Pierre Paul Reinhart, was appointed in 1875. The French were required to live outside the Citadel on the south bank of the Perfume river.

In 1882, Hanoi's citadel fell to the French a second time, this time to Henri Riviere. Hanoi's defeated governor, Hoang Dieu, committed suicide in despair. One can but feel sympathy for the Emperor Tu Duc, who watched his country's territory being seized militarily bit by bit without having sufficient military means to defend it, while former courtiers in Hanoi, of course, blamed him for letting it happen. The death of Emperor Tu Duc in 1883, marked the beginning of the darkest period of the Nguyen dynasty.

Having no children – his sterility thought to have been caused by having had smallpox as a child – Tu Duc had named three young nephews as successors. It was Tu Duc's wish, despite misgivings, that the eldest adopted nephew, Duc Duc, be crowned emperor. Tu Duc's will had stated his displeasure at the prince's 'bad manners and sexual activities,' a will that should have been read out by the prince at his coronation. Only four days after the coronation, one of the three mandarin regents, Nguyen Van Tuong, sent a petition to the Queen Mother Tu Du, asking her to dethrone Emperor Duc Duc for his four 'crimes': cutting a section from the royal will (the prince had refused to read out his father's rebuke written into the will at the coronation); receiving a Catholic father as assistant; wearing a coloured robe during the mourning period for his adopted father; and having sexual affairs with the late emperor's ladies-in-waiting. The queen mother must have complied. Duc Duc ruled for only three days; he was dethroned, imprisoned – and died of starvation: regicide one.

The regent mandarin bypassed Tu Duc's two remaining adopted sons, opting for Emperor Tu Duc's younger brother, who very reluctantly accepted the crown as Hiep Hoa. From that moment, Hiep Hoa lived with the thought of restraining the abuse of power of the two regicidal regents, Nguyen Van Tuong and Ton That Thuyet, and made a secret agreement with the French to protect himself – from the two regicidal mandarin.

On 23 July, 1883, no doubt under duress, a treaty was signed under Hiep Hoa's rule by two Vietnamese mandarin, Tranh Dinh Tuc and Nguyen Trong Hiep, and the French representatives, the Governor Harmand and the Chargé d'Affaires Champeau – giving France total authority over the remaining part of Vietnam – including Hue. This treaty became the legal basis for France subsequently to act as rulers of Vietnam.

Meanwhile, Emperor Hiep Hoa plotted with two trusted cousins to have the all-powerful regents assassinated, but his note to the cousins was intercepted by one of the regents, Nguyen Van Tuong. In a fury, Nguyen Van Tuong summoned a court of mandarin and despite strong objections, it was finally agreed that the Emperor Hiep Hoa should be granted the royal prerogatives of killing himself – by poison, sword or silk string. Awakened and told the verdict, he refused to drink the poison, so poison was forced down his throat and for good measure, he was clubbed to death. He had ruled for four months and ten days: regicide two.

Again, Tu Duc's second adopted son, Dong Khanh, was passed over. When Tu Duc's youngest adopted son, Kien Phuc, was awakened in the middle of the night at his adopted father's tomb where he was mourning and invited back to the Citadel to become emperor, the thirteen-year-old prince cried and refused to come. But he was forced into a palanquin and carried in heavy rain through the approaching dawn to the Imperial City. He was crowned 1 December 1883. Soon he caught smallpox and was being looked after by Lady Hoc Phi, the third lady of Tu Duc's former court. Seeing how influential she was with the young emperor, the regent, Nguyen Van Tuong, ingratiated himself with her and eventually, in the words of a discrete author, 'they fell in love.' However, overhearing their amorous exchanges, the young emperor became so outraged that he shouted out: 'When I recover, I will behead three clans of yours.'

That same night, after taking a bowl of medicine, the young emperor went to glory peacefully. He had reigned barely seven months: regicide three. In a short space of eleven months in 1883, the Nguyen court had crowned and lost three emperors.

In June 1884, the Treaty of Patenôtre, named after the negotiator and originally signed under Hiep Hoa, was ratified. This treaty relinquished sovereignty over all three regions: Cochin in the South, Annam in Central and Tonkin in North Vietnam. From that moment on, Vietnamese emperors in Hue – despite sporadic resistance – were reduced to puppets and their mandarin were forced to follow French orders.

Ignoring Tu Duc's second adopted son, Dong Khanh, once again, the regents Nguyen Van Tuong and Ton That Thuyet selected another young prince, also only thirteen, who perhaps they thought would be malleable. Ham Nghi was crowned on 1 August 1884.

On 1 July 1885, the French Governor General de Courcy arrived in Hue from Haiphong, putting forward new demands. In the small hours of 4 July, 1885, (22nd day of the fifth month of the lunar year of the Rooster), the mandarin regents, Ton That Thuyet and Nguyen Van Tuong, in the name of the young Emperor Ham Nghi, attacked the Fish Gill bastion at the north-east corner of the Citadel, occupied by the French troops, burning their bamboo barracks. When the French troops rallied, they burnt the Citadel and the fighting overflowed into the city of Hue, killing somewhere between 1,200 and 1,500 resistance fighters and civilians, an anniversary that is still observed in Hue to honour those who died.

Ham Nhi – some say that he was kidnapped by the regents – and the court fled to the hills. The court sent a representation to try to convince young Ham Nhi to return to the capital, but he refused. In his absence, Tu Duc's second adopted son, Dong Khanh, was crowned emperor, 14 September 1885. For a time, Vietnam had two emperors simultaneously.

After three years in the hills, Ham Nhi was captured, betrayed by one of his own men, who had been bribed by the French. He was exiled to Algeria. The regicidal regent, Nguyen Van Tuong, was imprisoned on Poulu Condor (Con Dao Island) in September 1885. When he continued to plot from prison, in November 1885, the French exiled him to Tahiti where he died the following year. It is thought that Ton That Thuyet escaped to China where he died.

In 1887, the French announced their Indo-Chinese Union consisting of Cochin, Annam, Tonkin and Cambodia. Laos was added in 1894. After a short war, also in 1887, the French obtained a trade agreement with China. The frontier between the two countries was marked and China relinquished any remnant of sovereignty remaining over Vietnam as a vassal state. Permission to build a railway to the Chinese frontier was also granted. The wily General de Negrier, commander of the French army, immediately following his victorious battle, demanded that a sign be painted in Chinese and affixed to the Friendly Gate reading: 'Borders are not protected by stone walls, but by the enforcement of treaties.'

The border agreed in the Treaty of Tianjin remains unchanged to this day, either by the establishment of the Republic of China in 1912, or later, when Vietnam gained independence from the French. The only time a border question has arisen was during the sixteen-day skirmish between Vietnam and China in 1979, when China set out 'to teach Vietnam a lesson,' following Vietnam's defeat of the Chinese-supported Pol Pot regime in Cambodia. In fact, it was the battle-hardened Vietnamese who sent the Chinese scurrying, according to Vietnamese sources, leaving an estimated 20,000 Chinese dead in just over two weeks.

The Treaty of Patenôtre signed in June of 1884 may have ended the legal existence of independent Vietnam, but active Vietnamese resistance against the French continued throughout the country right up to World War II when Vietnam was invaded by the Japanese and then, of course, afterwards throughout the French Indo-Chinese War that ended at Dien Bien Phu in 1954.

41

A DESCENDANT OF THE ROYAL FAMILY

A single drop of blood is worth a pond of clear water
– Vietnamese proverb

During my year in Vietnam, I had the privilege of meeting a man in Hue – amongst a few others he assured me – who might have become emperor. His name was Nguyen Phuoc Bao Hien, he was in his seventies and lived in the tomb of his grandfather, the tenth Nguyen emperor, Thanh Thai.

Nguyen Phuoc Bao Hien was neither a recluse nor an eccentric living amongst tombstones. A royal tomb in Hue is not a bad place to live, if you happen to have one, a complex of buildings and courtyards including temples dedicated to the dearly departed. In the case of Bao Hien, he was joined in the tomb complex by some thirty members of his family: his two wives, ten children, a son-in-law, a daughter-in-law and his grandchildren. He had ten children, six sons and four daughters ranging from thirty-nine to fifty-three years old. Each of his wives had five children.

'I tried to keep things balanced,' he said with a twinkle. How very Confucian of him.

There were thirteen emperors of the Nguyen dynasty. Bao Hien's home served as the burial place for three: the fifth emperor, Duc Duc; the tenth emperor, Thanh Thai (Duc Duc's son and Bao Hien's grandfather) and the eleventh emperor, Duy Tan (Bao Hien's uncle). Duy Tan's younger brother, the thirteenth son of the emperor Thanh Thai, was Bao Hien's father.

So much for primogeniture in Vietnam. An emperor's choice of successor, quite apart from his first-born, court intrigue and later, the intervention of the French, played havoc with anything like a simple, direct line of succession. The period encompassed by the rule of Bao Hien's ancestors between 1883 and 1916 was a turbulent epoch in the history of Vietnam, as the country struggled and finally succumbed to French domination in 1884.

Bao Hien received me in the temple dedicated to his grandfather. A lean man with taut skin, he gave a dignified impression of strength as he sat bolt upright, wearing khaki trousers and an open-necked white shirt with a biro in the pocket. Despite the gold frame glasses, he looked anything but meek, which is the meaning of his name, Hien. We sat in straight-backed, red and gold painted chairs that might have been lifted from a royal palace. He poured tea from a tray on a glass-topped table, beneath which were numerous colour photographs of smiling faces. Beside the tea tray was the brown, leather bound volume with gilt lettering of the Nguyen family tree (see appendix). The temple had an interior of dark wood and pillars. Around the corner I glimpsed a low wooden bed with a straw mat, presumably Bao Hien's. Two red ceremonial parasols stood propped in one corner. A revolving fan perched on a wooden box. Beyond the open door, a rooster strutted under a green brocade court robe, flapping on the clothesline.

Bao Hien started at the beginning of his family's history.

'Nguyen ancestors descended from the Dinh dynasty of the tenth century. Vietnam won freedom from the Chinese in 938 in the time of the Ngo dynasty. The Dinh reigned towards the end of the tenth century, having defeated twelve feudal lords. Later Nguyen descendants served under the Ly, Tran and Le dynasties' – in Thang Long (Hanoi).

I knew that Nguyen Hoang had moved from Hanoi as governor of the southern region in 1558 and that after nine generations and a long civil war, another Nguyen, Nguyen Phuoc Anh, had taken the throne in Hue in 1802 as the first Nguyen emperor, Gia Long. There were only four Nguyen emperors before the French forcibly occupied Hue in 1884 after which, like it or not, the Nguyen emperors were little more than puppets.

'At that time, more than a hundred people' – the families of Bao Hien's grandfather and uncle, emperors Thanh Thai and Duy Tan – 'were moved by the French into this tomb complex, held under guard and restricted from speaking to the common people. Even the servants who worked for the royal family were guarded by the Vietnamese secret police, controlled by the French.'

Bao Hien filled me in on these turbulent and terrible years for his family after the death of the fourth emperor, Tu Duc.

'As Tu Duc had no children – it is thought he became sterile through having had smallpox as a child – he adopted three nephews: Duc Duc, Dong Khanh and Kien Phuc. One was the son of his younger brother, the fourth son of the third emperor (Thieu Tri). The other two were sons of the twenty-sixth son of Emperor Thieu Tri.'

43

At the request of Bao Hien, a young relative, his 'uncle', he insisted – such are the convolutions of Vietnamese families where there are many wives – heaved a huge trunk onto a nearby table and rummaged through the piles of photographs, eventually unearthing a faded photo of three little boys encased in stiff court robes. These were Tu Duc's three adopted sons.

'The eldest of his adopted sons, Duc Duc, ruled for only three days in 1883 before two powerful, senior mandarin dethroned him and threw him into prison where he died of starvation. The second and third adopted sons were passed over and another brother (of Tu Duc), Hiep Hoa (aged thirty-eight) was crowned emperor. He met a similar fate – he was only allowed to rule for four months before the two senior mandarins forced him to drink poison.

'The second adopted son, Dong Khanh, was again passed over in favour of the third, Kien Phuoc, aged only thirteen, who ruled for seven months before dying of smallpox.'

Bao Hien continued the story.

'The next emperor . . . young Ham Nghi resisted as best he could, but was overwhelmed and fled to the mountains with the royal golden seal where he tried to raise support to resist.'

In October 1888, he was arrested by the French and exiled to Algiers where he was held in the village of Elbiar a few miles from the city. Much to the annoyance of the French, he had melted down the royal golden seal rather than surrender it to the French.

'At first the emperor refused to learn French, but on reflection, decided that if he were to understand his captors, he would have to learn the language. To pass the time, he painted. He continued to wear the traditional Vietnamese court robes and was known as the Prince of Annam. In Algeria, he was well liked and eventually married the daughter of the French Judge Laloe. They had one son and two daughters. One of his daughters, Nhu Mai, distinguished herself by becoming the first Vietnamese woman to graduate from a European university, *l'Institut d'Agronomie,* in 1927. Known as Mademoiselle d'Annam, when asked why she continued to wear the traditional Vietnamese *ao dai,* she replied, "To please my father the king, Ham Nhi."

At last, it was the turn of the second adopted son, Dong Khanh, to become emperor. His rule lasted less than four years from 1885 to 1889 when he died at the age of twenty-three of a brain disease.' Becoming emperor seemed to carry serious health hazards.

'The legend goes that before he ascended the throne, Dong Khanh asked his mother to go to Hon Chen temple to ask the goddess when he would become emperor. His mother dutifully went off and spent the night at the temple praying, and the goddess appeared, telling her that in six months her son would be crowned. The prophesy came true. Six months later, Dong Khanh was, indeed, crowned. In gratitude, the new emperor repaired Hon Chen temple and thereafter considered himself to be the "younger brother and student of the goddess." Previously, there had been pictures of seven students of the goddess in the temple. Dong Khanh added his own.'

Bao Hien then tells me the story of how his own branch of the family came to power, a curious tale not recorded by historians.

'When Dong Khanh died in 1889, Thanh Thai, the son of Duc Duc' – he who had been dethroned, imprisoned and starved to death by the mandarin – 'was placed on the throne. How it came to be he rather than the son of Dong Khanh, who was ten years old when his father died . . .

'By that time the succession was virtually controlled by the French. The royal family decided that Dong Khanh's son should become emperor, but they had to seek permission from the French resident superieur. The royal family duly sent a representative to meet the French resident. Because the French resident spoke no Vietnamese, he had an interpreter.

'As it happened, this interpreter's wife was the elder sister of Thanh Thai, son of Duc Duc (who had been starved to death). So the interpreter explained to the French resident that the royal family would like for the next emperor to be – not Dong Khanh's son – but his wife's brother, Thanh Thai. The royal representative duly returned to the royal family, saying that the resident would prefer for Thanh Thai to become emperor.'

Treacherous, these interpreters.

Such were the machinations of the succession during the Nguyen dynasty. Thanh Thai, Bao Hien's grandfather, was only eleven years old at the time he was crowned. He ruled for seventeen years from 1889 to 1906. Bao Hien handed me another photograph sealed in plastic of his grandfather as a wide-eyed boy in an enormous court robe. Despite his relatively long rule, the boy grew up to resist the French. He in turn was dethroned and imprisoned in South Vietnam at Cap St Jacques, now known as Vung Tau, sixty miles south-east of Ho Chi Minh City.

Bao Hien told the story of how, during one lunar New Year season, his grandfather, the Emperor Thanh Thai, dressed in ordinary clothes and went to Kim Long, a village known for its beautiful women, in search of a concubine.

'Finding no one he fancied, he took a sampan to return to the Imperial City. Getting into the boat, he noticed that the boat girl was around twenty, quite timid and blushing.

'He called out to the girl, "Say, Miss, how would you like to marry the emperor?"

'The girl regarded him with alarm, "Please don't joke. They will cut off our heads."

'Touched by her sweet voice and sincere manner, the emperor took another tone.

'I tell you sincerely, if you would like to marry the emperor, I will be your go-between.

'The young girl blushed even more and looked away. An old man passing, who had heard the exchange, called out to the girl, "Say yes, Miss, and see what happens."

'So with all her courage, the girl said yes.

'The emperor, enchanted, stood up and took the hand of the young girl, leading her to the bow of the boat saying, "Now, my dear lady, sit down and I will row in your place," and with these words, he began to row to the astonishment of everyone who recognised the emperor. Onlookers were delighted, but also apprehensive. The boat continued along the Perfume river to the Phu Van Lau pavilion (still there) in front of the Citadel where the emperor announced in front of everyone, "Leave the sampan now and come with me, my dear lady, to the court."'

The poor girl must have been terrified. But she accompanied him to the palace and remained a favourite wife of the Emperor Thanh Thai, Bao Hien's grandfather.

'Thanh Thai's son and successor, Duy Tan, who ruled from 1908 to 1916, also tried to raise a rebellion. When it was unsuccessful, in 1916 both he and his father, Thanh Thai, were exiled to the island of Reunion.' It was then that their families, one hundred eight people, were rounded up and moved into the tomb complex and kept under guard by the French. 'The later emperors are labelled as collaborators with the French, but in my opinion, the tenth and eleventh emperors were patriots. They didn't want the French to dominate, they wanted to resist, but lacked the power.'

'The two emperors who followed Duy Tan were from another branch of the Nguyen family. The son of Dong Khanh, Khai Dinh, ruled from 1916 to 1925, when he died a natural death at forty-one. The last emperor, his son Bao Dai, reigned from 1925 until 1945, when he abdicated in favour of Ho Chi Minh's Communist government, saying that he would far rather be a citizen of an independent country than the emperor of a country in slavery.

'Bao Dai was invited to act as adviser to the new Communist Government, but following a mission to China, fled to Hong Kong and waited to return to Vietnam, until it was once again occupied by the French in 1947. The French invited him back as chief of state, which he remained nominally from 1947 to 1954, (during the French Indo-China War), passing his time travelling, hunting around Dalat and relaxing in his villa overlooking the sea at Nha Trang. Following the French defeat at Dien Bien Phu, he went to live in France.'

He died there in 1997, during my year in Vietnam.

Bao Hien was born in 1927, 'and started school at seven under the French system and was taught to work for France until 1945.' Due to the Second World War with the Japanese, he was unable to continue his education, his deepest regret.

'Vietnam suffered greatly during World War II. The Japanese requisitioned so much rice in Vietnam that two million people, one out of five, died of starvation.'

Throughout the war, Bao Hien remained in the tomb looking after his grandmother, the empress widow of Thanh Thai. In 1945, his uncle, the eleventh emperor, Duy Tan, was killed in a plane crash flying from Africa to France.

'Some people say that he was assassinated.'

His grandfather, Thanh Thai, was only allowed to return to Vietnam in 1947, when the French freed him, but he was not allowed to return to Hue. He was made to stay in Cap St Jacques (Vung Tau), sixty miles (96 km) from Ho Chi Minh City, until just before he died – then and only then, was he allowed to return to Hue.

'The last emperor, Bao Dai, was Thanh Thai's nephew and although they had very different views, the two met to discuss the protection of the royal family tombs and how to preserve the royal palaces.' Bao Hien hands me a murky, black-and-white photograph sealed in plastic of his lean faced, high-browed, austere looking grandfather wearing a dark suit, seated beside a round faced Bao Dai, in a light sports jacket and black-and-white spectator shoes. The two

47

men look as different as two men can. The man who handed me the photograph looked remarkably like his grandfather, Thanh Thai.

'Up to 1945, although their movements were restricted, the French had supported the royal family financially. Members of the family were allowed to take part in court ceremonies, but the French always noted which princes took part. After the revolution in 1945, the royal family was very afraid that the Communists would turn against the monarchy.

To their enormous relief, 'the temporary government continued to pay an allowance to the old people in the family, who could no longer work. The family felt moved by this generosity and had second thoughts about the new government. When the French returned to Hue after 1945, the French once again supported the royal family financially.'

Bao Hien remained in Hue, under the French, under the Japanese during World War II, under the French again, and during the Vietnam War.

'I have lived under many regimes, but I have always helped the people. I am very happy that I could be useful, especially during the French War. There were very bloody battles in this city between the French and the Vietnamese. At that time I worked for a Buddhist charity organisation. Many soldiers were killed and I and some other people, after the battles were finished, we would take the bodies of both sides and organise the burial of the dead soldiers.

'I knew it was very dangerous but I was not frightened. At the time, I and some others carried a white flag so that both sides would know that we were working for charity. And I always thought, because what I was doing was a good thing, if I were killed, my spirit would go to heaven. During the wartime, I was very lucky because nobody shot me. At that time I thought if a person didn't help, if he had just stayed idle at home, surely he would go to hell. That thought gave me comfort.

'Before liberation in 1975, I worked for a state organisation concerned with relics management of the old regime and after liberation, I continued to work for the new organisation set up by the new government – until now. According to new government regulations, officers have to retire at sixty. Now I am in my seventies, but our office, the Hue Monuments Conservation Center, still agrees for me to work in the Center. I feel that it is a privilege to continue to work for the government.

'Many members of the royal family followed the Communists and many became leaders in the government. After the liberation, those who took part in the resistance of the country, the government still appreciates them.'

And the royal family now, how many members of the royal family continue to live in Hue?

Musing for a moment, Bao Hien estimated that perhaps around 60,000 people with royal blood over the age of eighteen lived in or around Hue, out of a population of a million in the province.

'The second emperor, Minh Mang, had so many children – one hundred forty-two', he explained, 'that he actually set down a system for naming and labelling each successive generation.'

Bao Hien's guess is that there are perhaps two million members of the royal Nguyen family alive and dispersed throughout the world. Not a very exclusive club.

Apart from his job in the Center, Bao Hien served as the master of ceremonies, the chief mandarin or minister of rites at the royal banquets staged for tourists, who don the golden robes of emperors for a royal banquet of Vietnamese food and music at the Huong Giang Hotel. Many an evening I had seen him clomping regally around the hotel grounds in his scroll-toed platform boots, wearing a brocade court robe and a winged mandarin hat, royal banquet guests none the wiser as to who he really was. All of his immediate family worked for the Hue Monuments Conservation Center, the Huong Giang Hotel or in the royal feasts business.

The colour photographs beneath the glass table top, it transpired, were pictures taken at the many royal feasts over which he had presided. He was pleased to tell me that he was also well known because he likes bonsai.

Our interview at an end, he gallantly invited me to lunch at a nearby restaurant. He clapped on a felt hat, hopped on the back of his young uncle's motor bike – a might-have-been emperor on a motor bike – and off we went, me in a cyclo.

At the Blue Sky Restaurant (Thien Thanh), the tannoy was playing *Besame Mucho*. As we sipped Heineken beers, Bao Hien insisted that I choose one dish. I skimmed the menu and finally pointed to grilled shrimp with garlic, salt and pepper. Imagine my chagrin when one shrimp arrived in the centre of a plate, prettily garnished with slices of tomato and cucumber. Clearly, I had ordered *the wrong thing.*

In a moment, another plate arrived bearing four tiny, well-browned birds, complete with their little round heads, beaks and fragile, stick-like legs. As though I were presented with a plateful of wee brown birds every day of the week, nonchalantly I grasped one in my chopsticks and dropped it into my bowl. Taking another long draught of beer, I picked up the tiny bird with my chopsticks, closed my eyes and thought of England, and took a bite out of one side. Very crunchy. After another large gulp of Heineken, I took a second bite. That was it. I simply could not bring myself to eat the pathetic looking little legs and head and left them lying forlornly in the bowl. Politely, nobody said anything.

By then a huge plate of delicious spring rolls *(nem)* stuffed with pork, bean sprouts, herbs and mushrooms, had arrived and I did my best to forget the tiny birds. Later, I asked the owner of the restaurant how they removed the feathers.

' Oh, by dropping them in boiling water,' she replied. 'They are sparrows and had to be ordered especially from the market.' I refrained from asking if they had arrived at the restaurant live.

During the course of the meal, Bao Hien told me that he had never been abroad and had no desire to leave his country. I asked if he were worried that as the country opened its doors to the world and rushed towards a market economy, that Vietnam might lose many of its long-held traditional cultural values?

For a man whose family had uniquely flourished in the past, then suffered and survived terrifying and distressing times, one might have expected him to take a conservative view.

Instead, lifting his arms wide, he replied with just three words: *'Ouvrez les portes'* (open the doors).

(Note: Bao Hien has since died.)

SERVANT TO THE QUEEN

To a frog at the bottom of a well,
the sky is as big as a lid
– Vietnamese proverb

Pham Van Thiet was a very old man. His eyes in his hollow-cheeked, bony face, had a faraway look. He welcomed me with a sinewy, outstretched arm in the garden of the large French-style villa where he lived, wearing a short-sleeved khaki shirt with a Ho Chi Minh collar and incongruously, Prince of Wales checked trousers. The villa was the home of the former queen mother Tu Cung, mother of the last emperor, Bao Dai. She died in 1980 at the age of ninety-one.

A photograph of the queen mother as a young woman took pride of place on the carved red and gilt altar that filled the entrance hall. Pham Van Thiet led me into a long, formal salon where two rows of threadbare silk-upholstered, gilt dining chairs stood rigidly to attention like mandarin, facing one another across a court of low tea tables. Elaborately carved, black and gold Vietnamese style, glass-front display cabinets lined the walls, holding the family photographs that would have been dear to a granny. Pham Van Thiet identified the subjects in the photographs. In the place of honour in the first cupboard were two tinted photographs of her son, Bao Dai, and his young wife, Nam Phuong, taken at the time of their wedding in 1934.

'He would have been twenty, she nineteen – and a Catholic. They met on board ship en route back from France where Bao Dai had been a student.

'On the death of his father, Khai Dinh, at the age of twelve Bao Dai was crowned emperor, then returned to France to continue his studies. During his years in France, four senior mandarin looked after the affairs of court – those not looked after by the French.'

The photographs of the young couple showed not the slightest hint of what transpired before they were allowed to marry.

'When Bao Dai told his mother that he wished to marry a Catholic, she was distraught. This would mean that the heir would be Catholic and therefore, unable to celebrate the cult of the ancestors to

51

the gods. The court had the same concerns. But despite the obstacles, Bao Dai was steadfastly determined to marry Nam Phuong.

'The wedding took place the 20th of March 1934 before the court and the representative of France within the Imperial City and Bao Dai immediately declared his new wife queen.'

In earlier times, the noble title would often not have been bestowed upon the favourite wife of an emperor until after his death.

'Bao Dai also created a new title for her, Perfume of the South, and proclaimed a new law permitting her to wear yellow, the colour previously reserved exclusively for emperors.'

Even more of a heresy, the marriage was celebrated in Can Chanh, the 'work palace' where two high ranks of mandarin stood to attention facing one another before the emperor. This was the first time in the history of the Nguyen dynasty – or Vietnam – that a woman had been presented to the mandarin at court. The bride wore a huge royal robe with scroll-toed shoes and a royal hat decorated with jewels and pearls. She came before the emperor and prostrated herself three times, then as instructed, seated herself on his right.

'The ceremony, lacking the ritual of precedent, was fairly quick.'

In one corner of the drawing room, a glazed pottery head of Bao Dai rested on a pedestal. Nearby was a family photograph of Bao Dai, his wife and their first two children, a boy and a girl, taken with granny around 1937.

'Bao Dai converted to Catholicism in 1980 – realizing his mother's worst fears – and thereafter, theoretically, was allowed only one wife. But he had several . . .'

Pham Van Thiet leaves me to find an appropriate word.

A large painting of Khai Dinh, the husband of Tu Cong, the queen mother, shared the wall above the cupboards with a 'matching' portrait of Tu Cong as a young queen – wearing a yellow court robe and a crown – painted in retrospect. She would never have been allowed to wear yellow during her husband's reign.

'The portraits were painted from photographs by a Japanese artist in 1944, Khai Dinh having died much earlier in 1925 at the age of forty-one.' Then I hear the most amazing story . . .

'Bao Dai was not the son of emperor Khai Dinh,' Pham Van Thiet confides – another fact not recorded by historians.

'He was the son of another member of the royal family. According to much evidence, Khai Dinh was a homosexual, but that hardly relieved him of the requirement for nine wives. His "escort" (a euphemism for lover) was well known in court circles and even attained the fifth rank.

'The story of Khai Dinh's first wife, De Nhat Giai Phi Truong, was rather tragic. The daughter of a mandarin, she married him before he attained the throne. As a crown prince, he had little money and like many a crown prince, was probably bored, took to gambling at cards and invariably turned to his wife to ask her father to pay his gambling debts. Her father, although he was a mandarin, was not particularly rich. What he had, he had saved judiciously through the years. Finally, in a true test of luck the prince wanted to go for broke, but his gambling friends refused unless he produced the wager in cash.

'He told his wife to ask her father for the money to save his face. His wife, despite her sadness at her husband's physical "incapacity", recognised equally his cowardliness and refused. He was furious, insulted and threatened her. Desperate and angry – she could not approach her father for money yet again – she felt obliged to leave everything, the palace, her life as a royal wife. She retired to a pagoda that she had built for herself on a hill in the village of Thanh Thuy in the district of Huong Thuy, two miles from Hue. Later, after he became emperor, Khai Dinh sent a mandarin to the pagoda to bring her back to the royal Forbidden Purple City, intending to give her the noble title of Wife of the First Rank, but she refused.

'Khai Dinh's second wife, Ho Thi Chi, was the ambitious daughter of an ambitious father who accepted the lonely, loveless life of a royal wife with the intention of gaining power and riches, and ultimately, the title of queen mother. It was to no avail. She died, childless, alienated and old in a Catholic monastery.

'Bao Dai's natural mother, Tu Cong, was not of a noble family. She was Khai Dinh's third wife, became queen and ultimately was honoured as queen mother, only because she had a child.'

Naturally, my romantic curiosity is stirred. Had the last emperor, Bao Dai, been the love child of some secret alliance, was he the product of a political ploy by another faction of the family, or a child born out of grim duty contrary to the strict Buddhist beliefs held by his mother? Naturally, I was intrigued to know who Bao Dai's real father was, but oriental discretion ruled the old servant, even years after the old lady's death.

Later, in a little book written by one Nguyen Dac Xuan, I found the most astonishing story. Khai Dinh, recognising the need for a successor, consulted a relative of his own age, concerning his difficult situation – 'with whom in the past he had had an intimate relationship and unforgettable good memories.' Together they concocted the story that 'one day, after taking a perfumed medicinal concoction laced with ginseng, Khai Dinh felt so strong and passionate that he desired a woman and took his third wife, who became pregnant.'

Then we have a most appalling trial of a woman, perpetrated by women. Not believing her story, Tu Cung's mothers-in-law, Khai Dinh's two 'mothers', the two wives of Dong Khanh, his natural mother, Thanh Cung, and his wet-nurse, Tien Cung, and others in the family, had a hole dug eight inches deep and made Hoang Tu Cung lie stomach down in the hole, beating her in turn to find out if she was truly pregnant by Khai Dinh. No matter how much they beat her, Tu Cung insisted that Khai Dinh had made love to her and made her pregnant. Finally satisfied, the grandmothers were delighted and proclaimed that their son was to become a father. Everyone had to accept the story, whether they believed it or not.

Much later, a mandarin of the fifth rank, Phan Van Dat, declared the concocted story untrue, saying that the pregnancy was by Huong D, the relative to whom Khai Dinh had turned for advice. He stated as evidence that when he became emperor, Khai Dinh bestowed power and wealth on Huong D. The mandarin took further evidence from the family history written by the son of Huong D, Ung Dong, who recorded that at royal family gatherings at the palace, his father was often referred to by the title, 'the professor brother of the former king,' thus proving that he, Ung Dong and Bao Dai were cousins, or half-brothers, of whom the father was Huong D.

The son, Ung Dong, often said, 'In 1912 my father and the prince (who became Khai Dinh) were two dear friends, eating and sleeping together on the same mat. In October 1913, the prince Bao Dai was born. A month and a half later, Ung Linh, the official son of Huong D was also born. These two children as adults resembled one another a great deal.'

Ung Dong also recorded that his maternal grandmother often went to visit the Queen Mother Tu Cung, the mother of Bao Dai, who always called her Di, grandmother, although his grandmother had no family tie with her whatsoever. This he maintained further proved that the mother of Bao Dai considered Huong D to be her husband. The queen mother would often say to the mother of Huong D, 'When his majesty returns, will you bring Linh (the son of Huong D) here, so that he can help him.' The two boys grew up together like brothers.

The following anecdote reinforces the story. In 1934 when Huong D attempted to visit Bao Dai in the Imperial City, the French guards refused to let him enter. Returning home, Huong D went into a rage and is reported to have shouted, 'Dogs, they have no respect for me – although I am the father of the king.'

As might be expected, there were many photographs of the eldest granddaughter and grandson, Bao Long. In one photograph, the handsome grandson stood erect in the white uniform of a French soldier, taken while he was a cadet at St Cyr.

Opposite was a photograph of him as a small boy of seven, almost choked by a heavy embroidered court robe, taken at the ceremony when he was named crown prince.

Bao Dai had five children and there were group photographs taken of them in Paris as well as individually, wearing royal robes when they were younger.

In open-handed fairness, the old servant pointed to the next cupboard, devoted to Bao Dai's second family, which held the photograph of his second wife, Mong Diep, by whom he had two more children.

Then he proudly handed me a black-and-white print taken in October 1945, developed from a negative he had only recently found. It was a group photograph of Bao Dai, Ho Chi Minh, an American officer, General Garogret, and several famous Vietnamese scholars.

How Pham Van Thiet came to live in the Forbidden Purple City was a very Vietnamese sequence of events.

'While the prince, Bao Dai, was still a child, his forward-thinking mother, Cu Tung, had gone to a pagoda and asked a Buddhist monk to look for a suitable little girl that she might adopt. The monk introduced her to one of his own nieces and the empress adopted the child, bringing her into the palace as a royal princess.'

However, the little girl missed her little brother so much that the queen asked her to introduce her brother. Obviously, a boy could not be adopted by the queen mother, so at the age of twelve, Pham Van Thiet joined the queen mother's royal household as her one close manservant, a neat Vietnamese solution. He must have been the only normal man (non-eunuch) apart from the emperor within the Forbidden Purple City, so quite a concession.

It had been the queen mother's fond desire that her son should marry her adopted daughter, Pham Van Thiet's sister. But the plan was thwarted when Bao Dai fell in love with Nam Phuong on board ship.

'There was even talk that Nam Phuong had been intentionally planted on the ship by the French, who wanted Bao Dai to marry a Catholic.' Pham Van Thiet's disappointed, intended sister later married a younger brother of the queen mother, thereby still making a royal alliance.

It was in 1937 that Pham Van Thiet first come to the royal palace in the Forbidden Purple City to serve the queen mother in the villa where now the steps lead to nowhere.

'In the mornings I attended school, in the afternoons I returned to the palace and learned to play classical musical instruments. In the evenings I studied the royal rites of the palace and at night, slept in the servants' quarters of the Forbidden Purple City.'

At that time the queen mother would have been about forty-eight. Once Pham Van Thiet had finished his education, he took up his full time duties. He finds it rather difficult to describe exactly what they were, 'something like a bellboy.' He was allowed to get up whenever he pleased, because mostly his duties involved going to houses to invite friends to come to play cards or *mat chuoc*, a Vietnamese form of *majong*. It was his duty to be there for the queen mother, to do whatever needed doing, whenever a pair of male hands was needed. Apart from Thiet, there were ten female servants: a cook, an ironer, a shopper, a driver.

'There were too many servants, so sometimes they were idle, but whenever the queen mother called, someone had to rush to her. Sometimes when the queen mother went out, a servant went with her to carry her box of betel leaves and areca nuts.

'Every night when the queen mother slept, there were usually four female servants on hand to massage and fan her, because she didn't like mosquito nets. She was rather strict.'

While serving the queen mother, Thiet wore a long black gown and a black headband. When he went to bed, he always kept the headband nearby because sometimes she would call for him during the night.

'There were female mandarin, who wore ivory tablets to indicate their ranks. Whenever the emperor wanted to see his mother, a female mandarin would bring the order from the emperor. A female mandarin was also charged with discipline of the female servants, having the authority to punish or sack them. There was an equivalent male mandarin in charge of male servants.'

Pham Van Thiet remembered very few instances when he was punished, rarely more than a reproach, when the queen mother had wanted him to do something and he had done something else, having misunderstood. At exactly eighteen, he married a girl to whom he had been introduced by the queen mother. His wife was not allowed to enter the Forbidden Purple City, so in the daytime from time to time, he was allowed to leave the palace to spend time with her. At night he had to sleep with the royal servants, although sometimes with special permission, he was 'permitted to stay outside.' Usually he 'had to stay at home' to await orders from the queen mother.

Until the August revolution of 1945, he lived inside the Forbidden Purple City with the servants and contact with other people was restricted.

'It was only after 1945 that the royal servants became freer to go out and began to learn about society.'

Pham Van Thiet's first wife left him after the August revolution. He later married another woman and had five children. She died in 1996. He had six children, three sons and three daughters. Some live in Hue, some in Ho Chi Minh City.

'After the revolution, the queen mother had to move out of the palace and into an enormous villa outside the Citadel.' In her changed circumstances, only Pham Van Thiet and one close female servant remained to serve her. 'She was given an allowance, as were all nine of Khai Dinh's former wives, most of whom were only from seventeen to nineteen years old when he died. Unlike in times past, they were even allowed to remarry, although they had to give up the allowance if they did. Six found new husbands. Of the three who never remarried, one was the queen mother. One went to live with relatives and the third went to a pagoda as a nun.'

Pham Van Thiet's own salary was not very much, so in addition to working for the queen mother, he worked as a building contractor – got estimates and supervised the work – to earn money.

'After Bao Dai's abdication and move to France, the former emperor tried many times to get his mother to join him. But she always refused, saying, "I was born in Vietnam and I will die in my birth place." She loved her country very much. She had come from a peasant family, she treated the servants well and tried to help the people. She was a very devout Buddhist.

'In 1956 the queen mother was forced to move once again when President Ngo Dien Diem of South Vietnam allocated her villa to his brother. She then bought this villa and had it repaired.'

Pham Van Thiet had lived there ever since, serving her until she died. Only a few things had been changed. After her death, he had moved the inlaid mother-of-pearl sofas and tables from the central hallway to the dining room where we stood, and installed the altar in the entrance hall. Musical instruments hung from the walls: a moon-shaped lute, a couple of fiddles, and at the far end of the room, a monochord lay on a low marble-topped divan bed *(sap)*, beneath a wall calendar. Yes, he used to play music for the queen mother, and she passed the time by visiting friends, playing cards.

'But every first, fourteenth, fifteenth, sixteenth and thirtieth of the lunar month, she would be upstairs at an altar praying to Buddha and her ancestors.'

Pham Van Thiet retained warm sentiments for the queen mother. He had lived with her and served her since he was a child and loved her almost as a mother. When she died, he wrote a poem expressing his grief, which was part of a carefully handwritten manuscript describing his life that one day he hoped his nephew in California would be able to have published.

Had he any regrets? The old man thought for a few moments before replying.

'I have not followed any regime, not the French, not the Japanese, not the American, nor the present. I have always felt comfort that I did not have to follow any government.'

He went on to explain that he felt fortunate that his position had been respected by the many regimes. Now, he raised birds – sparrows, bluebirds and parrots – because the queen mother as a devout Buddhist, wouldn't allow him to keep caged birds while she was alive. He took up the moon-shaped guitar and haltingly played a piece called *Flowing Water (Luu Thuy)*, once much loved by the queen mother. Then we moved to the far end of the room where he settled with one leg folded under the other, a toe resting on the instrument's soundboard as he played the monochord *(dan bau)*, my favourite traditional Vietnamese instrument. Several pairs of sandals lined up beneath the divan bed on which he sat.

'Southern melodies are melancholy.'

(Note: Pham Van Thiet has since died.)

PART II

A CITY CALLED HUE

THE PERFUME RIVER

The swallow skims over the ground
Rain will swell the pond
The swallow flies high
The shower will be short
– Vietnamese proverb

Soon enough when I first came to stay in Hue, I learned that foreigners are only allowed to sleep overnight in licensed premises, which is why hotels are required to ask for your passport – in order to take them to the local police station to be registered. That demolished all hopes of moving into a little house overlooking the river. It had to be a hotel – for me, on the river. Wandering along the southern river bank, I found the Huong Giang Hotel, named after the river, in those days a much more modest establishment than it is currently, and I bargained for a long-term rate for a room in an old annex that has now been torn down.

Overlooking the river and Con Hen island, the Huong Giang Hotel was built in the 1960s. A bullet hole, retained as a souvenir in one of the glass tiles in the stairwell between the second and third floors, testifies to its age (damage during the Tet Offensive, 1968). Built in what can only be described as royal Hue style, the ornate red lacquer pillars and beams, and the gilt chairs of the vast banqueting hall, were doubtless copied from the royal palaces. In an artistic *tour de force,* bamboo and woven cane decorate nearly every surface of the corridors and the top floor restaurant of the central building, looking out over the Perfume river.

My room did not look out over the river, but I never tired of watching life on the river. Each morning the chores of the boat people were different. Sometimes, two young boys harvested wild green convolvulus – river spinach. The younger brother, squatting in a slim sampan with what looked like a minnow-net, scooped up the green river weed from the water and flipped it into the boat after his elder brother, standing in the water, had plucked it from the river bed. Sometimes, a single fisherman, balancing on one foot on the curved stern of his sampan, would guide the rudder with the other foot as he drifted down river, dragging a long net. Once I saw a fisherman lift quite a big fish, but usually it was only a silvery minnow. Some mornings, a large square, yellow net attached to four poles was lowered into the river by a woman, winding a pulley from her perch on a rickety bamboo tower in the river. Then she would slowly wind up the net and her husband in a sampan would paddle beneath it, pushing any fish to one side where he could retrieve and drop them into his boat. Then the whole procedure of lowering and raising would be repeated.

Nearly every evening I would sit with a Huda beer on the terrace overlooking the river and Con Hen island, nearly the same view as that from Thien Mu pagoda, which had first attracted me to Hue. For a brief few minutes – sunsets last no more than five minutes – the billowing clouds provided a brilliant light show as they rolled and scudded, every shade from mauve to peach, indigo to violet, ignited by shafts of molten sunlight, turning the sparkling river from pewter to pink. A dark, narrow strip of town floated on the far shore, backed by the indigo of what Hueians call 'the screen' of the Truong Son mountains.

It was mesmerising. No two evenings were ever the same and it was never dull, even on an overcast night when the palette of the sky was limited to subtle shades of indigo – unless it was raining when the entire scene turned sepia. As the flaming sun sank, a sliver of a boat might glide past, a woman coming back from the market, a father rowing his toddler homeward from school, or the slightly larger, noisier ferryboat returning from the market on the far bank, silhouetted against the silvery water. And the river, dissolving from mauve or peach to platinum, flowed smoothly past.

Dragonflies zoomed above the terrace like so many mini-helicopters, their iridescent wings gleaming in the sunlight. Geckos chirped from the warm, white walls of the hotel. I had to laugh one balmy evening, inspired by a particularly pearlescent sunset, when two geckos playfully chased one another up a lamppost and overcome by the romance of the moment, clutched at one another. As the sky faded, tiny orange cooking fires would take spark on the boats, and lights along the shore of the island would begin to twinkle. It was a captivating sight, as twilight ebbed to darkness.

The chunter of the ferry from the causeway to the far shore continued, long after it was possible to make out its silhouette. Add a Huda beer at the end of a hot, heavy, humid day and the spell was utterly enchanting. Apropos of nothing, I learned that Huda beer, made in Hue, is Hue's top revenue earner. Entrance fees to Hue's tourist sites come second.

Upstream to be south, a sturdy, six-arch steel bridge designed by George Eiffel spans the river. It is picturesque in an industrial sort of way, especially when lit up at night. It has also achieved the status of a Hue icon, appearing in silk paintings and on postcards.

And so, my premonition that gazing out over the Perfume river would figure in my future became reality, and now it has again. And life along the river appears to be much the same. Sometimes, the mornings start with sparkling sunshine, sometimes the sun has to burn its way through a gauzy mist. As the sun ignites, the fishing stops and sampans and larger motor-junks with arched, thatch roofs move upstream. From the far end of the causeway beside the hotel, two flat-roofed, open-sided ferries splutter back and forth across the river to the market. Not since my childhood can I remember such blue skies and tumbling clouds. On windless days, tiny yellow birds flit amongst the fuchsia and salmon-coloured bougainvillea.

And now, once again, for a short time I will be staying at the Huong Giang Hotel – which has come to feel like my home in Hue.

On the first morning after my return, a solitary fisher women drops a line off the prow of her dark sliver of a boat, and a couple in only a slightly larger boat haul up their tubular net. Dragon boats glide sedately past to where they will pick up visitors bound for Thien Mu pagoda and the imperial tombs. To the foreign observer, the gentle life along the river feels almost eternal, unchanged from an earlier era, a dreamy, blissful escape from our modern Western world, a time before smart phones, the internet and ipads.

Later, strolling along the river towards the bridge, blinking into memory, I remember Hue's southern river bank as fairly scruffy, a motley string of ramshackle tourist stalls along the pavement, only here and there allowing access to the water where boats moored, hoping for chance-by trade. The boats are still there and the boat women are still persistent: 'You take boat, very cheap, one hour, to market, to Citadel, no tour today, very cheap.'

A paved promenade along the edge of the river has transformed the river bank. A rickety floating restaurant with

PepsiCola signs near the bridge has disappeared, replaced by a round, ultra-modern, floating restaurant, looped with circular hoops to resemble the petals of a lotus flower.

Curving paths now wind over grassy lawns of a park along the river bank, planted with chunky statues, unappealing to one who views most abstract art with scepticism. The one exception is a horizontal male nude figure holding his baby in his arms before him, his wife stretched out, clinging gracefully to his back. Beautiful, yet inexplicable. Is he swimming – armless – holding his child in his arms, his wife on his back? It is only later that I wonder if the sculptor is Phan Thi Binh, the professor of sculpture at Hue College of Fine Arts, whom I met years ago. Unfortunately, the plaque is too weather-worn to read.

A bronze tableau draws me across Le Loi Street. In the best neo-Socialist tradition, it depicts a crowd of peasants in a protest against taxation at 'the site of the former Palace of the French resident superior,' a protest in which Nguyen Tat Than, later to be known as Ho Chi Minh, participated in his youth. The tableau was erected in 2005 and recognized as a historic monument in 2007. Quick history.

Just before sunset, I find myself on Huong Giang's terrace beside the river under a canopy of dribbling mauve morning glory blossoms. Slim boats like curved black needles, skim the water. Dragon boats glide past sedately, heading homeward. Salmon-coloured clouds sweep like rumpled silk across the sky. Birds chatter, whistle and chuckle, then silence as they settle. From somewhere far away, a tapping, perhaps a monk at his evening prayers. Venus appears. Swallows flit low above the water, soundlessly.

High in the Truong Son mountains that form a curved spine down the length of Vietnam, Mount Lu is the source of five major rivers in this region, amongst them the Perfume river. Originally, it was called A Pang in the Cu Tu ethnic tribal language, which translates portentously as human life. Illusions were shattered on learning that the Perfume river is named, not poetically, but because some of the ingredients for perfume grow along its upper banks.

Hue is divided by the broad, slow flowing river, running from south-west to north-east. Upstream to the south is where the Nguyen emperors sited their imperial tombs, set in landscaped parks with ornamental lakes – royal palaces for the afterlife, although one was used as a rural retreat during the emperor's life.

A bit upstream in the centre of Hue, the Nguyen dynasty's Citadel sits four-square on the north bank of the river, the site partly chosen for its position, precisely three miles (5 km) in a straight line from Mount Ngu, whose symbolic role was to act as a screen to protect the Nguyen dynasty, both from winds and from the influences of evil – to ensure longevity. The north bank is known as the Left Bank. The chosen site was also strategically placed between two guardian islands: upriver White Tiger island (Con Da Vien), down river Blue Dragon island. Local people know the latter as Mussel island (Con Hen), as mussels for a much loved Hue mussel dish, *com hen,* come from its shores.

The newer town, some of it more than a century old, spreads over the south-east bank. Passing through Hue, the river meanders to the coast eight miles (14 km) downstream at a village called Thuan An where it joins the South China Sea. Having fought off aggression from China numerous times over the past two millennia, Vietnam remains wary of its huge northern neighbour.

HUE TODAY

Money can even buy fairies
– Vietnamese proverb

So very much has changed, Hue is barely recognisable. Apart from the river and the tree-lined streets – and the Citadel, of course – houses have shot up several storeys. Shops at street level no longer remain open at night; now, shutters come down. At first, small, family-owned, mini-hotels shot up five storeys, then larger hotels with lifts to seven or eight storeys, now numerous very large, multi-storey hotels stand at busy corners, although the international chains have yet to move in. Old hotels have been renovated and refurbished to a high standard. I pass two major building sites in the space of one city block. Cafes, restaurants and travel agents have proliferated, tiny family-run clothes shops and pharmacies have opened. And they are full of Vietnamese tourists, not just locals.

Vietnamese tourists now have more than enough money to drink coffee and the frozen fruit smoothies, once the prerogative of backpackers and foreign visitors. Whole families come out at night for ice cream confections and travelling Vietnamese fill the hotels – even the more expensive hotels. Some of them are rich, very rich, indeed. The car park of my hotel is tightly packed with large people carriers. When I first came to Hue, Vietnamese hotel guests were rare and then, they were usually on government business. Now, the Huong Giang Hotel is full of Vietnamese tourists, particularly from Ho Chi Minh City and Hanoi. The dining room at breakfast is overflowing with Vietnamese family groups, from grannies to toddlers, travelling for the first time. One morning I get on the lift to find a granny holding an infant, the mother spooning food into the baby, just like at home. Another morning, a youngster on roller blades was flitting around the breakfast tables. On yet another morning, I opened the door of my room to find a Buddhist monk in the corridor, brushing his teeth, the door to his hotel room wide open – in what is now a four-star hotel. So the Vietnamese are travelling as never before.

Girls walk around in smart trousers, short skirts, dresses and high heels. Some even wear shorts, unheard of only a few years ago. Most wear make-up, at least lipstick. Some even tint their hair. Young people sit in smart cafes and restaurants after school and of an evening with their friends. Bars and pubs with loud music have sprung up, but as far as I know, still no disco in Hue. Everyone has a smart phone or at least a mobile phone. Many have iPads. And everyone but everyone has a motorbike. First, it was cheap Chinese motorbikes; now motorbikes are made in Vietnam. A smart model I saw being admired cost eighty million dong (US$3,666, £2,900). A few years ago a smart Honda, imported from Japan, cost upwards from US$1,500, £1,200). Even allowing for inflation, the realm of the affordable has changed dramatically – for some.

Attitudes have also changed with rising incomes and exposure to international television and foreign visitors. A whole new generation of Vietnamese has no memories of past wars.

People in Hue – in Vietnam – are much, much better off than they were eighteen years ago. The narrow streets are clogged with motorbikes and anxiously competing red, green and yellow taxis, huge people carriers, countless air-conditioned minibuses and enormous luxury tour buses. The Citadel now charges the same rate, 150,000 dong (US$7, £5.60) for Vietnamese and foreigners alike. It is obviously felt that now, the Vietnamese can afford it.

However, some things in Hue have not changed. Many in Hue are still poor, very poor. Fishermen and women still pole their slim boats along the river. Women still sell fruit and vegetables from their baskets, swinging from their bamboo carrying poles every morning. Pushcart cafes still roam the streets, or wait opposite the backpacker hostel to sell a cheap sandwich *(ban mi)* or a hot steamed dumpling. Modest local restaurants still throw open their ground floors, where not so well off locals sit on low plastic chairs over their bowls of noodle soup or beers. Cyclo drivers still line up in front of hotels, hoping for trade. I passed a cyclo driver the other day, taking an afternoon snooze in a hammock strung up between trees, and my own old cyclo driver of eighteen years ago is still peddling at seventy-two. So many, most people in Hue, are still poor and struggle each day to get by.

In 1997, I had strolled around a slightly run-down, provincial city, frayed at its genteel edges, living on its regal past, a quiet backwater compared to Hanoi or Ho Chi Minh City. The streets were choked with swarms of bicycles eddying round heavily loaded cyclos, often carrying two people in a seat for one and rusty, old, rattling Russian buses, farting blue-black exhaust fumes. There were very few taxis, fewer cars. Hue's tree-lined streets were quiet and peaceful, a confusion of dust and broken pavements and come the monsoon season, awash with mud and puddles. I took a cyclo everywhere I went in town and a boat upriver to the royal tombs.

There were only three large hotels, the Huong Giang, the Century next-door, and the old French-built Morin facing Georges Eiffel's Truong Tien Bridge. Scruffy shop houses along the main tourist streets were one and two-storey and beyond, most family houses were one-storey.

People were poor. The daughter of two school teachers was very anxious when she lost one of two ballpoint pens, because her mother would be angry. Although her ambition at the time was to become a tour guide, and although she was a student at Hue University, she had never had the 5,000 Vietnamese dong, then worth about 30 US cents, charged to the Vietnamese, to visit her own royal heritage, the Citadel. (There was then a two-tier ticket charge, 30 cents for Vietnamese, US$5 for foreigners.)

Her parents had a television set, yet although she begged them to have cable to help her with English, her parents refused, probably on the basis of expense. Her ambition was 'to travel – to Danang, to Ho Chi Minh City.' Although Danang was only a three-and-a-half-hour bus ride away, costing three or four dollars in a tourist bus in those days, much less in a local bus used by the Vietnamese, she had never been beyond Hue. I remember her shock when I asked what she did in her spare time.

'I have no spare time. I go to school and I study. Boys, if they have spare time and get up early, can play football. After school they drink coffee with their friends. Girls have to stay at home. Sitting in cafes drinking coffee is bad. Some girls from wealthy families, they are bad. They drink coffee every day and go dancing with their boyfriends. Parents in Hue are very strict with girls. They have to come straight home after classes.'

Trying to get to grips with how poor is poor, how much did an ordinary Hue family need to live, I asked how much an *ao dai* (the national costume) cost, to which the reply was, 'New, or used?' There was a thriving market in used clothes on one side of Dong Ba market. The *ao dai* (pronounced ow as in ouch, and zeye as in eye) is a high-collared, long-sleeved, side-slit, calf-length tunic worn over flowing, often black or white trousers.

In those days, once out of the *ao dai* high school uniform, a girl's status symbol was a pair of trendy jeans, or two pairs if she were lucky – no make-up, not even lipstick. And sandals, usually plastic – no proper shoes, certainly no high heels.

I remember my young friend's astonishment at the luxury of my then very ordinary hotel room – 'And you live here all *alone?*

That I need not share the room with others was to her a whole new phenomenon as Vietnamese families, sometimes several generations, often shared one room. And she was astounded that I had books lying around. When I explained that I needed them for my research, her astonished response was, 'Did you *buy* them?' In those days, the hip business to be in was a photocopy shop and often, books were photocopied and are still (pirate copies of books are sold, wrapped to disguise their quality in cellophane). My short-wave radio seemed to her a miracle.

At the time, her family was very poor. Despite two teachers' salaries, with four children, her parents barely earned enough to exist. My cyclo driver and a waiter at the hotel had both been English teachers, but given up their teaching jobs because they could earn more as a cyclo driver and a waiter. A cyclo driver in those days could earn $5-7 a day.

Happily, Hue retains her distinctive charm as a provincial city. Once off the tourist streets, beyond the backpacker hostels and cafes – most in two small areas – Hue's gentle character shows itself in the open friendliness of the people, who live on their doorsteps or in their courtyards when temperatures rise. Get lost and someone will lead you to where you need to go. He may even invite you home to meet his family, as has happened to me. The gentle spirit of Hue lives on, despite radical, rapid change.

PART III

HUE'S UNIQUE ARCHITECTURE

HUE STYLE ARCHITECTURE

When the lamp goes out,
the hut and the brick house look alike
– Vietnamese proverb

Imagine a gate with three arched entrances. Add a smaller version of the same three-entrance gate as a second storey tower. Splash the gate with vermilion, cobalt blue and ochre paint. At each turned-up corner of the tubular tile roofs, perch a phoenix covered in chipped china 'feathers' about to take flight. Around each arched entrance, paint sharply-drawn red and yellow mouldings. In each of the recesses between the mouldings, install a colourful three-dimensional, chipped china mosaic – a bouquet, a bonsai, or vines and foliage. At the uppermost centre of each archway, fix a glaring dragon face with bulging eyes, radiating a halo of wavering rays – and you have Hien Nhon gate, the east gate of Hue's Imperial City. This is only the beginning of Nguyen-style decoration in the Citadel.

Or install a line of four bronze poles. Mount an ascending dragon over the two poles on the right and trail a descending dragon around the two poles on the left. Join the four poles with two tiers of blue and yellow enamel tableaux, each flourishing a finely drawn, colourful floral bouquet. Then at the top of each pole, affix a pink and white enamel lotus bud and you have Nghi Mon gate, one of two, at the entrance and exit of Trung Dao bridge over the Lake of Great Waters (Dai Tich) in the Imperial City.

To the Western eye, the Nguyen's colourful embellishment and decoration of their imperial architecture is so far over the top, so contrary to the clean lines of Scandinavian functionality or modern brutalism that were it not so finely balanced – Confucian – each facet so beautifully complementary, one part to another, it would be completely dizzying. Instead, the overall impression is one of utter

68

charm, in stark contrast to the heavy, grey stone buildings of Western officialdom – and it is on a human scale.

When Gia Long was crowned the first Nguyen emperor in 1802, much thought and consideration was devoted to the design and building of his imperial capital. The Nguyen placed the utmost importance on the advice of expert geomancers, adhering to the principles of *feng shui*. These geomancers sought out and chose the sites for the positioning of the Citadel, royal palaces and tombs, sometimes in the case of a royal tomb, taking several years to find exactly the right spot.

Adhering to Confucian principles, royal Nguyen palaces and temples were invariably placed in a strictly symmetrical format; in the case of the royal tombs in a sophisticated, vast landscape garden; or conversely, in the case of private residences, in contrived, miniature landscapes, offering a different scenic view at each turn of the path or along each step of a bridge.

So beautifully designed were the royal palaces and many of the pagodas that the third emperor, Thieu Tri, composed twenty poems praising his favourite Hue beauty spots. He also commissioned glass paintings of them, his poems surmounting the framed paintings. Sadly, most of these beauty spots, many of them in the Citadel, have now either disappeared or been vastly altered. But several of his glass paintings survive in the Citadel: in the queen mother's tea palace (Cung Dien Tho); in the temple dedicated to the Nguyen emperors (The Mieu); and in the temple of Dong Khanh's tomb.

Above all, Nguyen architecture had to be in harmony with nature, which explains why only Ngo Mon (gate), Mang Ca (fortress), the guardian miradors along the Citadel walls and one temple inside the Citadel, Hien Lam pavilion, are more than two storeys high. Even gates within the Citadel to the Imperial City rarely have more than a low, open tower, highly decorated.

Sites were chosen where mountains form 'screens' for the Citadel and the royal tombs, not only to protect them from the winds, but to provide romantic, poetic, scenic backdrops. In the view of Hue people, mountains link heaven and earth, reflecting a line of poetry by Tung Thien Vuong, a Hue poet during the Nguyen dynasty, 'Where the heaven and earth become one.'

The architecture of Nguyen palaces, temples, pagodas and even private houses can look remarkably similar in style. Wide, low, one-storey buildings have three or four openings across the front with multiple folding doors, up two or three steps, or in the case of an emperor's tomb, maybe up more than a hundred steps. These low-slung buildings rest beneath tiled, hipped roofs, one hipped roof behind the other.

The tile roofs carry colourful, elaborate decorations. In Hue, their vertical ridge lines are most often encrusted with brightly coloured, chipped ceramic mosaics of rollicking dragons, phoenix, carp, sun and moon. Pediments often feature bats, because the word for bat is the same word, *phuc,* as luck, so bats are considered as a sign of good luck.

Colourful enamelled tableaux featuring floral designs, alternating with poems, form cornices just beneath the ridge lines. Wide, over-hanging eaves to provide shelter from both sun and rain, turn up at the corners in an oriental manner, their ridge lines bearing dragons, phoenix, sometimes carp.

Inside, the interiors of royal palaces and tomb temples are alive with vermilion lacquer pillars and panels. Intricate, carved and lacquered fretwork beneath the beams might separate the pillars or be in the form of carved 'drapes' hanging from a beam, dazzling the eye and leaving an impression of extravagant red and gold exuberance and grandeur.

Royal palaces and temples, almost without exception, are built of precious hard woods: iron wood, *gu* (signora), Vietnamese oak or Tehran pine. Floors are of wood, sometimes tile. Rafters supporting the roofs are left to season to their natural, warm brown.

The use of screens is a unique characteristic of Hue architecture, small free-standing walls built just inside an entrance or a gate to a palace, pagoda, temple or even a private residence, blocking sight of the building within. Many are beautifully painted with fluid, colourful floral designs; others have extravagant ceramic mosaic decorations.

Gardens are a subject unto themselves, whether they be the gently rolling hills, lakes and lake pavilions, tiled paths and arched bridges – settings for a royal tomb – or the vast royal gardens of the Citadel, or the smaller private gardens of former princes and mandarin, planted with ornamental trees, contrived topiary and potted bonsai. Winds and water were taken into consideration. Where there was insufficient water, a river was diverted to form ornamental lakes and moats, or a canal was dug. According to my friend, Professor Buu I, 'For the people of Hue, their lives must be in harmony with nature. A garden house symbolizes a miniature universe. Its landscaping utilizes the science of winds and water, including the orientation of the house to the trees and plants, and if possible, contains a rock formation and a small pond.'

The importance of the garden was brought home to me one day, returning from the royal tombs, when we were stopped for half an hour while a fully grown tree was unloaded with a crane, lifted over a garden wall and carefully positioned in a private garden. The taxi driver showed not the least sign of surprise or impatience. Taking great care in designing one's garden, following oriental rules of geomancy, is accepted as normal behaviour. The entrance gate to a private garden house nearly always has a small roof and eaves wide enough to shelter passers-by from the sun or rain. Trees line the central path to the folding, front doors. Open verandas across the front hold potted bonsai and other flowering plants.

Planting in a Hue garden may look to be poetically random, but follows certain principles. Hedges are of bamboo, tea plants, wild pineapple or banana trees. Next come fruit trees: coconut, jack fruit, plum; then fruit trees that need more careful attention: orange, mandarin orange, persimmon, mangosteen. The innermost trees and plants are purely ornamental. If the above sounds regimented, the results look accidental. You would never guess that there are principles and rules in play. All are thoughtfully positioned to form scenic views from various vantage points.

Most Hue gardens contain a small pond, sometimes with an arched bridge or at least a rock garden, placed in a huge rectangular 'planter' full of water – what in the West might be called a water feature. The aim of a rock garden in Hue is to create a mini-universe. A rock garden starts with perhaps a couple of rough boulders to represent mountains, dotted with small plants to simulate trees, generously sprinkled with tiny arched bridges and pagodas, set in a 'lake' – a miniature world to contemplate from an open veranda.

The royal gardens of the Citadel hold several fine rock gardens. And also in the Citadel, there is an elaborate rock garden beside the Emperor Khai Dinh's library (Thai Binh pavilion) and two more at Truong Du pavilion, behind the queen mother's palaces. Nearly every Hue garden house has to have at least a small one.

Wandering through the streets of Hue, it is not obvious, but official statistics state that Hue boasts 1,778 'garden houses'. Many were built several hundred years ago, are privately owned and not open to the public, although several have opened as restaurants, notably: the Garden of Tranquillity (Tien Gia Vien), owned by Madame Ton Nu Ha, a Hue chef who 'sculpts' the four sacred animals; the Nguyen Xuan Hoa restaurant and the Y Thao restaurant, which serves a tasting menu of Hue specialities. All three are set in delightful, beautifully designed Hue gardens.

At first, the busy wealth of detailed architectural decoration in Hue can be a bit overwhelming to the Westerner, unaccustomed to so much embellishment. The plethora of exquisite details can melt into the larger image of a palace or a pagoda without conscious absorption. Nevertheless, the enduring impression is one of colour, charm and grandeur on a relatively small, human scale. The Nguyens built a grand, extravagant and enchanting environment. There is nowhere else in Vietnam – or the world – quite like it.

THE CITADEL

The mandarin passes by,
the people remain
– Vietnamese proverb

During Hue's feudal period, a huge yellow flag emblazoned with a red imperial dragon flapped from the flagpole that heralds Hue's royal city, the Citadel. Feudal times may have ended much earlier than the nineteenth century in Europe, but the reign of Vietnam's last feudal dynasty, the Nguyen, began late and lasted from 1802 well into modern times – ending in 1945. These days, a red flag with a yellow star flaps from atop the monumental, pyramid flag tower.

The Citadel is made up of three square, walled enclosures within enclosures: the outer city walls of the Citadel; the second walled enclosure protecting the Imperial City, also known as the Great Enclosure, where court ceremonies were held and mandarin went about their business; and the innermost sanctum, the Forbidden Purple City, reserved for the emperor and his extended family.

Built in the early years of the nineteenth century, the Citadel combines the architectural traditions of oriental geomancy and the techniques of Vauban-style fortifications of the West.

A hexagonal fort, Tran Binh Dai, surrounded by a moat, was built at the north-east corner of the Citadel to control boat traffic moving along the two branches of the Perfume river – the fort that was occupied by the French and attacked by the mandarin and their supporters under the Emperor Ham Nghi in 1885, to which the French responded by torching the Citadel and much of the city. The Vietnamese call the fort Mang Ca (Fish Gill), for its peculiar shape.

A moat sixty-six feet (23 m) wide separates the royal walled city, the Citadel, from the outer world. Occasionally, a fisherman in a slim sampan tries his luck in the moat, now carpeted with water lilies. Each entrance gate, guarded by a two-storey watch tower, is over one of ten humped bridges crossing the moat. The route then plunges through a tunnel under the city wall sixty-three feet (21 m) thick, the end of the dark tunnel opening into the royal air of the Citadel. The original Citadel walls, built in 1805 by the first Nguyen emperor, Gia

Long, were of earth. The second emperor, Minh Mang, covered them with brick to a height of roughly eighteen feet (6 m).

Reflected by day or floodlit by night in the second moat that surrounds the (middle) Imperial City, Ngo Mon, the main ceremonial gate, is one of the most imposing structures remaining of the Nguyen Dynasty. Its square, U-shaped, stone base, 'signifying the open arms of welcome,' looms like a massive fortress – you could scarcely imagine a more forbidding gate. London has Big Ben, Paris has the *Arc de Triomphe,* Hue has Ngo Mon (Noon Gate). Hanoi has, well, Ho Chi Minh's Mausoleum.

Air and light filter through the open, two-storey Five Phoenix pavilion that floats above Ngo Mon's heavy stone base. Its yellow and green glazed roof tiles gleam in the sun, the corners of the roofs turned up in proper oriental fashion. As timeless as it looks, Ngo Mon was built as recently as 1833.

Beneath the imperial, yellow tiled roof, the central entrance was formerly reserved exclusively for the emperor and presumably, his palanquin bearers. Civil mandarin filed through the left archway, military mandarin through the right, under ordinary green tiled roofs. The two entrances in the wings were reserved for horses, elephants and soldiers, men and animals dressed up in colourful silk court regalia, a spectacle recreated in even years during the bi-annual Hue Festivals. In the odd years, Hue stages a craft festival.

Only emperors were permitted to wear yellow. Only yellow tiles could be used for palaces of the emperor. So why, the Forbidden Purple City? The answer is simple: because the walls of the royal enclosure, the innermost sanctum, the Forbidden City, were originally painted purple. So purple is synonymous with and symbolic of Hue: official guides to the Citadel still wear purple *ao dais;* Hue girls attending the high school formerly wore violet *ao dais,* now white.

The innermost Forbidden Purple City was also known by several other names: Dien Tho, which translates as the Great Within; Cung Thanh, which means Strict; and the Everlasting Longevity Palace. Only the emperor and the royal family, his wives and concubines, servants and eunuchs, albeit a crowd of several hundred, were allowed inside this third, innermost sanctum. Even mandarin were excluded and there came a time in the life of every young royal prince – at sixteen – and for princesses at thirteen, when they were thrust out of the Forbidden Purple City to be educated in the (middle) Imperial City. Probably not a bad idea to separate royal princes from the numerous lovely, idle and bored, nubile young wives and concubines of the royal household.

When speaking English, the Vietnamese refer to this crowd of court ladies as 'wives', although to the Western mind, such a multitude might well be thought of as concubines.

When I first visited the Citadel, little girls waited in ambush outside Ngo Mon, selling note cards with delicately painted landscapes on silk and strings of miniature conical straw hats. Now, the little girls have grown up or the authorities have abolished street vendors from around the gate. Hue's beautifully painted, watercolour landscapes on silk are sold now in a stand beside Thien Mu pagoda, by souvenir shops in town and by a couple of roving vendors.

Ngo Mon retains its monumental, majestic stance, a barrier to intruders. Through another brick tunnel under Ngo Mon gate, now open to visitors, you enter the Imperial City.

My guide during one of my visits to the Citadel was a knowledgeable young graduate music student named Phan Thuan Thao, daughter of a distinguished historian, Phan Thuan An. Thao started with a lecture on dragon-ology.

'Dragons, simultaneously represent the symbol of power and the power of the emperor.'

Therefore, it is little wonder that stone dragons, mosaic dragons and carved, wooden dragons embellish the ridge lines of nearly every temple, pagoda, palace and pillar in Vietnam.

Naturally, dragons exult heraldically over the yellow and green tile roofs of Ngo Mon, where no women were allowed to pass through. During royal ceremonies, only a few female members of the royal household, the queen mother, the queen and perhaps a few privileged wives, were permitted to watch discreetly from behind the bamboo screens of the second storey Five Phoenix pavilion, where they could not be seen. Common people had to watch from beyond the lotus ponds of the moat.

Climbing the wide flight of stairs to the airy Five Phoenix pavilion, we found ourselves amongst a multitude – a hundred – thick, gleaming, carmine lacquered columns, flourishing rampant, golden dragons.

On my first visit to the Five Phoenix pavilion, I was suddenly reminded of a jewellery box I had been given as a child by a sailor in the family. It was a lacquered box with a few brush-strokes to evoke a branch of bamboo and inside the hinged lid were thin-walled compartments, cushioned and lined with bright pink silk. Could that long forgotten, precious childhood treasure have been the source of my fascination with Asia? The subconscious is a strange country.

Thao placed me at the centre of the Five Phoenix pavilion in the exact position where the last emperor, Bao Dai, had stood to abdicate in 1945. I looked out over the empty court and the lotus-covered moat towards the flag tower, wondering what it felt like to be an emperor? As worried, no doubt, as any politician before or since, wishing to retain power, absolute power. By 1945, of course, it had been a long time under French domination since any Vietnamese emperor had enjoyed much power at all, let alone absolute power.

An enormous drum that was struck whenever the emperor arrived or departed, stood at one end of the pavilion. Formerly, its boom had also signalled to the sentries to fire the cannons by the flag tower to announce the closing of the gates to the Citadel at the end of each day. Years ago, there was a slash in the drumhead, hardly unexpected in a city that had survived three major military conflicts – or perhaps deliberately slashed to mark the end of feudalism.

Having been built of wood, only a few of the original buildings of the Forbidden Purple City remain. Those that survive or have been restored or rebuilt are a glory to behold, and today, the drum head has been replaced.

'A masterpiece of urban poetry,' is how Amadou-Mahtar-M'Bow, Director General of UNESCO, described Hue in 1983. Yet it took ten years until 1993, before UNESCO declared Hue a Site of World Cultural Heritage to be preserved for mankind. A huge bronze bell cast in 1823, during the third year of Minh Mang's reign, rests at one end of the pavilion. There is no clapper; it was struck like a gong.

A framed, jade and marble collage mounted on one wall, depicts a scene that took place here many times, the Proclaiming the List Ceremony – the reading out of the names of candidates, who had successfully passed the triennial doctoral examinations. Four rows of candidates in the collage kneel in the courtyard expectantly, facing Ngo Mon, the successful few, destined to become mandarin, their ranks dependent upon their exam results.

Elaborately caparisoned elephants stand at the four corners of the courtyard, flanked by orderly lines of musicians, soldiers and mandarin, naturally, placed in perfectly symmetrical Confucian balance. The last such ceremony took place here under the Emperor Khai Dinh in 1919.

The main royal palaces of the Citadel lie in a straight line along a central axis. From Ngo Mon, beyond a broad, sun-baked courtyard, the Central Path bridge (Trung Dao) crosses the Lake of Great Waters (Dai Tich), the bridge creating two exactly symmetrical square 'lakes' on either side of the bridge. In the Confucian ideal, each part of the whole must be equally and harmoniously balanced by another. Fragrant, white-flowering frangipani trees soften the squared, paved banks of the lake. Green lily pads float on the surface like stepping stones, dry but for a few droplets of dew that glisten like mercury, here and there a bright pink lotus blossom. Despite having been nurtured in the more casual Western landscape garden tradition, there is something immensely satisfying in these strictly ordered, soft, well-balanced scenes.

Dragon-in-clouds designs ascend and descend the four bronze columns that form Nghi Mon, one gateway at the entrance to the bridge, another identical gateway marking the end of the bridge in perfect Confucian balance, each bronze column topped by a colourful enamel lotus bud. The Nguyen left no surface, no pillar nor post undecorated, and decorated finely, with elaborately carved, cast, gilt, painted, enamelled or mosaic designs. Yet the excess of embellishment culminates in a harmonious whole, one part setting off and complementing another.

The Great Rites Court (Dai Triu Nghi), also known as the Esplanade of Great Salutation, opens at the far end of the Central Path bridge. Two bronze *kylins,* translated by the Vietnamese as 'unicorns' (English not having a wide choice of mythical beasts to choose from), glare at visitors from the far corners of the courtyard, bearing not the least resemblance to single-horned unicorns. The role of these beasts – part lion, part crocodile, part dragon – despite their obvious ferocity, 'is to act as harbingers of peace and as reminders of ritual solemnity.' To the uninitiated, they look like rather savage temple dogs, their like to be found throughout the Far East.

The Esplanade of Great Salutation faces the expansive Supreme Harmony palace (Thai Hoa). As recently as only seventy years ago (1945), scores of mandarin lined up at dawn in this Esplanade of Great Salutation, standing in ranks to greet and kowtow to their emperor during royal ceremonies. Stone tablets along each side of the courtyard mark the guide lines where the nine ranks of mandarin took their places, grades one to three on the upper level nearest the emperor, grades four to nine in the lower courtyard.

The colours of their court robes and their headgear indicated rank: civil mandarin to the left, military mandarin to the right. Topiary life-sized elephants flank the steps to the Palace of Supreme Harmony, a one-storey building that stretches majestically across the entire width of the Great Rites Court, its yellow tiled roofs gleaming in the sun. Immediately beneath each of the roof ridges, like hardened, colourful ribbons, stretch cornices of enamelled tableaux of red, yellow and green, alternate tableaux decorated with flowers or inscribed with poems in Chinese characters *(chu nha)*. The Nguyen dynasty valued scholarly poetry – nearly as highly as religion.

Built in 1805 by the first Nguyen emperor, the Palace of Harmony, Thai Hoa, is the most eminent royal palace in the Citadel; it is also the throne palace. Inside, isolated in the centre, dwarfed between a four-tiered dais and an elaborately carved, two-tiered gilt canopy, stands the smallish carved, red lacquer and gilt, open-armed chair that served as the throne for thirteen Nguyen emperors. It is said that from this throne, the emperor could distinctly hear sounds made from anywhere within the palace, a phenomenon so far no acoustics expert has been able to explain. No one is allowed to pose for photographs seated on the former royal throne.

The longest reign of any Nguyen emperor was that of Tu Duc, thirty-six years (1847-1883). The shortest was that of his adopted son, Duc Duc, who ruled for only three days before two mandarin removed him from the throne, imprisoned and starved him to death – there was considerable risk in becoming emperor in 1883.

Years ago, I came upon a workman, up a ladder, re-gilding the canopy. Feudalism might have ended, but craftsmen continue to do the same work; only the master has changed. Each of the eighty iron wood columns carries more than ten gleaming layers of red lacquer and splendid, rollicking, golden dragons.

One old discarded column has been preserved to show the damage done by termites, eating from within. Decorative panels, alternating poems and flowers, ring the walls in a high cornice just beneath the ceiling. The poems were composed by emperors and their mandarin, the subjects of the poems, praising the landscape. Pale yellow lacquer panels, set in red lacquer and gilt frames, cover the walls. Apart from coronations, the emperor's birthday anniversary and the receiving of ambassadors, large meetings of mandarin were held here twice a month; smaller meetings took place in the emperor's 'working palace' further on.

As recently as 1910, a Frenchman, Robert de la Susse, described a grand court ceremony held in the Palace of Supreme Harmony under the Emperor Duy Tan.

'The Emperor sat on the throne, frozen in a formulated posture. He wore a golden crown, a yellow silk robe and was separated as a sacred man from the court by a wisp of smoke which arose from the incense-burner in the dim light below the canopy . . .

'Outside, in a brick-paved court, about two hundred high-ranking mandarin, all in court robes, lined up in strict order according to their ranks and titles. On both sides of the court were several persons holding parasols, musicians, singers and soldiers. Farther away stood richly adorned elephants, then the imperial sentinels and finally, the massive background of the Noon gate, magnificent with the Royal Screen mount looming on the horizon in the hilly area beyond Hue.

'Suddenly in the lingering silence, arose a singsong tune, wafted by a melody with a strange rising and falling rhythm. Then in a unanimous movement, all princes and mandarin bowed, knelt down, prostrated themselves on the ground and resumed their position. These prostrations were repeated several times during the ceremony. What an imposing and significant scene! High-ranking mandarin, most of them were white-haired elders, attired in court robes of precious silk, blazing in the sun, prostrated themselves in respect to an existent and remote monarchy.'

Nine imperial dragons graced the emperor's crown. His attire included a gold embroidered court robe, a jade belt and scroll-toed, silk brocade platform boots. He held in one hand a thin jade tablet, a *tran que,* a mirror on one side to emphasise the solemnity of the ceremonies – perhaps also to ascertain that everything about his person was in place or that no one was lurking behind him.

Only four high-ranking mandarin and princes were allowed to stand inside the throne palace, the others outside in the sunny courtyard. Fortunately for the mandarin, most such ceremonies were held very early in the morning and ended at sunrise. Otherwise, they would have sweltered in their court finery.

These days there is a very fine video with English subtitles, explaining the building and the layout of the Citadel, also a huge model showing the positions of the numerous royal palaces, many of which no longer survive. Both are excellent aids in getting your bearings and realizing just how vastly spread out it was.

When originally completed, there were more than a hundred buildings within the Imperial City.

Passing through and out the back of the Palace of Supreme Harmony, the buildings facing one another across the courtyard, left and right, were originally used as offices for the mandarin: civil mandarin left, military mandarin right. It seems a trifle ironic that their ceramic window screens were formed in the shape of the Chinese character for longevity – a futile hope as it turned out. In the profusely painted interior of the building on the left, visitors can dress up in court robes to have their photos taken, seated on a replica throne. Surprisingly, a good many Vietnamese do.

Beyond the courtyard behind the Palace of Supreme Harmony (the throne palace), two enormous bronze cauldrons rest in the grass where the Palace of Audiences (Can Chanh), the emperor's 'working palace', once stood. Ten or more of these 'victory' cauldrons are strewn around Hue, cast from Dutch canons, collected and melted down 'to celebrate the defeat of the Dutch navy in the mid-eighteenth century.' Now, only the foundations of the old palace are discernible in the open, grassy space. One story goes that the origin of large urns as an emperor's symbol of power derived from the Emperor Dinh Bo Linh (923-979, (from whom Bao Hien traced his ancestry), one of the first rulers of the newly independent Vietnam after the Chinese were ousted in 938. In the courtyard of his palace in Hoa Lu, then capital, south-west of Hanoi, the emperor Dinh Bo Linh displayed a huge kettle and a caged tiger, having decreed that: 'Those who violate the laws will be boiled and gnawed.' Well, that's one story that historians adamantly refute and remain unable to verify from written records.

A lone potted palm marks the former position of the Great Golden Gate (Dai Cung Mon), the gilded gate once the entrance to the Forbidden Purple City. Apart from eunuchs and the emperor himself, no men were allowed to enter and women, brought here to work, were never allowed to leave.

There have been many discussions concerning the possibility of reconstructing the Great Golden Gate (Dai Cung Mon) and the emperor's working palace (Can Chanh). The emperor's private residential palace, Can Thanh, stood directly behind the working palace. Inside the gate to the right stood Quang Minh Palace, the residence of the crown prince. Nearby, opposite on the left, stood Trinh Minh, residence of the emperor's concubines, Quy Phi.

Behind the emperor's residential palace stood Khon Thai, the palace of the emperor's 'main wife', the Most Favoured Lady. To the east of Khon Thai Palace was Thuan Huy Palace, reserved for the emperor's other wives. And to the west of Thuan Huy Palace were five more palaces – residences for the emperor's lesser wives. To the east of Khon Thai Palace (residence for the emperor's 'senior' wives), was a small theatre called Tinh Quan Palace, where his lesser wives, *cung nhon,* performed for the emperor's pleasure. The working palace and the residential palaces of the emperor and his Most Favoured Lady were destroyed by bombs during World War II, quarters of the royal wives, during the Tet Offensive of 1968. In recent years, covered passageways running along the inside walls of the Forbidden Purple City have been rebuilt, evoking the feeling that here, emperors and royal wives lived and breathed in the not so distant past. Strolling along these passages, open on the inner side, the interior walls covered in red lacquer and gilt panelling, doors echo through doors, beckoning one back towards a dream-like, earlier and more elegant imperial age. In the far reaches of the grassy field, two tiny tea houses, symmetrically left and right, have been reconstructed, china mosaic dragons flouncing on their roofs. Beyond the tea houses, two stone lions guard a flight of forlorn stairs leading to nowhere, where the European style villa of the last but one emperor, Khai Dinh, once stood – where Pham Van Thiet came to serve the queen mother. Just beyond, at the far end of the central axis, just before the North gate (Hoa Binh), up a long flight of mysterious stairs, past a glittering life-sized deer on the lawn, stands a two-storey wooden pavilion, sporting imperial dragons on the roof. To my relief, a sign indicates that this is Tu Phuong Vo Su pavilion, the site originally of the north sentry bastion, which was replaced by the last but one emperor, Khai Dinh, who used it for 'fresh air and enjoying the scenic landscape.'

Combining European and Asian styles, an arched, colonnaded verandah provides shelter at the lower level; terraces at the upper level are open to the sky. Rather surprisingly in what is now a tea house, I am asked to remove my shoes before mounting the very narrow, rather steep, wooden steps – steps that would have been climbed by the last but one emperor – to the second floor where pale, beautifully grained wooden settees stand rigidly beside a low tea table of matching grained wood. From here, the Emperor Khai Dinh would have enjoyed a fine view over the moat, lined by frangipani trees, and the yellow tiled rooftops of the Forbidden Purple City.

LIFE OF THE EMPERORS

The king's son will become king,
the guard's son will sweep the pagoda,
but when the people rise up,
the deposed prince will sweep the pagoda
— Vietnamese proverb

An emperor's ordinary day, if there was anything ordinary about the lives of the Nguyen emperors, began by waking in Can Thanh palace at about six in the morning. Immediately, the emperor was asked to write how he felt in red ink on the prince's health inquiry card, presented to him each morning by a eunuch. The card informed the court of his state of health.

Breakfast was served at half past six, lunch at eleven and dinner at five. Each dish at every meal, prepared by a different cook, was presented in a tightly covered pot with a label. The rejected dishes were sent to the imperial wives.

The emperor ate alone, almost alone. Certain emperors were tended by five imperial ladies kneeling to one side, others by a mandarin who not only served but kept him company. With their meals, Nguyen emperors often drank alcohol soaked in medicinal herbs, allegedly to strengthen their health.

Emperor Dong Khanh liked a tipple of strong alcohol made from dried lotus seeds and he was the first emperor to drink Bordeaux – on French doctor's orders, of course.

If an emperor felt 'uneasy', he sent for the chief royal physician. When the Chinese herbal medicine for the emperor was ready, it would be poured into a container, shut and sealed, and placed in a wooden box that was also sealed. The box would then be carried by imperial guards, shaded by a parasol and accompanied by the royal physician.

But before the emperor would drink the medicine, the royal physician had to make three bows before the emperor and drink a small cup of the medicine himself, watched by the emperor, to prove it wasn't poison.

When the emperor held a feast for courtiers, foreign envoys and the successful doctoral candidates, the emperor never attended the banquet, but appointed the minister of rites to entertain his guests. Even in his absence, however, protocol demanded that before eating, all guests should stand, hold their chopsticks in a horizontal position and make three bows to show respect and gratitude to the emperor. These feasts might last for half a day and on leaving, each guest was given a present to take home to his children – going home gifts, rather like a birthday party.

An emperor often worked 'alone' at one end of Can Chanh palace, the working palace, attended only by a beautiful royal servant standing by to bring tea or light cigarettes. Every other day the emperor Tu Duc was carried by palanquin to visit his mother, a duty he honoured throughout the thirty-six years of his reign.

The emperor's wardrobe was the duty of five maid servants, who helped him to dress, who brushed every crease, styled his hair, polished every fingernail and arranged his immediate surroundings in an aesthetically pleasing manner.

Within the Forbidden Purple City, royal gardens were created where the emperor and the imperial wives could stroll among trees, flowers and plants around lakes, pavilions and man-made mountains.

The Nguyen emperors also went hunting and sightseeing outside the Forbidden Purple City. Emperors Minh Mang and Thieu Tri loved the sea and Emperor Tu Duc loved hunting in the Thuan Truc forest, nine miles (15 km) from the Citadel.

There were two theatres, one within the Forbidden Purple City, Tinh Quang palace, exclusively for the emperor and the imperial wives, and a larger theatre in the Imperial City, Duyet Thi Duong, where the emperor watched classical dramas together with mandarin of the higher ranks, the royal family and honoured foreign guests.

In the springtime, the Nguyen emperors often took pleasure excursions on the Perfume river. The emperor's dragon boat must have been quite a majestic and impressive floating palace – pulled by six to eight boats, each manned by fifty to sixty oarsmen.

In the hot days of summer, the emperor and his imperial wives often bathed in the Perfume river – fully dressed, of course, to prevent curious eyes from prying – off the boat house, Nghinh Luong pavilion, which stood half in the water in front of the Citadel.

Whenever the emperor was resting, five imperial concubines stood by: one cooling him with a fan, one massaging him, one singing him to sleep, one preparing cigarettes and betels to chew and one to await further orders. It is even said that at night certain emperors, in addition to the royal guards (eunuchs, of course), required thirty imperial wives to lie beside the royal bed like guardian angels to watch over his sleep. Well, maybe . . .

Because there were so many imperial wives, each night the emperor ordered the eunuchs to call for only a few of his favourites. Those he favoured most would be called many times. The rest, poor dears, languished. At least once, eunuchs caught two beautiful wives, desperate for affection, making love to one another.

Usually, only daughters of high-ranking mandarin were presented to the emperor and there was an expression in royal Hue, 'taking one's daughter to the Imperial City,' which meant that the girl would never again be allowed to return home to lead a normal life. Once having nominated his daughter to the emperor in the hope of being offered a high position if she became a favourite or queen, a father was never again allowed to cast eyes upon her. He might stand outside in the courtyard where his daughter could see him, but not vice versa. Mothers were sometimes granted compassionate visits for a brief and limited time.

Moreover, the royal wives held ranks, in the first instance dependent upon the mandarin ranks of their fathers, eventually upon length – and presumably, quality – of service and favour. The top ranking wife was considered to be, but might not be named Most Favoured Lady – queen (or empress); there might even be two 'queens', naturally the two top-ranking wives. Since imperial wives numbered from dozens to hundreds, envy and jealousy was rampant amongst them. These conflicts caused many an emperor a headache. Emperor Gia Long often said that he found it easier to rule the country than his wives.

'Whenever I enter the harem, I meet the wicked devils. They quarrel, make violent combat with each other and then come to me to judge. Their cries deafen me.' A list of 'engagements' was carefully kept by the eunuchs to confirm that the children born were those of the emperor. Every morning, wearing loose-fitting robes and headbands, the wives took turns to go to Can Thanh palace to the emperor's private apartment to wish him well. The lives of the wives were full of restrictions. All references to the emperor's activities were described in euphemisms. Wives were forbidden to use 'rude' words such as: ill, blind, lame, death, blood. The taboos were so numerous that often newcomers to the Forbidden Purple City were so afraid of erring that they kept completely silent for the first few months (what bliss for the emperor). If a wife fell ill, she was only allowed to extend an arm wrapped in silk from behind a screen so that the doctor could take her pulse through the silk. No verbal communication was allowed; the doctor was not allowed to see, much less to examine his patient, because once she had joined the royal harem, all contact with men was strictly forbidden. Even the clothes of wives were strictly regulated. In essence, they wore royal uniforms, mostly of coloured fabric, especially red and green. Black was forbidden. Yellow was exclusively reserved for the emperor. Their hair had a regulation parting in the middle and when they wore headbands, their front locks were loosened to form two curves over their brows. Their teeth were lacquered black – then considered a sign of civilised style; white teeth were considered to be vulgar, like an animal. Although the emperor had many wives, not all were beautiful. It is said that some were very ugly indeed. Those who were most beautiful – or who appealed – were most often summoned. The emperor's main wife, ranking highest among the wives, would be crowned queen, but not always immediately. Sometimes she was not named queen until after an emperor's death, then being named queen *mother*, if her son became king. However, if she were designated as Most Favoured Lady, once named, I wonder if she was so imbued in her culture that she took a hundred other wives in her stride with equanimity and understanding, or if she, too, was vexed by jealousy.

Twice during the Nguyen dynasty, the wives were released. The first time was in the sixth year of Minh Mang's reign when the country was struck by drought. The emperor attributed the disaster to the confined sorrows of his wives, so he released a hundred of them to put an end to it. The second time was in 1885, when Hue surrendered to French troops and all of the wives escaped from the Forbidden Purple City. Many returned home to resume normal lives. Even after an emperor's death, his wives were kept secluded for the rest of their lives – within his tomb temple complex – to fulfil worshipful services. Remarriage, of course, was out of the question.

The lot of eunuchs was not much better, considering that it was their job to organise and control up to several hundred gossipy women in the three palaces and six chambers where the wives lived. Scores of eunuchs performed these functions. One of the eunuch's most important tasks was to keep records of the most propitious time for the king to make love, if he wanted an heir from a particular wife and of those with whom he had made love – to assure royal paternity.

There were two kinds of eunuchs: those who were born asexual, having neither the sexual organs of a man nor a woman; and castrated eunuchs, who volunteered to be de-manned in order to be selected to live in the world of beautiful women at the emperor's side. If a natural eunuch were born in a village, his parents had to inform the local authorities, who would report the event to the Ministry of Rites. The Ministry would order the child to be brought up and educated according to the royal rites so that when he was grown, he was brought to the royal court as a eunuch. Such a child was referred to as Mr Ministry and considered to bring good luck, because when such a child was recommended to the palace, his village received three years of tax exemption.

Oddly, in a country where homosexuality is buried deeply in the closet, sometimes two eunuchs were allowed to 'marry' to comfort one another in the sadness of their lonely lives – not a liberty extended to the wives. Eunuchs even raised adopted children to give them joy and heirs in a society where one needed heirs to provide food and ancestral worship after death.

When Nguyen Anh came to the throne as the first Nguyen emperor, Gia Long (1802), a man named Le Van Duyet (1763-1832), a natural eunuch, was appointed as eunuch to the court. Eunuchs, once chosen, served successive emperors. As one of the emperor's inner circle, Le Van Duyet came to be hated in certain court circles. Eunuchs sometimes used their positions in the royal household to create political ferment. In 1836, the second emperor, Minh Mang, proclaimed that eunuchs were to have absolutely no further role in political affairs, that in future they were to be employed only in the 'back palace' occupied by the royal family and henceforth, wives and eunuchs were to be divided into five ranks. A case of divide and rule.

Eunuchs were required to wear a special blue silk *ao dai* with a flower embroidered on the chest, to be easily identified from a distance from other mandarin. They also wore different hats, a kind of black pillbox. Most eunuchs lived in the Forbidden Purple City, but some served the widows after an emperor's death in their mourning and worship in the emperor's tomb complex.

When eunuchs grew old or sick, they had to leave the Forbidden Purple City and reside in the Palace of Eunuchs at the northern corner of the (middle) Imperial City.

They could never be allowed to die in the Forbidden Purple City or within an emperor's tomb complex, the sacred abodes of royalty. In 1843, they were allowed to establish a monastery near Tu Duc's tomb, Tu Hien pagoda, where still a community of monks live in tranquil grounds surrounding a courtyard of orchids and a century-old star fruit vine – honouring the former royal eunuchs.

TO THE SACRED URNS

One must raise children to understand one's parents
— Vietnamese proverb

Hue's Citadel is far too expansive to see and easily assimilate in a day. It must be remembered that between sixty and eighty thousand people lived within the city walls of the Citadel. Even the (middle) Imperial City and the Forbidden Purple City are spread over a fairly vast area. So I nibble and savour rather than trying to gulp it all down in one exhausting feast.

Off both sides of the central axis of the Imperial City stand some of the most historically significant and impressive royal buildings. Off to the left from the courtyard at the back of the Palace of Supreme Harmony, the throne palace (Thai Hoa), I pass beneath another bronze pole gate and stroll down a leafy, walled lane.

Past a very welcome refreshment pavilion, some way along on the walkway on the right, behind a mysterious, three-entrance gate and a protective screen, lurk the raised foundations, all that remain of Phung Tien temple. Curiously, its sole purpose was to honour Nguyen emperors and their empresses from Gia Long to Khai Dinh – on their birthdays and on their death anniversaries – ceremonies that female members of the royal family were permitted to attend. Built in 1814, the temple was destroyed in 1947.

A few steps further on the left, a somewhat insignificant, narrow doorway through the wall leads to three truly important, historic, renovated temples. The terracotta tile path passes bonsai after bonsai and numerous mini-rock gardens.

The first temple, Hung To Mieu, was built in 1804 by the first Nguyen emperor, Gia Long, rather touchingly, to honour his parents. The stories of court intrigue extend right back to the time of the Nguyen lords, long before they became emperors. Gia Long's father, Nguyen Phuc Thuan, had been cheated out of the succession to the Nguyen lordship (governorship) by a conniving mandarin, who had favoured his uncle – the same mandarin who had raised taxes so high that the Tay Son brothers rebelled and massacred the Nguyen clan, sending young Nguyen Anh fleeing to Ha Tien, where he accepted aid from the French priest.

So only naturally, after twenty-five long years of military struggle, as a good Confucian, having finally gained power, one of Nguyen Anh's (Emperor Gia Long's) first acts was to build a memorial temple to commemorate both of his parents. It had been recently restored when I first visited. Now, years later, its gleaming red lacquer has mellowed.

Next door to Hung To Mieu Temple is the almost identical The To Mieu Temple, constructed during the reign of the second Nguyen emperor, Minh Mang, in 1821-1822, and dedicated to all of the Nguyen emperors – keeping in mind that at the time, there had been only two Nguyen emperors – Gia Long and himself!

Under French domination (1884 to 1954), only seven emperors were honoured in The To Mieu temple: Gia Long, Minh Mang, Thieu Tri, Tu Duc, Kien Phuoc, Dong Khanh and Khai Dinh. The three anti-French emperors – Ham Nghi, Thanh Thai and Duy Tan – were excluded until 1959, after the French had left. I walk along the row of red lacquer and gilt altars, each dedicated to a Nguyen emperor, where when possible, a framed photograph is displayed – making one realise with a slight shock just how recently feudalism in Vietnam existed.

First in the line of altars is that of emperor Duy Tan, (whose ceremony the Frenchman described), eleventh to reign and the third from last emperor. He stares from a ghostly, black-and-white photograph, his young, royal face looking somewhat overwhelmed. Not surprisingly, as he was only eight when he was crowned. Duy Tan and his father, the tenth emperor, Thanh Thai, (Bao Hien's uncle and grandfather, respectively), were both exiled by the French to the island of Reunion.

The second altar displays a photo of the rather full-faced Khai Dinh, the penultimate emperor, the gay husband of Tu Cung, the queen mother served by the old manservant, Pham Van Thiet.

At the third altar, poor Emperor Kien Phuc has neither commemorative photo nor portrait. Crowned at thirteen, he occupied the throne for only eight months before he died – not from smallpox as Bao Hien had said – but of the poison administered to him by an angry mandarin, Nguyen Van Tuong, who the young emperor had discovered in an illicit love affair with one of the widows of Emperor Tu Duc, who was caring for him in his illness.

Nor does Thieu Tri, remembered as the poet king and honoured at the fourth altar, have either a photo or a portrait. The third Nguyen emperor, son of Minh Mang, built the tower at Thien Mu pagoda and composed the book of poems describing his favourite Hue beauty spots, now mostly destroyed, apart from the Perfume River and Thien Mu pagoda. He also built the beautiful Long An palace that houses the Hue Museum of Ancient Objects.

The first Nguyen emperor, Gia Long, is commemorated in the centre of the temple with a painted portrait, wearing what one might assume to be a 'working crown', a tight-fitting hat with a high gilt topknot. At the next altar dedicated to his son, the second emperor, Minh Mang, there is also a painted portrait, wearing a similar 'working crown', with what look like two topknots, perhaps to indicate that he was the second Nguyen emperor?

Dong Khanh, Tu Duc's second adopted son, who so yearned to become emperor that he sent his mother to Hon Chen Temple to ask the goddess when he would be crowned, sits on the throne in his photo, at last, looking immensely pleased. However, the reign of this rather vain, wine and perfume-loving emperor was to last only three years before he died at the age of twenty-three, of what is described as a brain disease.

At the next altar is a photograph of Ham Nghi, a portrait in profile with a faint moustache. No doubt his young shoulders were weighed down by the sad affairs of state. Having attained the throne at only fourteen, two mandarin regents mounted a rebellion against the French in his name, and when it failed and the Citadel and much of the city were burnt (1885), he was forced to flee with them to the mountains to rally resistance against the French, taking much of the royal court with him. After a short time, the queen mother and her retinue returned to Hue. After all, what use was a bunch of women in resisting the French?

It is said that Ham Nghi's brother, Dong Khanh, came to the mountains to try to convince him to return, but that Ham Nghi obdurately refused to see him. Or did the ruling mandarin prevent them from meeting? During his absence, Dong Khanh was crowned emperor – so there were two emperors simultaneously for a time. Finally, three years after fleeing, Ham Nghi was captured in the mountains by the French, betrayed by one of his own men and exiled to Algiers.

Thanh Thai, the tenth emperor (Bao Hien's grandfather) was only eleven when he was crowned. The portrait is of a handsome lad wearing what looks rather like a military hat. During his reign (1889-

1907), he founded Quoc Hoc high school, which is still educating Hue's youth. Son of the short-reigning Duc Duc, imprisoned and starved to death, Thanh Thai was removed from the throne by the French, who put it about that he was feeble-minded – but not so feeble-minded that they were so wary of him that both he and his son, Duy Tan, were exiled to the far away island of Reunion. Thanh Thai was only allowed to return to Vietnam in his very old age, and then only to Vung Tau, south of Saigon – not to Hue until he was on the brink of dying.

Leaving Hung To Mieu temple and crossing the blazingly sunny courtyard, the tower of Hien Lam Pavilion rises thirty-nine feet (12 m), the height of its second-storey tower marking the upper limit for any building within the Citadel. It is dedicated to all of the civil and military mandarin, who have supported the Nguyen dynasty throughout their reign.

Oddly, it had been a photograph of the nine sacred dynastic urns in front of Hien Lam pavilion that first tweaked my curiosity about Vietnam. Those immense bronze urns, head-high on their sturdy legs, looked so forbidding, so alien, so eternal. To what purpose? Strange, how a photograph can niggle at the mind. That was long before the days of Google, and it was years before I actually laid eyes on them. The much-photographed line of nine imperial urns still stands tall in front of Hien Lam pavilion.

The casting of each urn (1835-1837), dedicated to the emperors of the Nguyen dynasty, required approximately two tonnes of bronze at a time when melting pots held just over a pound of molten liquid. A good many melting pots were therefore needed to produce the necessary quantity of liquid to cast one of these urns. Each melting pot required two craftsmen, one to operate the bellows by hand, the other to supply the fuel and metal. To heat so many pots to exactly the proper melting point simultaneously must have been a delicate task. Modern moulders think it likely that the mould for an urn was turned upside down and the molten bronze poured through the openings for the three slender feet.

Casting of the urns was ordered by Emperor Minh Mang, whose remarks at the time were recorded: 'Now the carvings of the nine dynastic urns are being done, and though they have not been finished, when coming there in my leisure time to see how the people are working, I see that the urns are being prepared with great dexterity quite worth praising. Therefore, among the goldsmiths

91

working, those who are the original members of the handicraft unit who came from the region of Binh Dinh to Thua Thien province are to be rewarded one *quan*. The remainder called up by the provinces as supplementary personnel for the unit are to be rewarded two *quan* in the case of those who came from Ha Tinh or Nghe An, and three *quan* in the case of those who came from Ha Noi.'

Today no one seems to know the contemporary value then represented by a *quan*.

The decoration around the sides of the urns – bats, tortoises, dragons, cranes, carriages, trees and flowers – were cast separately and riveted to the surface. The idea of casting nine commemorative urns derives from China.

Minh Mang had optimistically – rather as he had built a temple to honour future Nguyen rulers – named each of the nine urns in advance, so that the posthumous name of each future Nguyen emperor had to incorporate the name of the urn waiting in turn. For instance, Minh Mang's own urn was named Nhan; therefore his posthumous name became Thai To Nhan Hoang De. Tu Duc's urn was named Anh; his posthumous name became Duc Tong Anh Hoang De.

These days the urns have adapted to political correctness and honour the reunification of Vietnam.

Retracing my steps back along the shady lane towards the Palace of Supreme Harmony and turning left at the first junction, I follow the signs to Dien Tho, residence of the queen mothers.

At one time it was a complex of ten wooden buildings, built in 1804. A roofed corridor connected them to the Forbidden Purple City. The original residence, Trinh Minh palace, built for the queen mother by Minh Mang, was replaced in 1927 by a palace, which was used as a medical clinic for the Empress Thanh Cung, Dong Khanh's first wife, in her later years.

But in 1950, it was completely rebuilt and renovated to become the last emperor, Bao Dai's private residence, the villa we see today. It was partially restored 1998-2001.

The gate to the queen mothers' quarters, fittingly, is painted with a colourful phoenix, symbol of the queen mothers and queens. A wide screen with painted enamel panels protects the villa from view. Layered bonsai stand formally along the edge of the paved courtyard beside the European-style villa, a covered veranda on the ground floor, open terraces surrounding the building on the second floor.

Snarling dragon bannisters guard the stairs. Pillars supporting the square porch are decorated with ceramic mosaics. Inside, the walls are hung with old photos of the royal family: the last Emperor Bao Dai's empress, Nam Phuong, who he met on board ship returning from France, photographed with their small children; a photo of her in a rickshaw in front of this very villa; and another taken in her court robes in a rickshaw on her wedding day in 1934.

On the side wall hangs a photo of the Queen Mother Tu Minh, Emperor Thanh Thai's mother, whose rickshaw was recently purchased at auction in France. Unfortunately, the photo is not of her in the rickshaw. And there is a photo of the interior of this very palace with its formal furnishings, taken in the early twentieth century.

A little further on is a blurry photo of the queen mother, Lady Tu Cung, wife of the Emperor Khai Dinh and mother of Bao Dai, who was put through such an ordeal to make her confess that Khai Dinh was not the father of her child.

On the back wall hangs a photo of Lady Nguyen Huu Thi Nhan, the official wife of Emperor Dong Khanh – by my reckoning, one of his two wives who beat Tu Cung to make her tell the truth about who had made her pregnant. A bit further along is a better photo of Tu Cung, mother of Bao Dai, here giving her full name and regal titles: Queen Nung, Queen Mother Doan Huy Hoang Thi Cuc.

I leave the villa in the footsteps of the queen mothers and walk beneath a covered corridor around the courtyard to Cung Dien Tho, a long, low traditional palace, where a black lacquer and gilt rectangular table and stiff square chairs await a queen mother's tea party, or perhaps a game in the evening.

Several of the Emperor Thieu Tri's commissioned paintings on glass of his favourite scenes in the Forbidden Purple City hang attached to the beams above. Parallel sentences, gilt on red lacquer, embellish nearly every pillar. Some of the objects are original, from the time of Cu Tung, some are replicas – I wonder which. This was, indeed, the queen mother's tea house, a very large tea house, but then, it served two purposes. As well as serving as a tea house, former queen mothers were worshipped at the back altar, so it also served as a temple (built 1804, restored 2002).

Continuing my meander through history along a covered, half-open corridor through a series of red lacquer and gilt doors, the recently purchased rickshaw stands in silhouette at the end of the corridor, inside Ta Tra palace. Also a long, low traditional building, facing the queen mother's villa, Ta Tra palace was used as a waiting hall for those granted an audience with the queen mother. Damaged in the Vietnam War in 1968 and again by a typhoon in 1985, it has now been completely restored.

Turning right again – it begins to feel like a maze – I find myself in a courtyard with an ornamental pond where two huge rock gardens loom up out of the water. Continuing straight ahead under the covered corridor, through yet another open door, along another corridor I come upon a display of photos of rickshaws, which first appeared in Hanoi in 1883, having been invented in Japan in 1868. The later cyclo, short for the French, *cyclo-pousse,* (a chair on wheels with a bicycle behind to push it), didn't appear until the 1940s.

Here is a photo of the Emperor Bao Dai on his palanquin en route to his wedding in 1934, and another photo of him in his palanquin at his coronation in 1926. So while Europe was puttering around in motor cars, on the far side of the world, Vietnamese emperors were still being carried about on palanquins. Here is a photo of the crown prince, Bao Dai's son, Bao Long, this time in a rickshaw at the time of his investiture in 1939 – and a photo of a line-up of rickshaws for tourists in the early twentieth century. Cyclos still wait every morning outside my hotel. At least, they use peddle-power.

Looking back, I note that all of the queen mothers' palaces have yellow tiled roofs. So not only the emperor had the privilege of yellow tiles.

I retrace my steps and turn right to visit the pretty lake pavilion I had earlier passed by. Called Truong Du and built in 1849, the pavilion, fittingly, is now a cafe. The pavilion looks out over a pond, containing not one, but two impressive rock gardens – if you couldn't get out into the countryside, the country could come to you. Turning to leave, beautifully carved, dark wooden filigree forms a screen around the doorway and above, delicate inlaid mother-of-pearl tableaux decorate the pediment beneath the rafters. What a beautifully crafted building, facing its small pond, another architectural gem.

Leaving from the far end of Ta Tra palace (the queen mother's waiting room), I notice a door to yet another covered corridor, around three sides of the vast grassy field where the emperors' residential palaces and those of his concubines once stood. The panelled walls of the corridors display enlarged replicas of Nguyen dynasty records, listed in 2013 by UNESCO as 'Documentary Heritage belonging to the programme of the World Memory of the Asia-Pacific Region.'

In the first half of the nineteenth century, under the reigns of Gia Long, Minh Mang, Thieu Tri and Tu Duc, imperial records were written in Sino-Vietnamese, *chu nom* (Chinese) ideograms. In the late Nguyen dynasty, during the latter nineteenth and early twentieth century, they were mainly written in French and the romanized version of Vietnamese, *quoc ngu.*

The earliest, written in the old *chu nom* script, have been translated into romanized *quoc ngu* Vietnamese, as well as into English and French. Here, official Nguyen documents affirm the country's sovereignty over seas and islands and set out to prove that the two contested groups of islands, the Paracel (Hoang Sa) and Spratly (Truong Sa) Islands, have been under Vietnamese sovereignty for some considerable time.

The earliest Vietnamese maps, a map of Ly Thanh Tong dated 1490, and a map compiled by Do Ba Cong Dao in 1686, show Hoang Sa (the Paracels), expressed as Golden Sands in the old *chu nom* script under the name of Ba Cat Vang.

The documents explain that from the seventeenth to the nineteenth centuries, Vietnam's feudal dynasties claimed sovereignty over the Hoang Sa and Truong Sa islands. Furthermore, under the early Nguyen lords (governors), teams of mandarin and soldiers took part in managing and exploiting these islands. As acknowledgement, presumably of the hardship of living away from their families, those who worked on the islands were exempt from taxes and entitled to 'special treatment regime of the court.'

The documents go on to explain that their task was to salvage whatever they could from ship wrecks, to exploit rare sea products: sea turtles, dolphins, six types of rare fish. Later documents show that throughout the Nguyen dynasty, Vietnamese children were taught in schools that the Paracel and Spratly Islands belonged to Vietnam. The records could hardly be more explicit.

Unfortunately, Vietnam's age-old enemy, their mammoth, encroaching neighbour to the north, clearly has other ideas.

A little further along is mention of the Haimond Treaty, signed with the French in 1880, and the later death knell of feudal Vietnam, the Paternôtre Treaty, signed in 1884, that made Vietnam a Protectorate of France

ROYAL THEATRE AND GARDENS

Royal edicts yield to village customs
– Vietnamese proverb

Two of the most delightful buildings and imperial gardens lie to the east of the Citadel's central axis. From the steps behind the throne palace, the Palace of Supreme Harmony (Thai Hoa Palace), crossing the courtyard diagonally to the right, I find myself under a recently rebuilt, red lacquer and gilt, covered corridor. At the first corner, an open doorway to a terracotta path leads to Duyet Thi Duong theatre, one of the most splendid, fairly recently renovated and rebuilt buildings, and admittedly, my favourite. Inside, its red lacquered pillars are alive with dragons and gilt clouds. This is how palaces must have looked when they were new.

In former days, a long, covered corridor connected the Duyet Thi Duong theatre in the east to Dien Tho, the queen mother's palaces in the west. Using this covered corridor, the royal family could visit the queen mother or stroll to a performance in the Duyet Thi Duong theatre, sheltered from the monsoon rain or the blazing sun.

The two-storey Duyet Thi Duong theatre was built by the second emperor, Minh Mang, in the seventh year of his reign (1826), reflecting the importance in which the Nguyen emperors and before them, the Nguyen lords, held the performing arts. It is the oldest traditional theatre remaining in Vietnam and two parallel sentences composed by Minh Mang himself express his feelings towards music:

Music is composed not only to harmonize the mind,
but it must also foster the will
Everything is done not only to support the right,
but also to stop the wrong.

The rectangular theatre is a warm riot of red lacquer, red pillars, red carpeting and red chairs. A red demon head in a halo of wavy clouds screams from the flamboyant red lacquer screen at the centre of the stage. The red carpeted stage is only two steps above the

96

seating. Across the back of the stage, two stairways from either side meet at a small, high, central platform, their bannisters rippling with ceramic mosaic dragons, gazing at the moon – or sun – in the centre.

White, diamond-shaped, paper lanterns dangle like beads from the ceiling along both sides and above the back of the stage. Painted bamboo screens hang in front of the upper balconies, running along both sides of the theatre. Royal wives and concubines would have been sequestered behind these screens, through which they could view the performance without themselves being seen by the mandarin and foreign guests.

From the theatre I walk back to the covered corridor and turn right, strolling along the covered corridor through a series of red lacquer and gilt doors to the emperor's former private library and study, Thai Binh pavilion (on the right). Approaching the library, the path passes alongside an ornamental pond in the middle of which rises an immense Vietnamese rock garden – huge craggy rocks, mini-mountains, planted with ornamental trees, a trick of perspective viewed from the pavilion, a miniature landscape.

Thai Binh pavilion was built by Minh Mang and rebuilt later by Emperor Khai Dinh. It has been recently restored. Approaching from the rock garden, it feels like a closed sanctum within a sanctum. Dark wooden doors to a passage within surround the square building. Inside, another layer of doors prevents the visitor from reaching the interior. Then surprisingly, walking around the building, the east side of the pavilion stands completely open, revealing a low, red lacquer and gilt dais, upon which the emperor would have sat cross-legged to read or write at a tilted lectern, contemplating the graceful tendrils of painted plants adorning the outer pillars and the amazing topiary dragons guarding the eastern courtyard.

Leaving through the courtyard and turning left, then right, brings me to the entrance of Vuon Co Ha gardens. A hedge 'screen' has been planted to mimic the wall screens that block the view from the entrance of many royal palaces, this one artfully trimmed to form lotus buds at the top of each side of the hedge. It is a masterpiece of extraordinarily delicate topiary: topiary cranes stand on the backs of topiary turtles, facing a sacred topiary urn, the urn standing on spindly, topiary legs – all grown in low pots.

More shallow containers hold bonsai, spaced along the path leading to a pavilion, jutting out into an ornamental lake. All is plucked, pruned, trimmed, shaped, tweaked, trained, tempered and arranged. An enchanted imperial garden. Low hedgerows edge the path that emperors walked with their queens and concubines, like me, seeking a breath of cool air in the heat. How many gardeners must there have been in Tu Duc's time? And how many now?

One can only imagine the thoughts of Citadel restorers, faced with rebuilding their ruined palaces at the end of three wars. When they had no money to rebuild, they must have replanted – and such splendid results. As I gaze out from the open lake pavilion, gardeners stand at work in the shallow lake, dead-leafing lotus plants.

In Buddhism, the ubiquitous lotus represents purity, fidelity, compassion, wisdom and enlightenment. A recent exhibition on the theme of the lotus's significance in Vietnam's culture at the Hanoi History Museum explained: 'The lotus is symbolic of transparency in the Vietnamese culture.'

Albeit fascinating, I have never found Vietnamese culture in the least bit transparent. 'It also represents the refined and unyielding spirit of the Vietnamese people' – as in, it is very difficult to break a lotus stem, a fact well known by Vietnamese people.

Suddenly, I recall an essay written by Hanoi scholar, Huu Ngoc, explaining the varieties of love in Vietnam. He quoted a passage from Nguyen Du's epic poem, *The Tale of Kieu,* describing the tenacious tendrils of love, whatever may happen later in life . . .

> *Our love is lost and it is bitterly regretted*
> *But our hearts, like a broken lotus stem,*
> *remain bound by the straggling filaments.*

Lotus buds and petals appear on teacups and teapots, plates, bowls, lidded boxes, censors, sword hilts, candle sticks, pillar bases, furniture, an elegant silver Nguyen bowl around which a lotus vine and pod are wrapped, lotus petals around the mouths of wells, statues holding lotus buds, particularly statues of Buddha, who often sits upon a lotus, and most recently, I have just read that the seats on Hanoi's new urban transport train will be in the shape of lotuses!

Dating from considerably earlier than the Nguyen dynasty, another recent exhibition displayed a splendid Cham 'hat' – it must have been a crown – made of carefully lined-up lotus petals above a head band – made of solid gold. The lotus symbol goes back at least two thousand years. Inside the lake pavilion is a helpful sign in Vietnamese, French and English, describing a game much enjoyed by the emperors, particularly at *Tet*, the Vietnamese New Year. Called Bai Vu, the game was played with one 'roller', presumably, one dice, carrying the pictures of eight animals. The board had eight animals. At each turn, a player would select a box (with an animal on it) and place a card on it. The 'games person' would use a plate upside down to rotate the bowl, presumably, to shake the single dice. 'Face up' on the side of the roller (dice) won. 'The game moved very fast, only three to five minutes from the time the players placed their cards, until the games person gave the card to the winner and losers card collection.' The full name of the game was Tro Cho'I Bai Vu.

I sit for a time staring at the peaceful lake, enjoying the tranquillity. A curved, red bamboo bridge beckons. I skirt round the square lake and over the bridge. To the left is a small brick ruin. What was it, I wonder? Beyond lies a larger lake, the lake of the Serene Heart (Ho Tinh Tam), its banks feathered with a grove of fine-leafed bamboo. Potted bonsai on each side of the gravel path lead to another open lake pavilion, surrounded by pink, petunia-like flowers and red and yellow hibiscus. The pavilion extends out into the lake, facing a thickly forested, artificial, mini-mountain of an island. All is quiet, not another soul about.

On leaving the pavilion I notice a tiny ceramic figure the size of a finger, sitting amongst the roots of a bonsai beside the steps – an entire, miniature world in one bonsai.

The path leads to another lake pavilion with tables and chairs and a cool drinks machine. I sit with an iced lemonade – 'Please buy, we go' – as the waitresses depart for lunch, leaving me to a solitary emperor's view from his lake front pavilion.

ROYAL TOMBS

Living, each has his house
Dead, each has his tomb
– Vietnamese proverb

On my first visit to Hue, I took a dragon boat along the Perfume river, upriver to the royal tombs, and you still can. To book the boat tour for the following morning, I took a cyclo to where the dragon boats moor just downstream from Tuong Tien bridge The cyclo was a giant step forward from the palanquin. A collapsible cloth cover protects the passenger from sun or rain; if it rains, the driver wears a mac. Given the lithe stature of the Vietnamese, it is not unusual to see two women sitting side by side in a cyclo and often, the chair is piled high with a couple of children or produce.

Westerners sometimes object to taking cyclos, having sensitive scruples about being pushed around by the muscle-power of another human being. Long ago, I came to the conclusion that it is far better to leave one's Western values at home and abide by local customs. In Vietnam, one of the ways men have to earn a living is by peddling cyclos. To refuse to take cyclos is therefore to deprive them of earnings. So until cyclos are replaced by taxis, I take cyclos.

The boat was perhaps thirty feet long with an engine in the middle and another smaller area astern that doubled as a galley. A striped, straw mat covered the plank deck and a cheerful floral cotton cloth hid the under side of the straw roof. Aboard were three young French tourists, a Japanese girl and me. With four plastic chairs for the five of us, we took turns sitting on the mat. A youngish Vietnamese couple ran the boat. The woman's first task was to set out wordlessly, a crowd of small metal figurines in front of each of us in turn: a bronze fisherman, a women carrying baskets from a shoulder pole, a buffalo, a Buddha. It didn't take long to realise that this was a one-to-one sales tactic aimed at a totally captive audience, cunningly based on embarrassing each individual into buying without much bargaining. After the statues, she tried paintings. Hard-nosed, sales resistant lot that we were, no one succumbed to purchase.

Not ten minutes out, we drew up to a floating mid-river platform and it took a few uneasy minutes to realize that we were merely refuelling and not about to be handed over to the river police as punishment for not buying souvenirs.

My first visit to Thien Mu pagoda had been one of the reasons for my return to Vietnam. On this, my second visit, the Emperor Thieu Tri's seven-tiered tower, Thap Phuoc Duyen, stood like a sentinel at the entrance. It is an especially lovely way to approach Thien Mu – by boat from the Perfume river. A pony-tailed backpacker ambled past, wearing a T-shirt reading: 'Christianity is nutty' – very appropriate for pagoda viewing, especially in Hue where Christians were persecuted by the early Nguyen emperors. A tiny Vietnamese doll in a frilly pink dress and button-strap shoes skipped amongst the monks' bonsai pots in the wide courtyard.

More recently, I have visited Thien Mu in the late afternoon, when the sun seared the edges of the billowing clouds reflected in the Perfume river, which had turned to silver. Four o'clock is ideal, the time for evening prayers. Behind the fat, laughing, brass Buddha in a glass case, who seems to be scratching his ear with one hand and amiably holding out his other hand for alms, a monk in saffron chanted as he knelt before the altar, striking a small gong. On either side of him a young monk, head shaved, but for the tonsure of hair that hung over his brow, sang in falsetto unison as they struck a wooden knocker *(mo)* and the gong.

Regarding their devotions was a group of Japanese tourists. Behind the altar sat the statue of a huge Buddha, watched over from behind by a higher trilogy of Buddhas of past, present and future, their heads illuminated by back-lit haloes, the gloom of the pagoda just managing to prevent them from looking garish.

Back on board the boat, ice cold tinned drinks with straws were handed round from a cold box by a young boy, who to our astonishment, said he was fourteen and that his wee sister was seven. The Vietnamese, man, woman and child, always look much younger than they are – until old age finally hits them. The noisy engine – so much for the romance of dragon boats – moved us up river past slim, canoe-sized sampans, each with a woman overboard, heaving baskets of sand into the boat. Were they dredging the river or were they going to sell the sand? The answer was both. Later we saw boats where women were lifting coarse gravel by the same method. I spied a thatch-roofed junk with a TV aerial.

101

Along the river bank stood thatched, wooden houses in vegetable plots of corn stalks and neat rows of pepper vine pyramids. Fish traps pricked the river's surface. Higher up the hillside, white headstones of cemetery after cemetery studded the crests of hillsides along the western shore. Many died in Hue in that early resistance against the French, later during bombings in the Second World War, and still later, during the French Indo-Chinese War, and later still, during the Tet Offensive (1968) of the Vietnam War.

On the next leg of the voyage, a new, clean mat was laid on the deck and bowls, plates and chopsticks were set out along with chopped cabbage, soup, rice, fish and boiled greens. Lunch in Vietnam is early, at eleven or eleven-thirty, quite reasonable if you have had breakfast just after six. Also, it is clever to cook before the worst heat of the day. The lunch was delicious, but how on earth had she produced it on one clay pot charcoal 'burner'?

Unlike anything resembling a tomb in the west, the tomb of a Nguyen emperor covers many acres and is a modest replica of an imperial palace complex. In fact, they were designed to be exactly that, an emperor's imperial living quarters in the next world. Naturally then, it had to include all of the majestic accoutrements and mod cons of the emperor's living world at that time. The tomb of the penultimate emperor, Khai Dinh, was built between 1920 and 1931. The Vietnamese like it least of all the royal tombs for departing from pure indigenous architecture. It has been under-whelmingly described as a synthesis of Vietnamese and European elements.

The worst of it was, to get there you had to entrust your precious body to the back seat of a stranger's motorbike and take a very bumpy dirt track uphill. We were told that the tomb was more than three miles (6 km) away, not a distance to be undertaken lightly, walking in the heat of the day. (These days there are numerous bus tours to the tombs that drop you at the entrances.)

Having heard the story of Khai Dinh's widow, the Queen Mother Tu Cong, I was eager to visit her husband's tomb. Khai Dinh, who reigned from 1916 to 1925, had adopted the western habit of living in the same new 'palace' as his wife. Actually, it was the Western-style villa at the far end of the central axis of the Citadel, where now, only the steps remain, leading to nowhere – the villa where the old servant, Pham Van Thiet, had come to serve the queen mother as a young boy.

102

Khai Dinh's tomb looks like something Hollywood might have turned out for a B-movie. Steep steps between four heavy stone dragon handrails lead to an oriental gate, the openings barred by very French wrought iron gates. The ostentation starts here. But for the oriental ornamentation of the pillars, it might be a gate to a chateau.

The Honour Court is well-peopled by a double chorus line of stone mandarin, horses and elephants, left and right. Plopped at either end of this stone throng is a chunky obelisk, placed off-centre in a very unbalanced, un-Confucian manner. Clearly Khai Dinh had visions of European-style grandeur. The stele pavilion – charitably, it looks like moulded plaster, less charitably, like fibreglass – has been painted to look like bronze. Grotesque dragons with bulging eyeballs glare from the deep-relief pillars, looking simultaneously both mad and comic, thus setting the tone for what is to come. A steep flight of steps leads to the first terrace, then another equally steep flight of steps leads to a second terrace. Khai Dinh clearly wanted visitors to his tomb to know that he was high and mighty – literally – at least at the end, though in reality he was no more than a French puppet. Finally, at the top of the third flight of steps, one arrives rather breathlessly at a terrace facing an odd pastiche of a temple.

The facade of the long, low building facing the courtyard has moulded plaster pillars decorated with deep relief dragons. So far, more or less Vietnamese. The arched openings – the arch does not appear in Vietnamese architecture except in gates – might have been the French doors opening onto a chateau terrace or a park. Their art deco-ish coloured glass is protected by very ordinary looking, curly wrought iron, the sort that might protect the windows of a basement flat in London. I can appreciate that they might need protecting.

The exterior walls of the temple are covered with *bas relief* oriental motifs in plaster, the motif turned diagonally as a fabric designer might use written words in the abstract. Accustomed to seeing temples where every detail has been exactly duplicated to balance and every architectural line is on the square, this diagonal motif looks askew. As a saving grace, these walls are painted white. Already one can begin to see what the magnificently weird Cao Dai cathedral near Ho Chi Minh City was derived from. This temple is an addled, mad-cap mixture of cultures, of Asian tradition and European modernity, as conceived through the oriental eyes of a bedazzled emperor meeting the West for the first time and taking a few tricks home with him.

Inside, the walls of the entrance hall are painted in a *trompe l'oeil* marble effect, perhaps borrowed from a French provincial church; the floors are of modern grey institutional composite marble tiles. So far, subdued. But in the main room of the temple, every surface inch of wall, pillars and head-high altar is encrusted with coloured glass and ceramic mosaic panels, representing scenes of oriental splendour. It made me think of those little houses made of shells sold as souvenirs at the English seaside. Except that this is a grand-scale, walk-in model.

Behind the enormous altar, a life-sized, gold-painted statue of the last-but-one emperor sits on a throne beneath a threateningly heavy canopy. This whole assemblage, seen after a succession of now, seemingly sober, wooden temple interiors with delicately carved, painted and gilt columns, jars the sensibility silly. Khai Dinh probably would have thought it absolutely splendid.

On the west bank of the river, seven miles (12 km) south-east of Hue, the tomb of Minh Mang, the second emperor, is the most classical, grand and stately of the tombs. Here the local women had discovered that tourists simply could not resist the photo opportunity of snapping a baby sitting in a basket dangling from a carrying pole. One woman, who had two babies on offer, one in each basket, rather hoped for double the tip from any passing photographer.

Nearing the tomb complex, one side of the sky turned bruise blue, a wind came up and it began to thunder. The disappearance of the sun and the cooling breeze were welcome. I couldn't help thinking how welcome that breeze would have been to the nearly 10,000 craftsmen and soldiers, forced to work in such difficult conditions to build the tomb in 1841. Three thousand of them contracted dysentery and died. Minh Mang, son of Gia Long, was arguably the greatest emperor. After three hundred years of intermittent civil war, his father, Gia Long, had finally succeeded in defeating the Trinh and unifying the nation. It fell to Minh Mang to rebuild it. During his reign, Vietnam flourished, the times were prosperous and relatively peaceful, apart from the Catholic uprising in the South, a rare occurrence in Vietnam's two thousand years of tumultuous history.

Minh Mang stabilised the recently united country by reorganising local and regional administration and called for the first palace examinations since those held under the Le dynasty of Hanoi in order to appoint able and qualified men to the mandarinate.

Those who passed the examinations, before taking office, were commended by Minh Mang to consider: 'In guiding the masses, first of all, one has to love his people, has to discriminate good persons and bad, has to approach state affairs impartially, judge and decide as it should be. If the clerk acts right within his function, the people will be at peace. Moreover, to make policies one must now be flexible, now firm, depending upon circumstances. It is no policy at all if you impose your authority uselessly or grant favours without consequences. Consider it for yourself carefully.'

Minh Mang was also a great builder, ordering the construction of the major part of the Citadel. Consequently, he was a strong supporter of handicrafts and the arts. The performing arts also thrived during his reign. Classical opera, royal music and other theatrical genres, singing and dancing were encouraged on a large scale. He ordered the building of Duyet Thi theatre in the Forbidden Purple City, as well as a house of worship known as the Peaceful temple (Thanh Binh Tu Duong), to honour the founders of classical drama, *tuong*. Defensively, he restructured the armed forces, extended border areas and established a navy. He also had canals dug and resettled the poor on reclaimed land to build new villages.

Like any monarch, absolute or otherwise, he made mistakes. To him, the war against the invaders (French) – although French adventurers had helped his father to gain power – was linked to his struggle against the Catholic missionaries. Thinking to eliminate the Christian pagans, who honoured an unknown foreign god, having no respect for king and father as the supreme authorities respected by Confucians, he imprisoned and executed priests, thus drawing down upon himself the wrath and vengeance of the French.

It was also Minh Mang who divided the eunuchs into five ranks and restricted their employment exclusively to the back, private royal enclosure, effectively prohibiting them from dabbling in political affairs of court.

Minh Mang was quite the family man, the father of one hundred forty-two children, seventy-eight sons and sixty-four daughters. But it must be understood that by having a large 'harem' of concubines, mostly the daughters of high-ranking mandarin, an emperor built a strong network of loyalty through these close family relationships. In the case of Minh Mang, no one seems to know exactly how many wives and concubines were involved. Some historians venture an estimate of between four and five hundred.

It is said that every night he chose five concubines, one for each two-hour night watch and the saying came into vogue: 'Having relations with five concubines a night and four of them pregnant.'

So much dithering and disagreement went on over the years, while Minh Mang's mandarin tried to agree on the perfect tomb site, that although he made plans for his tomb and its oval wall was finally started during his lifetime, he suddenly fell ill and died in December 1840 at the age of fifty-one, before it was finished. This left his son and successor, Thieu Thi, to oversee most of its building between 1841 and 1843. The tomb construction was a monumental task. Apart from illnesses caused by working so close to the jungle, special troops were required to chase tigers – it took several months to rid the surrounding forests of the beasts.

On completion, Thieu Thi named his father's tomb Hieu Son, the Mountain of Filial Piety. Only then, nearly three years after he had died, could Minh Mang be buried amidst the pomp and ceremony due. Historians say that his corpse was escorted to its final burial position through three gates of an underground tunnel. If so, no one has yet found the entrances to the tunnels.

Minh Mang's tomb laid the template for imperial tomb design: a gateway, sometimes of ornately carved posts connected by enamel friezes; a central paved path leading to a large paved honour courtyard along the sides of which stand stone statues of civil mandarin to one side, military mandarin opposite and the stone horses and elephants intended for the stylish transport of the mandarin in the celestial world. Further on is a lotus pond, a temple dedicated to the emperor and empress, a stele pavilion in which the emperor's achievements were recorded by his successor, and a sepulchre enclosure, often under planted shade trees.

Minh Mang's tomb had all of these features on a grand scale built along a central axis within an oval wall approximately one hundred fifty yards from the Perfume river. From the Honour Courtyard, three carved granite dragon staircases lead up to the level of the Stele pavilion. Up three more terraces, the gate of Glorious Virtue (Cua Hien Duc) leads to the temple of Venerable Benefaction (Sung An), dedicated to the emperor and empress. Inside the temple, a bonsai tree, preserved in red and black lacquer, made me wonder if the emperor did not entirely trust the gardener to look after it following his demise. Or perhaps it was his own favourite bonsai and he wanted it with him in the next world.

When I first visited, Japanese architects and Vietnamese workers were busy reconstructing the two side buildings beyond the main temple, funded by the Japanese Government and the Toyoto Foundation. Beyond, three stone bridges across the lake of Impeccable Clarity lead towards the pavilion of Enlightenment (Minh Lau), up three more terraces that represent humanity at the lowest level, earth at the second, the heavens at the highest. The high and airy Minh Lau pavilion has such an atmosphere of cool tranquillity that it tempts you to linger and linger, looking out over the lake in the shade of this breezy, open temple. What a pity that Minh Mang did not live to enjoy it for a few years before his demise.

A single stone bridge crosses the crescent-shaped lake of the New Moon to the walls of the sacred round enclosure, the emperor's burial mound, a hill covered by murmuring pines, protected by an encircling wall. Breathing in the fresh pine aroma and gazing across the water, it seems an ideal resting place, temporary or eternal.

Once again back on the boat, the young boy and his sister were gleefully bouncing a small red ball to one another, until it bounced down a hole in the deck. While the boy lifted a deck plank to retrieve it, his sister playfully pretended to beat on him while he good-naturedly held her off. I could not help comparing their simple pleasures to the wheedling demands of Western youngsters for expensive computer games. Their next activity involved a tin of foreign coins, which the boy solemnly showed to each of us, presumably collected from previous passengers. Efficient tourists that we were, stripped to bare essentials, not one of us was carrying a single coin from our home countries. Not to be put off, he then asked directly for Vietnamese money – in English.

Nearly everyone's favourite tomb is that of the fourth emperor, Tu Duc, the son and successor to Thieu Tri, who succeeded Minh Mang. From the boat, we climbed aboard the back of motorbikes and bounced up a bumpy, winding path. Tu Duc's reign of thirty-six years from 1847 to 1883 was the longest of any Nguyen emperor. He died at the age of fifty-five, having come to the throne at the age of fifteen. The stories surrounding Tu Duc are legion. Some say he killed his elder brother in order to become emperor. False, say the historians. In fact, his father, Thieu Tri, decided that he should succeed instead of his elder, playboy brother. The elder brother mounted a coup against him, was thrown into prison and hanged himself.

107

Tu Duc is said to have been a short man, measuring only about four feet tall and his court robes in the Hue museum confirm this small stature. His own throne, therefore, was smaller than that of his empress. Childless, despite having one hundred and three wives, it is said that he had probably been rendered sterile by severe smallpox as a child. Tu Duc lived a life of utter luxury. Legend has it that at every meal, fifty chefs were ordered to prepare fifty dishes to be served by fifty servants, from which the emperor would choose. His tea allegedly was made from the dewdrops collected from the leaves of lotus plants.

It may seem an odd thing to say, but fortunately for Tu Duc, he had the pleasure of his tomb set amongst pines and frangipani trees during his lifetime. Tu Duc used his waiting tomb as a country retreat. It is not difficult to imagine the emperor and his colourfully dressed entourage strolling along the winding, tiled path lined with balustrades, beside Luu Khiem lake. I can hardly think of a picturesque scene more evocative of Vietnam's imperial past than the view of the lake pavilion from across the lotus carpeted lake, viewed from the tiny boat landing pavilion (Du Khiem). The emperor used to sit on the terrace of that far pavilion built out over the lake, composing poetry amongst his wives, who entertained him with music and singing.

It took three thousand soldiers and workmen three years to build Tu Duc's tomb (1864 to 1867) in conditions so harsh that the soldier-builders revolted and nearly succeeded in overthrowing the emperor before the plot was discovered and suppressed (1866). His mother, Tu Du, to whom he was deeply devoted, warned him against his luxurious excesses, but he paid no heed. Yet I can forgive an emperor almost anything, who designed such an exquisite retreat and such a romantic as one who could write this lament on the death of one of his favourites:

> *I want to break the mirror that held her face,*
> *I want to touch her clothes to keep her scent*

Through a gate beyond the Honour Courtyard, Hoa Khiem temple was used as a palace by the emperor and the empress, Le Thien Anh, while they lived; this is where they are now worshipped. Behind the palace to the right is Minh Khiem theatre, in such a perfect state that Tu Duc might have just stepped out from a performance, staged by his wives and concubines. Pretty floral patterns decorate the struts supporting the rafters of the roof. This is one of the two oldest classical theatres in Vietnam and it cries out to be used once more for public performances of traditional music, opera and dance.

Facing the Hoa Khiem temple is the palace used by Tu Duc's mother, the queen mother, who he visited every other day of his reign of thirty-six years. His mother, Tu Du, whose proper name was Pham Thi Hang, was the eldest daughter of a mandarin, who had first come to the palace at the age of fourteen to serve the second wife of Emperor Gia Long. When Minh Mang's son, Thieu Tri, took the throne, she was chosen as a concubine for the emperor. Eight years later, he declared her first wife, wanting to give her the title of queen, but unfortunately, Thieu Tri died before his wish could be fulfilled.

The Emperor Tu Duc was very close to his mother, lavishing gifts upon her, which she always placed in the State Treasury saying, 'By the grace of heaven, the earth and the country have become rich, but each thread of silk, each grain of rice has come from the people. Therefore, don't spend so much. Useless spending will bring poverty and unhappiness.' Considering history, it is a pity that Tu Duc did not heed his mother's advice.

Seeming to anticipate the short reign of his adopted son, Duc Duc – whose rule lasted only three days in 1883 – Tu Duc undertook to compose the words for his own memorial stele. On the one hand, it was the largest stone stele in Vietnam and took four years to move from Thanh Hoa, three hundred miles (480 km) to the north, but the inscriptions he drafted were touching. He admitted that he had made many mistakes – it was he who had finally been forced to succumb to French rule and who signed away the sovereignty of Cochin-China, the South, and who granted the French a military land concession in Hanoi. He named his entire tomb complex Khiem, which translates as modest. Despite the location of the sepulchre on the far side of a lake shaped like a half moon, Tu Duc was not actually buried there. To keep his final resting place and his burial treasure safe – from the French? – for his own use in the next world, the real burial spot was kept secret and it is said that every one of the two hundred servants who helped to bury him was beheaded. Historians dispute this story, saying that there is nothing recorded to verify it, pointing out that the Nguyen were strict Confucians, thereby placing great importance on the relationship between king and subjects, father and son, husband

and wife, brothers and friends. Another cruelty that certainly did occur, also the custom, was that all one hundred and three of his 'widows' were forced to live in the tomb complex in order to mourn and carry out worshipful duties to the emperor for the remainder of their lives, some as young as seventeen at the time. Sometimes, it is difficult to remain non-judgemental, even in regard to another culture in another time.

Once again on board the boat, this time turning back towards Hue, the French girl read a novel, *La Morte Double de Linda*. Imagine being bored amidst this enchanting riverscape. The little girl played hopscotch on three deck planks. A rainbow shimmered over the location of the royal tombs. The boatman steered casually with one foot. Tiring of hopscotch, the little girl disappeared, suddenly to reappear, hanging upside down from the roof, giggling through the window of the cabin.

> *A hundred years wear out stone stelae*
> *A thousand years will not change*
> *the judgement of public opinion*
> – Vietnamese proverb

A NEW GARDEN HOUSE

For old bamboo, new growth
– Vietnamese proverb

The brick, temple style entrance gate is finished, but not the paved walk. So for the moment, the entrance is along a narrow, muddy lane along the side wall. Then stepping onto a raised brick path, I enter another world. This new garden house is in Kim Long, slightly upstream from Thien Mu pagoda.

'There are five houses in the complex,' Truong Dinh Ngo explains, greeting me. Ngo is a retired Swiss-Vietnamese banker, who after living in Europe for forty years, has returned to Vietnam to retire with his Hue-born wife, Nguyen Ton Nu Huyen-Camille. She is an artist and a singer, and a member of the former royal family. They first met in Paris when they were young, where she was living with her family, when he travelled to Paris for a conference.

They have only been back in Hue for two months with their container of belongings from Switzerland. Retirement, however, is not something that either Truong Dinh Ngo nor Ton Nu Huyen-Camille does very well. He has formed a joint company, BioFarming Viet, in partnership with a professor from Hue University, to encourage the planting of a short-grain Japanese rice, which they have given the brand name, Hue Number One.

It took six years of research to create. Convincing Hue rice farmers not to use chemicals, pesticides nor herbicides – no 9MO – on the weeds in their paddies is rather an uphill project. The partners are starting to market their product by selling the high quality rice to chefs in five-star hotels. Having convinced the chefs, they then hope to move downmarket to the farmers.

Hue Number One rice has been especially developed to thrive in the tropical Hue climate, one of its advantages being a higher yield. Also, it is more nutritious in iron and vitamins than the locally grown, long-grain rice – with less sugar, and therefore, beneficial to diabetics. Furthermore, it has a shorter growing cycle, maturing for harvest in only eighty-five days, compared to local rice, which requires ninety-five to one hundred days. Truong Dinh Ngo calculates

111

that Hue rice farmers could produce three crops a year instead of two by using the new variety. Moreover, as it is a higher quality rice; it sells for three times the price paid for the local variety.

This sounds like a win-win situation, but no. Farmers and local authorities are reluctant to change. They are doubtful of its advantages. And there are conflicts of interest – the chemical and pesticide sellers. Even though Truong Dinh Ngo's company offers to give the farmers the new seeds and organic fertilizer, and would pay three times the market price for the new short-grain rice over the price of the local rice, still the farmers resist change.

'It is easier to spray than to do weeding. We have to change attitudes. Planting the seedlings is with a machine in straight rows, very deep, so the plants are very strong – in straight rows so a weeding machine can go through and remove the weeds between the rows. It aerates the plants, the rice plants get more air to grow. There are fewer plants, but they yield far more.'

Moreover, there is no need for transplanting, a major step in saving labour.

'The problem is the weeding,' says Truong Dinh Ngo. 'There is not one weeding machine in all of Vietnam,' he tells me with a mixture of astonishment and frustration.

'The weeding machines are made in Japan by Kubota. They use them both in Japan and Korea. And without a weeding machine to dig up the weeds between the rows, the weeding would have to be done by hand. What the farmer does now, he puts a cannister of chemicals or herbicide on his back and sprays. That's lots less work than weeding by hand.'

He leads me along a central path to the bank of the Perfume river. At the river's edge, on both sides of the path, is a small, rectangular paddy of bright green rice.

'Here we grow our own rice,' he says proudly, later showing me two bags of rice. Purple flowers border the path dividing the two paddies – 'Crows flying home,' says Ngo casually, translating the name of the flower. At the lower level is the boat landing. Beneath a ceramic mosaic railing, the insignia BX for Ben Xuan (Spring Shore), the name of their new garden house, serves as a welcome to those arriving from the river.

Turning our backs to the river, the brick path rises from between the paddies, straight to a paved brick, half-moon-shaped courtyard opening out in front of – a palace, a pagoda, a temple?

112

Dragon bannisters on each side of the steps lead to the open side of a wide, low building. Dark wooden pillars rest on stone lotus pedestals. Carved fretwork beneath the beams links the pillars. Along the roof ridge, colourful, floral-decorated, enamel tableaux echo those along the tile roofs of the royal palaces in the Citadel. And above the enamel cornice, chipped ceramic mosaics embellish the ridge line of the building, again, a reflection of the royal palaces.

'This is the theatre,' says Ngo. Inside, the building smells of freshly cut wood. Rows of wooden spindles, high near the ceiling, allow air to circulate. From the ceiling hangs a pretty sunflower lamp, 'designed by Huyen-Camille.' Doors, inlaid with mother-of-pearl, open to a comfortable sitting room backstage for the artists, waiting to appear. A dragon made of broken, blue and white porcelain chips, allows air through an open fretwork window.

'From ship wrecks, there is lots of broken porcelain and they didn't know what to do with it,' says Ngo. 'We use old bricks and old wood, whenever we can. When people tear down a pagoda and replace the pillars with concrete ones, we use the old pillars. But whenever we cannot get enough bricks or wood, we use new.'

The couple are ingenious at re-cycling and re-using old materials – to very stylish effect – to give their buildings a traditional, timeless quality, materials that would otherwise be rubbish.

Ngo tells me that he and his wife built their first house on the site, a holiday home, sixteen years ago. Obtaining permissions to build and the construction of the five buildings in the complex has taken that long. Clearly, they are a couple of very determined, indomitable people. It was not easy to convince the authorities to accept their building plans. 'We explained to them, my wife is from the royal family. We would not wish to do anything that would ruin the traditional style of Hue. We love Hue. My wife is a part of Hue.'

In their new theatre, Ngo and his wife plan to host musical evenings, chamber music, both Western and Vietnamese. As a singer, Huyen-Camille participated in the last two Hue Festivals. 'People can arrive by boat and walk straight up into the theatre.'

He then leads me across an arched brick bridge over a lily pond to a smaller, open building beside the theatre, 'the poetry pavilion. Huyen-Camille designed the intricate pattern of the bricks for the bridge and showed the bricklayers how to lay them.' Purple flowers *(bang lang)* line the curved, raised brick path set in separated blocks 'so the rain water can pass through.'

113

Here, the garden has a young avocado tree, beside newly-planted sunflowers. 'We use old fruit trees,' by which I think he means that they have bought old trees, had them uprooted and moved here, as I have seen in process on several occasions. Ngo names the trees as we pass: pamplemouse *(tranh tra),* lychee, tamarind, mangosteen, bitter apples *(trai vai),* ambarella apple *(coc),* all unknown to me. The purple flowering tree, dropping its petals picturesquely, is the elegant ornamental star gooseberry *(thanh nha, chum ruot).*

Puffy tufts of dark green grass soften a corner beside the path.

'Lemon grass. We plant it everywhere. There were lots of snakes, but snakes don't like lemon grass.'

Looking back towards the brick entrance gate, Ngo explains, 'It's a Zen gate. Can you see the head and shoulders?' And indeed, there is a round head, rounded shoulders and even the knees of a figure sitting cross-legged. Subtle, understated.

In the dining house on the far side of the theatre stand two large hardwood tables, surrounded by chairs and at one end, a tiny high-chair for their grandson, Thi Joa Kim.

'We call him Kim – Sweetheart.' Kim is busy drawing geckos at a small, low table facing an open doorway. Page after page of geckos lie on the black and white tile floor, at least a dozen of them. He counts them proudly in English. He must be about three or four.

Two plump temple dogs *(kylins)* play with 'balls' at the extremities of the ridge line of the kitchen house roof behind, again, built in the style of a temple. 'The globe,' says Huyen-Camille, at last joining us. 'They have an old face, but a young, innocent smile.' She has been rushing around, preparing for a French TV crew.

'They are dancing on the moon,' she explains, and suddenly, I see that the ridge line of the building is indeed curved, a bit like a new moon. Fish leap from the turned-up finials near the eaves – 'happy fish.' Inside is a large, rectangular, modern European kitchen, the cupboards made of beautiful local wood – 'and the oven, still in the packing case.'

Ngo leads me down steep wooden stairs to – surprise – a wine cellar, brick walls lined with two concentric squares of brick wine bins, those nearest the walls not touching, to allow air to circulate. In Hue's warm, humid climate, an air conditioner will control the temperature.

'We will have French and German wines for wine tastings; it will accommodate four thousand bottles.'

He then leads me back upstairs and up more stairs to the roof, surrounded by a rollicking fretwork of low railings covered with broken blue and white ceramic chips.

'The rooftop (pavilion) will be used after dinner, on a moonlight night' – with a glass in hand, gazing out over the garden to the Perfume river and the grassy river banks opposite.

Ngo points to the upper storey of the theatre, next door. 'Above the theatre is the library.'

Back downstairs, Ngo shows me the line drawings carved on the doors of the dining house.

'Do you know the work of Paul Klee? Huyen-Camille drew the designs, then the lines were carved.'

The graceful, stylized designs on each door have a musical theme. On one door is a figure with a pear-shaped lute *(dan ty ba);* another has a woman playing a sixteen-string *dan tranh.* On the opposite side of the building, doors pay tribute to friends in Zurich: a bass viol player, Fumio Shirato; a violinist, Noriko Kakamura and a guitarist, Walter Giger.

'Huyen-Camille also drew the intricate designs for the fretted, wooden shutters of the dining house; then they were cut out by a craftsman. In the Vietnamese alphabet there are twenty-four characters. Huyen-Camille created images with the letters.'

A delicate carpet of tiny yellow flowers spreads in front of the dining house.

'Wild peanut grass. It doesn't produce peanuts, only flowers.'

You have created a paradise here, I say.

'Yes, but we had to go through hell first,' says Ngo ruefully with a chuckle.

PART IV

ROYAL PERFORMING ARTS

TRADITIONAL OPERA AND BALLET

It's easier to speak well than to act well
– Vietnamese proverb

During the year I spent in Vietnam, I had a chance to see a rare performance of the Royal Ballet – courtesy of a group of French tourists for whom the programme had been staged. Performances had to be booked in advance for a sufficient number to cover the costs. Happily, times have changed. At the time, I knew nothing about these colourfully elaborate costumes and synchronized choreographies.

It was much later that I learned that royal court dance in Vietnam originated at least as early as the eleventh century under the Dinh dynasty in the still new Die Viet nation's capital, Hoa Lu, south of present day Hanoi. Court dance evolved through the dynasties and the centuries in the North – Le, Ly, Tran, the later Le and even the revolutionary Tay Son in Hue.

The early Nguyen lords of Hue, long before they became emperors, embraced and supported dance and the performing arts. In Hue, Dao Duy Tu (1572-1634) is considered to be the father of classical dance. The story of his rise from Thanh Hoa province, one hundred-fifty miles (240 km) south of Hanoi, to his position as a mandarin in the Nguyen court reflects the mores of his time.

In 1437, stage performances were so out of favour in the strict Confucian Le court in Thang Long (Hanoi), that the emperor, Le Thai Tong prohibited traditional stage and popular folklore performances on the royal stages, considering them libertine. Performers were regarded to be on a par with burglars and thieves. So no matter how talented, a performer was prohibited from sitting the royal examinations to become a mandarin. Nor could his nor her children – nor grandchildren – sit the exams! What's more, even high ranking mandarin who married singers or stage performers were fined and flogged with a rod seventy times and exiled to remote postings.

116

Even the sons of mandarin who married singing performers were beaten with a rod sixty times and compelled to divorce!

So because his father was an actor, Dao Duy Tu was banned from sitting the official examinations. He therefore offered his services to the second Nguyen lord in the South, Nguyen Phuc Nguyen in 1625. Not only did Dao Duy Tu create a dance troupe, as a mandarin he is also credited with building ramparts and writing a warfare manual.

Starting with the traditional dance forms from Thang Long, taken from folk dance, religious dance and *tuong* (Vietnamese classical opera), Dao Duy Tu formalised contemporary Vietnamese traditional court dance and established a new system of ritual music and court music for the southern court.

He created the Hoa Thanh Thu orchestra and three musical troupes: the first and third squads were musicians, the second did singing and dancing – a total of three hundred sixty artists who performed at sacred ceremonies and for the Nguyen lord's entertainment. During his last nine years, he created a genre of ritual and court music for the southern court, including eleven royal ceremonial dances:

Eight Lines Dance *(Bat dat)*
Six (Times) Offerings Dance *(Luc cung hoa dang)*
Three Star Gods' Wishes for Longevity Dance *(Tam tinh chuc tho)*
Eight Immortal Offerings Longevity Dance *(Bat tien hien tho)*
Four Scrolls Dance *(Trinh tuong tap kanh)*
Dance of the Four Supernatural Creatures: Dragon, Kylin, Turtle,
        Phoenix *(Tu Linh)*
Departure of the Women Warriors Dance *(Nu tuong xuat quan)*
Fan Dance *(Vu phien)*
Three Kingdoms and Travel to the West Dance *(Tam quoc tay du)*
Horse Dance *(Luc triet hao ma dang)*
Monkey King Dance *(Dau-chien-thang-phat)*

By far, the most important was the Eight Lines Dance, performed every three years as part of the Sacrificial Rites Ceremony at Nam Giao Esplanade, a three-day ceremony during which the emperor offered up sacrifices to the gods to preserve the nation. It had been the queen mother Tu Cung's greatest fear that if her son, Bao Dai, married a Catholic and was converted to Catholicism, that he would no longer be able to perform this all important royal ceremony. The Eight Lines Dance was performed by sixty-four dancers, divided into military and civil mandarin. (A shorten version of the dance is now performed every two years during the Hue Festival.)

The Four Supernatural Creatures Dance included the *kylin* (unicorn) parents and their baby, celebrating family happiness.

The Six Times Offerings Dance *(Luc cung hoa dang)* is considered to be the second most important Nguyen royal court dance, the dancers carrying lotus blossom lanterns in each hand.

The dances performed these days, twice daily, at Duyet Thi Duong theatre in the Citadel are, in fact, excerpts from these authentic royal Nguyen court dances, dances that would have been enjoyed by at least ten (of eleven) Nguyen lords and thirteen Nguyen emperors – created four hundred years ago!

Sacred ceremonial songs were also a component of royal ceremonies. For the three-day Sacrificial Rites Ceremony at Nam Giao Esplanade, there were nine sacred songs, all of which employed the word 'accomplished' *(thanh)* in the titles.

Another nine sacred songs, sung at ceremonies at the shrines honouring Nguyen emperors and meritorious mandarin, contained the word 'harmonious' *(hoa)* in the titles. The six sacred songs sung at shrines dedicated to national heroes, also used the word 'harmonious' *(hoa)* in their titles. Six more sacred songs sung at the shrines of Nguyen emperors, used the word 'beautiful' *(huy)* in their titles.

At ceremonies to worship the spirits of the crops and the earth, seven sacred songs used the word 'prosperous' *(phong)* in the titles. The six sacred songs sung at shrines dedicated to Confucius, used the word 'literature' *(van)* in their titles.

At royal banquets, five songs were sung using the word 'completing' *(thanh)* in their titles. And at the regular gatherings of the royal court, five sacred songs using the word 'peaceful' *(binh)* in their titles were sung. In the royal palace, five more ceremonial songs were sung, each with the word *khanh* in the title, which translates as 'joyous wishes'. It is not known, how often – perhaps, every morning?

So singing in the Nguyen court was not only for entertainment, but served a serious, worshipful, ritualistic purpose, perhaps similar to Christian church hymns.

It is said that *tuong,* Vietnam's traditional classical opera, derives from China, although very early on in the villages of north Vietnam, there was folk opera, *hat cheo,* combining music, singing and dance, farce and mime. It is more or less accepted that the form evolved into *tuong* in Hanoi after General Tran Hung Dao captured a famous classical Chinese actor, Ly Nguyen Cat, during the thirteenth century Mongol invasions.

However, as it was explained to me some years ago by then director of Hanoi's National Tuong Theatre, once in Vietnam, *tuong* evolved into a distinctly Vietnamese theatrical form. Yet even she admitted that *tuong* reached its greatest achievement in Hue under the Nguyen dynasty. That Hue produced the greatest scripts in the history of Vietnamese *tuong* or *hat boi,* and that *tuong* reached its pinnacle of excellence in Hue is generally acknowledged by people in the North.

Certainly, Chinese and Vietnamese classical opera have much in common. The stories are taken from Chinese or Vietnamese history and legends, the costumes are extravagant and flamboyant, the movements and gestures are highly stylized and symbolic, the make-up is dramatic and tells the audience instantly whether the character is a hero or a villain, and the musical instruments have much in common with those of China. Moreover, the acting is unrealistic, melodramatically exaggerated, so that even the spectator without a word of *chu nha* – used in poetry until the late nineteenth century – can follow the action.

This is why any child and I love it for the spectacle and the exotic music, despite missing the poetry – not so different from attending an opera in a foreign language in the West, having neglected to read the libretto. In fact, most contemporary Vietnamese would have trouble understanding the poetry as it is written in *chu nha* – early Vietnamese – the equivalent perhaps of early English. So young, modern Vietnamese have gone right off *tuong* – it's neither pop nor cool.

Tuong, often called *hat boi* in central and south Vietnam, reached its height of development in the court of the Nguyen emperors under Dao Tan (1843-1907), a *hat boi* artist and a composer of *tuong* from Binh Dinh province. Strangely, no trace of written scripts of *hat boi* have ever been found. One theory is that up to then, there had been no involvement of intellectuals in *tuong.* When Dao Tan composed the *tuong* play, *Son Hau,* it was the first to have a written libretto.

Under the second Nguyen emperor, Minh Mang, Dao Tan formed the Than Binh Thu (music editorial staff), which also recruited and trained young performers in *tuong* – a classical opera company. Performing artists were paid salaries and given titles; some even attained the rank of mandarin.

The fourth emperor, Tu Duc, considered a brilliant poet himself, formed another group called Ban Hieu Thu to collect folklore stories to be incorporated into new *tuong* libretti. Ban Hieu Thu also included a division of 'elegant music' *(nha nhac),* the division of royal dance and the division of royal classical opera, *tuong.* Ban Hieu Thu proved to be extremely productive. One source states that five hundred works of royal *tuong* are stored in the Elizabeth Library (England); another source says fifty-two volumes of *tuong* libretti, considered to be an invaluable treasure of Viet Nam's traditional performing arts. Well, there appears to be no Elizabeth Library in England. On a hunch, I found that the Vietnamese Department of the British Library in London holds 'ten volumes of Vietnamese plays,' about to be digitized. Could they be any other than *tuong* manuscripts?

The *tuong* opera, *Van Buu Trinh Tuong,* required one hundred nights to perform – making Wagner's ring cycle and the lengthy *Gotterdammerung* look like a case of attention deficiency. Another *tuong* play, *Quan Phuong Hien Thuy,* required a measly forty-three nights. I wonder if the composers created cliffhangers at the end of each performance to tempt their audiences back?

Most Nguyen emperors had intimate knowledge of *tuong* and several – Minh Mang, Thieu Tri, Tu Duc – wrote poetry and sometimes contributed to *tuong* libretti. Duyet Thi Duong theatre was built by the second Nguyen emperor, Minh Mang, in 1826. The fourth Nguyen emperor, Tu Duc, built the Minh Khiem theatre in his tomb complex as he used it as a retreat – and presumably, wished to continue enjoying *tuong* even in his afterlife. These two theatres are the oldest traditional theatres in the country. So popular was *tuong,* that certain mandarin residences in Hue even had their own performing troupes to entertain their aristocratic friends. The common people had their own popular *tuong* theatres – everyone loved *tuong.* One scholar goes so far as to say, *'Tuong* is the blood and flesh of our ancestors' cultural treasure.'

As recently as the early twentieth century, a national poet as well as a *tuong* composer, Ung Binh-Thuc Da Thi (born 1887), adapted *Le Cid,* by the French author, Pierre Corneille, into a *tuong* opera, *Dong Lo Dich.* Sadly, wars have nearly brought an end to *tuong* as gifted performers die off and young people are little interested, either in watching or training to perform. Yet there are still a sufficient number of professional *tuong* performers in Hue for a lady named Thai Kim Lan to have taken a full troupe of *tuong* actors to Munich to perform the play based on *Le Cid* a few years ago. And if Beijing's traditional opera can pack them in every night, surely so could Hue's.

Tuong may be on the brink of extinction, but another genre of unique Hue music, *ca Hue,* is alive and floating on the Perfume river. *Ca Hue,* which I first heard at musical evenings years ago at the home of Professor Buu I, translates as Hue singing, or Hue songs. It is said, perhaps generously, that *ca Hue* 'has inherited and adapted the nuances of many other distinct regions – from the ten ancient Chinese songs of the North to the plaintiff songs of Champa.' However, these are not folk songs.

The late Professor Tran Van Khe, who was possibly the world authority on Asian music before he died recently, and who I was fortunate enough to meet during my first stay in Hue, has written: 'There have not been any historical documents on the date of birth of *ca Hue.* It is only known that this is not folk music because it was performed only among noble circles or in the royal palace. Therefore, it can be said that this is royal music, not folk music.'

Ca Hue are of two different types, the first: joyful songs of the North, songs of spring *(ban xuan),* ancient songs *(co ban),* songs of butterflies *(long diep),* and poetic songs *(phu luc).*

The second type is southern songs *(dieu nam)* or *(deu ai)* sadness songs. These fall into further categories: southern melancholy melodies *(nam binh),* the widow *(qua phu),* love-sickness or missing husband *(tuong tu* or *vong phu),* spring in the South *(nam xuan).* Other *ca Hue* describe mixed feelings: elegy of the dragon *(long ngam),* scenery of the four seasons *(tu dai canh).*

As *ca Hue* is always chamber music, performed for a small group of friends, few instruments are required, most commonly the sixteen-string *dan tranh* zither, the two-string *dan nhi* fiddle and the two-string moon-shaped *dan nguyet* lute. Or an ensemble of five instruments, adding to the above, the four-string pear-shaped *dan ty ba* lute, the three-string rectangular *dan tam* lute or the one-string *dan*

121

bau monochord. The singer taps the rhythm with two pieces of wood – no drums. Most importantly, *ca Hue* can only be sung by a singer from Hue. The poet, Ung Binh Thuc Gia Thi (1877-1961) has written: 'It is called *ca Hue* because only the Hue people's accent is suitable for these songs. People from Quang Tri and Quang Binh (nearby provinces), as well as people from other localities around Hue, from Linh Giang in the North to Hai Van in the South, are also able to sing *ca Hue;* however, no matter what efforts they make, they can rarely attain an excellent singing voice because of their heavy accent. This is common knowledge.'

Words cannot convey the emotional appeal of these intimate, plaintiff songs. The Vietnamese live close to their hearts and the people of Hue express their emotions through their poetry and *ca Hue*. Although *ca Hue* languished during the war years, international tourism has contributed to its revival. Dragon boats take tourists on cruises every evening along the misty Perfume river at sunset and later, beneath twinkling stars, during which *ca Hue* singers and musicians perform their poetic, melancholy, romantic songs. The elderly mistress of *ca Hue,* Minh Man, is still singing and teaching young singers *ca Hue*. When I asked her some years ago how many *ca Hue* she knew, her reply was simple – 'all of them.'

GRAND COURT MUSIC

Spoken words fly by
– Vietnamese proverb

Hue may no longer be capital of the country, but the people of Hue still know how to stage a superbly grand ceremony.

Hue's Golden Tourism Crafts Week, held every even year in late April and early May, includes a series of ceremonial opening events redolent of imperial times past, demonstrating how even now, the people of Hue still hold tenaciously to their formal royal traditions. At 7.15 a.m. sharp I climb out of a taxi and follow the moat along the outer wall of the Imperial City to the public entrance of Ngo Mon (Noon gate).

The ticket taker glances at my invitation and starts shouting for an underling, who appears and leads me across the vast, already sun-baked courtyard. We pass beneath the colourful enamel panels spanning the four bronze columns of Nghi Mon (gate), straight on over Trung Dao bridge, dividing Thai Dich lake, on along the straight, central walkway to the two-level, paved courtyard, the Esplanade of Great Salutations.

A stage edged in pleated silk has been installed beneath a banner proclaiming in Vietnamese and English: Golden Tourism Week. Above the backdrop for the stage, loom the double, imperial yellow, tiled roofs of the Palace of Supreme Harmony (Thai Hoa).

I find myself chatting to a grey-haired Vietnamese gentlemen and his wife. This was when I first met Truong Dinh Ngo and his Hue-born wife, Nguyen Ton Nu Huyen- Camille, who retired to Hue and built their garden house.

The banker had organized the fund-raising from *Viet kieu* (Vietnamese people living abroad) to help purchase at auction in France, the rickshaw of the mother of the tenth Nguyen emperor, Thanh Thai, whose grandson, Bao Hien, I had met years ago. It is thought that the dethroned Emperor Thanh Thai, most probably sold or gave away several personal items as gifts to his chief French guard, Prosper Jourdan, before he was exiled to Reunion in 1907. Finding myself at the upper of the two levels as people begin to be seated, I suggest that perhaps I am on the wrong level.

'Oh no, you can sit with us,' the retired banker assured me. We seat ourselves in the second row. At the other end of the row sits the retired, former Minister of Culture, Nguyen Khoa Diem, who I met years ago in Hanoi, and who had invited me to visit the Vietnam Writers Society in Hanoi (I am definitely in the wrong place).

To the right of the stage, a band of *nha nhac* court musicians is assembling. *Nha nhac* – grand court music – recently recognized as part of Hue's Intangible Heritage by UNESCO, is fairly boisterous and nearly always performed for ceremonies outdoors. This morning, the musicians are sporting round black hats with curled rims, edged in gold; red dragons lear from their yellow tunics over white trousers. Seven of them march onto the stage to start the proceedings: two traditional Vietnamese oboe-like instruments, a couple of small drums, symbols and wooden tappers. For so few, they can make an unearthly din, particularly the piercing oboes.

Dr Phan Thanh Hai, director of the Hue Monuments Conservation Center, introduces the programme. To my dismay and no little embarrassment, amidst the unintelligible Vietnamese, as dignitaries and honoured guests are being introduced, I hear my name and Mr Ngo, the retired banker, nudges me to stand up.

The speech over, four extravagantly costumed generals leap onto the stage – *tuong* – Vietnam's traditional classical opera. This is an unexpected treat as Vietnamese *tuong* is so rarely seen. And never before have I seen *tuong* performed in Hue, which is where it reached its zenith. So I am giddy with pleasure.

The four generals are wearing elaborate crown-like headdresses, heavily embroidered gold, green and red tunics and embroidered silk platform boots with scrolled toes. Two flags sprout from each of their shoulders – quite a sight, stomping, strutting and leaping about the stage to the reedy, rhythmic music.

The generals are followed by a line of ladies wearing moon-like crowns *(khan vanh),* that traditionally framed the pretty faces of Nguyen court ladies. Their costumes are layers of gossamer silk: gold over green, over white, over chartreuse, wrapped round with red sashes. A female singer in a green brocade *ao dai* sings *ca Hue,* extolling the beauties of Hue, while her companions circle elegantly round a large terrine of fruit, and rather like castanets, tap two china teacups together in each hand, a delightful tinkling sound. My new friends are led amongst the dignitaries to the stage where four young women in stunning indigo and purple *ao dais,* hand out bouquets to

124

the dignitaries. The indigo bodices of their *ao dai* tunics melt into a design of traditional Vietnamese houses in the deep purple of their lower tunics, deep purple symbolic of Hue.

Then hearing music from behind, we turn to see another larger *nha nhac* band marching through Ngo Mon toward us, this time wearing red and gold silk uniforms and carrying pikes: the Changing of the Guard, a ceremony that occurs daily.

Golf carts (which visitors to the Citadel can rent) whiz us round to Cung Dien Tho palace, the former residence of the queen mothers, where another *nha nhac* ensemble has added several more traditional instruments: a moon-shaped lute *(dan nguyet);* a square, reptile-covered, three-string lute with a long neck *(dan tam);* a pear-shaped lute *(dan ty ba);* and a two-string fiddle *(dan nhi).*

Potted bonsai trees flank the wide entrance doors to Phung Tien palace, the queen mother's reception palace. Girls in crimson *ao dais* carry a mysterious long streamer of red silk across the front of the entrance. An official appears between each girl with scissors in hand and they simultaneously cut the silk, revealing that each girl is holding a framed certificate hidden beneath the silk. The certificates are presented to the honoured dignitaries. Recognition plays a significant role in the Vietnamese psyche. I have attended numerous concerts of amateur musicians performing traditional music through the years, and after each performance, the musician is invariably presented with a bouquet. Now, the certificates will outlast the bouquets as tokens of recognition and appreciation.

The newly retrieved, black lacquer rickshaw, its slender staves inlaid with mother-of-pearl, has been installed on a low dais at one end of the palace. The staves extend two meters long, between which the servant would have walked or run, pulling the rickshaw. It was purchased in Tours (France) at a Rouilac Auction from Chateau Cheverny for Euros 55,800 ($76,000, £61,000). Thua Thien-Hue, the province in which Hue finds itself, contributed Euros 42,800 towards its purchase. The rest was raised from public donations and from *Viet kieu,* Vietnamese ex-pats. Unhappily, Emperor Thanh Thai's bed was sold at the same auction for Euros 124,000 ($168,000, £134,000), too rich for Hue's resources. It is thought to have been bought by a mysterious royal descendant. The tenth Nguyen emperor, Thanh Thai (Bao Hien's grandfather, reign 1889-1907), ordered this fine rickshaw to be made in Hanoi from rare *tac* hardwood for his mother, queen

125

mother Tu Minh. In Vietnam, Emperor Thanh Thai is counted as one of the 'patriotic' kings, that is, one of the three anti-French emperors, who included his brief predecessor, Emperor Ham Nghi, and his son, Emperor Duy Tan.

Vietnam lost thousands of royal antiques and valuable relics, including much furniture and the imperial golden books – looted by the French when they seized control of the Citadel and Hue in July 1885 – most of which ended up in France.

According to Dr Phan Thanh Hai, director of Hue Monuments Conservation Center, a French priest, Pere Siefert, who witnessed the start of the attack and recorded the events, wrote that French soldiers stole whatever they could: jewellery inlaid with diamonds and pearls, crowns and royal costumes, beds and tables, teapots, embroidered curtains – even toothpicks.

The rickshaw is the first relic that Vietnam has managed to recover from abroad. Concerning the return of the rickshaw, Dr Hai believes, 'This success has great meaning. It will bolster the national spirit and hopefully bring about efforts to get back more precious Vietnamese relics from other countries.'

The elegant rickshaw stands more than four feet (136 cms) high and measures more than seven feet (2 m) long. The slender arms of the chair are inlaid with delicate mother-of-pearl flowers as is the back of the seat. Small lamps attached to the chair arms would have lit the way should the queen mother find herself out after dusk. Apart from having a man on foot pulling it, I quite fancied a ride.

At the opposite end of the palace stands a red lacquer and gilt palanquin, which would have been carried by sixteen men. Phoenix heads, indicating an empress, form the finials of the front staves; tails of the phoenix form the finials at the back: three tail feathers for a queen, five tail feathers for a queen mother – who enjoyed greater prestige. Phoenix finials for queens and queen mothers, dragon finials for emperors. This particular palanquin belonged to Tu Du, mother of the fourth Nguyen emperor, Tu Duc, he who practised such great filial piety, visiting his mother every second day and always seeking her advice (though he didn't always take it). She considerably outlived him, reaching the age of ninety-one, and was noted for her charitable works; a hospital in Ho Chi Minh City is named after her.

Her palanquin is utterly feminine. Golden fringes edge the curved roof and more fringes line the open windows where pleated silk screens prevented the queen mother from being observed – a palanquin with a fringe on top. Four pretty Citadel guides wearing Hue royal purple *ao dais* sit gracefully on a mat playing a game with wooden staves, *xam huong*. Dice are thrown into a small bowl to determine how many points each player gets. The winner is the one with the highest score, so not much skill involved.

At the far end of the room, four more Citadel guides sit playing another royal game. The board has eight paintings of animals and the players spin an eight-sided dice – the game described in the royal garden pavilion. Suddenly I realize that these games, being played by court ladies where they might well have been played by the queen mother and her guests, afford a glimpse into imperial life not even a century ago.

DUYET THI DUONG PERFORMANCE

He who laughs at others today
will be laughed at by others tomorrow
– Vietnamese proverb

It is nearly ten in the morning – I have timed my arrival in the Citadel for a performance of the court musicians and the royal ballet company at the royal Duyet Thi Duong theatre. Removing my shoes (the theatre and stage are carpeted), I take a seat. Unlike the queen mothers and court ladies, I am not obliged to sit in one of the upstairs balconies, watching from behind a bamboo screen, but downstairs in the stalls where the emperor and his mandarin would have sat.

A beautiful young Vietnamese lady in a glittering, green *ao dai* announces the programme, first in Vietnamese, then in English. In case anyone is feeling drowsy, we are startled awake by loud *nha nhac* court music. This time the court musicians are wearing royal blue and red brocade tunics over white trousers and black helmet-like hats covering their ears. I can't help wondering, maliciously, if the ear covers are to protect their hearing. Instruments this time are two 'oboes', two drums beaten with sticks, one symbols player, one hand drum and one wood knocker.

The dances performed in Duyet Thi Duong theatre at these morning and afternoon performances are in fact, excerpts from authentic court dances, formerly performed on special designated royal occasions:

The first number is the *kylin* (unicorn) dance. Each of the two huge, gorgeous *kylins* are animated by two male dancers – think giant stuffed toys. They prance and bounce about the stage, tossing their comical heads, rolling their silver ball eyes, flapping their big red mouths. The two *kylins,* one yellow and one green, express their affection for one another through playful nudges and what looks like a bit of affectionate licking – a romance between two mythical creatures? After a few minutes of antics, suddenly the two *kylins* stand quite still for a few seconds, then part, and a small 'ball' begins to unwrap itself and stretch its paws – a baby *kylin* has been born.

128

The name of the dance, *A Mother Kylin Giving Birth to Her Baby (Lan au squat lan ni),* rather gives the game away. This time the musical ensemble has added three lutes (pear-shaped, moon-shaped and rectangular), a flute and cymbals.

The *kylin* dance, one part of a longer dance suite entitled the Four Mythical Creatures Dance *(Tu li),* was performed on the occasion of the emperor's birthday, the queen mother's birthday, the second queen mother's birthday, the spring ceremony and the royal godmother ceremony.

For the Fan Dance *(Vu lien),* each of the ten female dancers carries a large pink and white fan. They are wearing turquoise, moon-shaped court hats *(khan vanh),* bright pink and green tunics, trimmed with green and navy over long white skirts. The Vietnamese love bright colours and mix them quite dramatically. This is formation dancing, lining up, peering flirtatiously over their fans, leaning sideways, leaning backwards, fans flicking open and closing. Although danced in flat red slippers not unlike ballet slippers, it has far more in common with folk dancing than the Western ballet tradition. Royal court dancing in Hue is said to have been influenced by the Chams. This dance was performed at royal feasts before the emperor's mother, the queen, princesses and royal concubines.

On comes a different musical ensemble, this time nine instruments playing Big Court Music. Ad a wooden knocker and sticks, a coin clapper, a moon-shaped lute, a two-string fiddle, a pear-shaped lute and a square lute, a flute and a drum. Once the ear has adjusted to the five-tone scale . . .

Then to my delight, we have another rare performance, a scene from Vietnam's classical opera, *tuong.* I had seen short scenes of *tuong* in Hanoi, but only once a performance of an entire *tuong* traditional opera – during *Tet* in Hanoi. Yet it was here in Hue that *tuong* reached its apogee, and despite many visits, apart from the short scene at the opening ceremony for Crafts Week, this is only the second time that I have seen *tuong* in Hue. To the uninitiated Westerner, *tuong* is so obviously melodramatic that the action and the acrobatic antics are extremely entertaining. We may miss the intricacies of the story and the poetry, but the energetic dancing, the flamboyant costumes and vivid make-up more than compensate.

The lights come up on a human-shaped, painted wooden monster in the centre of the stage, with flaming red hair, a glaring face mask, yellow silk sleeves and a red velvet tunic. A dancer in a

129

glittering black skeleton costume, black pompoms spewing from the top of his head, crawls onto the stage through the out-stretched legs of the monster and leaps about – no need to translate that this is a demon, who lives in a cave.

The good general, wearing a ceremonial crown, a red velvet costume and black, scroll-toed boots, struts about the stage, carrying a tufted lance, singing. He approaches the static, masked monster with some hint of trepidation. He has been sent to kill the monster. The black skeleton demon, with great agility, lurks behind him, rather like the street performers who shadow passers-by and imitate their actions in Europe.

First, the black demon tries to wrest the general's lance from him, but the general is too strong. Clearly, clever tactics are required.

In a moment, a beautiful woman in a pale pink and green tunic over a white skirt, appears and flirts with the general. Who could look more innocent? But no, it is the demon, disguised as a woman. She, too, tries to wrest the general's lance from him. When she fails, she disappears and the general continues his strut with a bit of bravado singing to give himself courage.

Then a poor old man with a long, white beard appears, the demon again, disguised. The general must be slightly surprised at how strong the old man is, trying to wrest his lance from him. When the old man fails, he also disappears. The general, then taking courage and lance in both hands, bangs the mask of the cave demon and it splits – to reveal the true, ugly demon that it hid before. This is an excerpt, *Invisible Variation (Huu bien vo hinh)* from a *tuong* play, *The Goodness in Cruelty (Thien trong ac)*. Considering the title, I would love to know the rest of the plot!

What I had previously thought of as the Lantern Dance turns out to be part of the *Six Times Offerings Dance (Luc cung hoa dang)*, considered to be the second most important of the Nguyen royal court dances. In each hand, the dancer carries a candle in a silk lotus blossom lantern. The costumes are a riot of colour – green, yellow and pink brocade streamers over green trousers, red gaiters (shin covers) and red shoes. This is an intricate formation dance, dancers weaving in and out amongst one another, the finale, a human pyramid to form a lotus blossom, each dancer still holding the lighted lotus-blossom lanterns in each hand – the same colourful performance that would have been enjoyed by Nguyen lords and emperors four hundred years ago.

SURPRISE PARTY

When having a party, go first,
when walking in water, go after
– Vietnamese proverb

It was the owner of the new garden house, Truong Dinh Ngo, who first mentioned Thai Kim Lan, the lady who had taken an entire *tuong* troupe to Munich to perform the *tuong* based on *Le Cid.* Naturally, I was eager to meet her, so I set off with my French professor friend, Buu I, to interview her. They are very old friends.

As we have been invited to her house at five, this maybe suggests dinner. Like in the days of the old royal court, the Vietnamese in Hue still have breakfast very early. They often start work at half past seven, have lunch at eleven, and supper at five. Thai Kim Lan's house stands in a tightly-packed row of traditional houses, east of the Citadel, facing Huynh Thuc Khang canal. No doubt, a prime piece of property in one of the oldest residential sectors of Hue.

The front door stands open so we walk into a gracious, old wooden house. Two carved, black wooden horses stand beside an inner door; parallel sentences hang from the pillars. Antique furniture fills the first room. Glass-front bookcases, stuffed full of earthenware pots, cover each of the side walls. A light and bright, small inner garden beckons from an opening to the right of the central doorway to the next room.

In the sitting-dining room we are greeted by a middle-aged lady – Lan? – who disappears to the kitchen. It's a huge, high ceilinged room. Two large rectangular tables run along the centre, wooden chairs round the walls. Fresh lotus buds stand in a large jug – no paper flowers here. More vases hold spiky orange flowers resembling Indian paint brush and branches of red buds a bit like pussy willows. A full length, oil portrait hangs on one wall of a young woman in a slightly wind-blown, white, swirling *ao dai.* Below it on a low table to one side, are several photos of a youngish man, perhaps in his forties. Her husband? The photographs, placed as they are on a low table, as photographs might be placed on an

131

ancestral altar, suggest perhaps that he is dead. Opposite are two photographs of the same young woman in western clothes, clothes with long, flowing skirts. At the far end of the room hangs a large painting, a view of the Perfume river from an unusual, high angle, presumably from the Five Phoenix Pavilion above Ngo Mon – precisely the emperor's view at the moment of his abdication.

We sit on a wooden bench and I notice stacks of glass tumblers and wine glasses on the low table in front of us, a loud speaker to one side of the room and what looks like an electric keyboard in one corner. One of the large tables holds plates of sliced French bread, a stack of plates and on one corner, a highly decorated cake in a presentation box. A closer look at the cake and Buu I explains that indeed, it is a birthday cake. So, we are the first guests at a party? I thought I was coming for an interview on the subject of *tuong*. One is often surprised by what transpires unexpectedly in Vietnam, due to a casual lack of communication.

A distinguished, slim, grey-haired gentleman in a red silk shirt and white trousers appears and introduces himself as Hoa. He offers us a sweet wine aperitif and I notice that several bottles of French wine have appeared on the low table. Hoa explains that he left Vietnam as a small boy and was educated in Paris, so we speak French. He tells me that he is a member of the royal family, as are many people in Hue, the second emperor, Minh Mang, having had so many children. And it is his birthday. But he disappears before I can ask where he fits into the royal family. Later in the evening, I discover that he was an architect.

At least twenty minutes pass before a slightly older version of the woman in the painting and photographs, Thai Kim Lan, appears on the stairs in a white silk *ao dai* and pearl earrings, her black hair pulled back sleekly in a bun. She has lived much of her life in Germany and speaks fluent German, and prefers French to English.

Professor Buu I had filled me in on her activities en route. She not only owned a restaurant in Germany, but also a kind of spa. She studied philosophy, particularly Kant, taught Zen meditation – and fencing. She has also written a cookbook and worked as a translator, German to Vietnamese and vice versa. A lady of many talents. What he neglected to tell me was that she had been a professor of Philosophy at a university in Munich.

Thai Kim Lan is graciousness itself. We are offered another aperitif and more guests begin to arrive, carrying bouquets or bottles of wine for Hoa. Inwardly, I shudder, having come empty-handed. Each guest in turn is introduced to me, some speaking English, some French, and throughout the evening, the guests themselves politely make certain that someone who speaks English or French is always sitting next to the foreigner.

There is a predominance of francophone speakers, but also several who lived for many years in the US – in the states of Washington, California and Tennessee – before returning to their homes in Hue. One, a former officer in the army of the South, spent seven years in a hard labour camp before being allowed to leave Vietnam. When most of the guests have arrived, our hostess takes a microphone to welcome her guests and to introduce each one of us, between thirty and forty people, all in Western dress apart from our hostess, the ladies in heels, many perched two to a chair, such is the slenderness of Vietnamese ladies, even Vietnamese ladies of a certain age. I feel quite under-dressed, having come in a pair of trousers, a loose blouse and sandals.

By the by, food is being brought from the kitchen to the table and a cover comes off: a suckling pig. There is a call in Vietnamese – to the table – and I am handed a tiny round saucer of *banh beo,* a transparent cassava jelly with grated shrimp and herbs on top, one of Hue's specialities, thankfully eaten with a tiny spoon. Another guest kindly loosens it from the saucer with the spoon before handing it to me, a stroke of infinite politesse to a foreign visitor. After the *ban beo,* there is a gentle, polite free-for-all at the buffet, which might have been choreographed, so synchronized is the in-and-out, unlike the elbowing and immovable bodies that sometimes hulk around a buffet in the West. The table is brimming with bite-sized pieces of pork (there are forks and knives, but most people are using chopsticks), a cucumber and pineapple salad, tiny fried fish, sliced bites of what in the West would be called frankfurters, a bowl of loose yellow rice, round tightly packed white rice cakes, along with wine and beer, or fruit juice for the ladies. Polite, properly brought up Vietnamese ladies do not drink alcohol, certainly not Vietnamese ladies of a certain age.

As the empty plates are put aside, a young woman takes the microphone and invites one of the gentleman guests to sing. He has a word with the keyboard player and they're off in an emotional rendering of *La Vie en Rose.* The person sitting beside me tells me that the singer is nearly eighty. Whatever his age, he sings very well.

133

To my surprise, the lady MC invites guest after guest to sing, romantic ballads of the sort that used to be transmitted every night on Vietnamese TV when I first came to Vietnam. They all sing well, yet they are all amateur singers, says the lady sitting next to me. Then nearly all of the ladies get up, form a line and sing a chorus, the lady MC having handed out song sheets, just in case. Afterwards, the solos continue, some of the singers quite professional. The man now next to me tells me that I would be surprised, perhaps to know the ages of most of those singing, several approaching eighty. And indeed, I am surprised when he indicates which ones – I would have taken them for their lively sixties.

Then our host and hostess, Lan and Hoa, take to the dance floor and dance elegantly together, neat little steps, pivoting and turning in what I think might be called the two-step, which I encountered years ago in Hanoi. Others join in, women sometimes dancing together. Lan drags me onto the floor to join a circle of ladies in a semblance of a *cha cha.* It's so hot that I am relieved to retreat at the end of the dance to watch. To cool down I move to the front room where Buu I and several men are drinking beer and join them until they suggest the Vietnamese tradition of *cent percent* – bottoms up. This is never a one-time exercise, so knowing I'm beaten before I begin, I escape with my glass of beer back to the dining room, suddenly remembering that nice Vietnamese ladies don't drink alcohol. There are two or three more ladies' chorus numbers, lots of mobile phones and iPads held up to take photos, a camera snapping and more solo singers as people dance. I ask the lady next to me what time parties usually end, explaining that I don't want to be impolite by leaving too early, nor too late. She says, usually about ten, but that as she lives a long way away that she must leave at nine.

At half past nine, I approach Buu I and ask if it might be time to leave and he replies with astonishment in French – 'Not before the cake!' So I resettle in the dining room as our hostess takes the microphone to make another speech in Vietnamese, this time I deduce, honouring Buu I, who this week received the *Plume d'Or* from the French Government for his contribution to French literature. Everyone claps and he takes the microphone to thank her, reciting a poem, and the other guests chuckle at his comments. Then I hear amongst his scramble of Vietnamese, the words *ca Hue,* traditional Hue songs, and to my delight an elderly woman stands up and sings two beautiful *ca Hue* – for Buu I.

134

More singing, more dancing, a candle on the cake is lit and Hoa, the birthday boy, carefully slices it. Quite how it is to be divided amongst nearly forty guests, I cannot imagine, but somehow they do it, garnished with tiny bites of fresh pineapple. Cake finished, guests begin to leave, most on their motorbikes, Buu I and I in a taxi. So having set out to do an interview, as so often happens in Vietnam, something quite else occurs.

But what a lovely party, and to hear so many people sing who could sing well, a totally unexpected pleasure.

A PASSIONATE *TUONG* ENTHUSIAST

A hundred things heard are not worth one seen
– Vietnamese proverb

Next morning I arrive at Thai Kim Lan's home a quarter of an hour early for our postponed interview, so to pass the time I stroll along Huynh Thuc Khang canal. About a city block further along is a walled park. One entrance of the triple gate, which tells me it is a pagoda, is open. Later, I discover that this is Dieu De, one of Hue's oldest and most venerated pagodas. From the left, I hear chanting from what look like monks' dormatories. At the far end of the central paved walk, up a few steps, the doors of the pagoda are firmly closed. Yet from within, I hear the tap of a *mo* and the chanting of prayers.

Back at Thai Kim Lan's door, this time at the right time, there is no doorbell or knocker and the door is closed. Resorting to modern technology, I ring her mobile. The door is opened by Hoa.

Having a few minutes to ourselves, I ask about his family.

His family name is Nguyen Phuc – 'Phuc' translates as grace, he tells me.

His grandfather was the tenth emperor, Thanh Thai, 'the direct line.' Like Hoa himself, his father had been an architect. His mother, he told me in French – *'être une grosse tête'* – she was very bright, director (headmistress) of a school – and an artist.

After his grandfather, the dethroned Emperor Thanh Thai, was exiled, his son, Hoa's father, went to Hanoi to study. There he married a local girl and practised architecture. Hoa came from a family of ten children. Although born in Hanoi, Hoa and his elder brother spent part of their boyhood from 1944 to 1949 in Hue – 'at a pagoda, Du Quang, founded by my family.'

These were troubled times, immediately following the end of World War II in 1945. The Japanese had left, Ho Chi Minh had declared an independent Vietnam, but the French thought otherwise and resistance against the French – the French Indo-Chinese War – began in earnest, only ending at Dien Bien Phu in 1954.

136

Perhaps fearing that his sons would be drawn into the conflict, Hoa's father took a momentous, radical decision – to send his two young sons off to France unaccompanied at the ages of only fifteen and seventeen. In 1952, Nguyen Phuc Anh Bao Hoa and his elder brother arrived in Paris, knowing only a few words of French, a foreign country where they had no relatives, where the family knew no one, no one to help them. Somehow, the two young boys survived. They found odd jobs, washing dishes, and eventually, Anh Bao Hoa managed to qualify as an architect. His elder brother qualified as a civil engineer and still lives in Paris.

A radiant Thai Kim Lan appears with outstretched arms – we have already discovered that we share a mutual passion for Vietnam's traditional classical opera, *tuong*. Today she is wearing a beautifully tailored white silk trouser suit, but instead of the flowing trousers worn under an *ao dai,* these are lean, tapered trousers under a short *ao dai*-like tunic. With heels. Very chic.

She serves tea in shallow, ceramic bowls, and insists that I try a Japanese delicacy, wrapped in tiny packets – chestnut cakes.

Thai Kim Lan's family came to Hue from the North with the Nguyen lords, three hundred years ago, she tells me. Her family home was near the Citadel. Her paternal grandmother was a great influence, she explains, a member of the royal family. It was her grandmother who told her many stories of the royal family and stories of *tuong*.

'She was an inspiration.'

Hoa interrupts to say that Thai Kim Lan can recite all 3,254 lines of Nguyen Du's *Tale of Kieu,* which she learnt from her grandmother. *Kieu* is Vietnam's epic poem, as highly revered in Vietnam as Shakespeare in the West and it has been said that if you do not understand the story of *Kieu,* you cannot understand the Vietnamese. *Kieu* was composed by Nguyen Du (1766-1830), who was known to have remained loyal to his king, the weak Le king in Thang Long, the king first defeated by Nguyen Hue of the Tay Son brothers, who in turn was defeated by Nguyen Anh, who became Emperor Gia Long. As piety towards one's king and filial piety are the most highly esteemed moral tenets of Confucianism, when Nguyen Du was invited – commanded – to join the new Nguyen government, he had no choice but to agree. But in his remorse at his own disloyalty to the former Le king, it is said that he wrote the heartbreaking poem as an allegory of his own sufferings from self-guilt. *Kieu* is the story of a young girl who sells herself out of filial piety to protect her father and brother from going to jail for unpaid debts. He wrote it in *chu nom* characters, which helped to popularize the old-new, Chinese-Vietnamese script in Vietnamese literature.

Thai Kim Lan's paternal grandmother could read *chu nom,* the old Chinese characters adopted by the Vietnamese to express their own language – at a time when it was very rare for a woman even to learn to read, much less, *chu nom.*

'But they taught the ladies of the court. Attitudes and poems, I received much from my grandmother.'

Thai Kim Lan's mother was also a member of the royal family, but not literary. Her maternal grandfather had been a military mandarin, a colonel.

Our mutual friend, Professor Buu I, had told me en route to Hoa's birthday party that Thai Kim Lan had owned a restaurant and 'some sort of spa,' that she had taught Zen Buddhist meditation – and fencing – also that she had written a cook book and done translations, German to Vietnamese and vice versa.

She has recently published 'a small book on the German author, Hermann Hesse, in Vietnamese.'

Thai Kim Lan left Hue in 1965 (at the beginning of the Vietnam War) to study in Munich. She had attended the Dong Khanh School for Girls in Hue where she learned German, then studied Philosophy at the University of Hue, before going to Germany to continue her studies. There, she obtained her doctorate. She remained in Germany, teaching at Ludwig Maximilian University in Munich until she retired.

Reminiscing about her childhood in Hue, 'There were even few bicycles, we walked to school,' which on the far side of the river from her family home near the Citadel, would have been a long walk, especially in hot months or under monsoon rains. Hoa tells me that Lan and her classmates wore white *ao dais* as the school uniform.

Her father was assassinated – he had been sympathetic to the French – when she was only four, leaving her mother a widow with four young children aged thirteen, eight, four, and a toddler.

'It was very difficult for my mother.'

Much later, in happier times in 2002, Thai Kim Lan took seventeen professional *tuong* actors and five other professionals to a theatre in Munich 'to explain *tuong'* – among them, Professor Tran Van Khe (1921-2015), the world authority on Asian music and a former professor at the Sorbonne, born in Saigon.

138

'A Vietnamese, Ung Binh, had translated *Le Sid* into Vietnamese and composed a *tuong,* using the story. 'The reason I took them was that I wanted to encourage them – here! I wanted to bring about a revival of *tuong.* I wanted to call attention here, to make them understand *tuong* in Hue! It is my wish, my dream, I would like to construct a *tuong* theatre – of wood – here. There was an opera house, opposite the market. It was destroyed in the Tet Offensive of 1968.'

Considering Thai Kim Lan's immense passion and energy, I have great hopes for the revival of *tuong* in Hue.

Then she brings out a beautiful book, explaining modestly that it is a history of the *ao dai.* I soon discover that it describes her own personal collection of *au dai xua,* the court robes that were the precursor of today's *ao dais.* Covered in royal yellow fabric with a pale ginkgo leaf on the cover, the title of the book translates as *Imperial Yellow Walking on Pale Leaves.*

She wrote it in Vietnamese and in German, illustrating and explaining the exhibition of the Vietnamese Nguyen dynasty court robes she has collected – twelve of them – an exhibition that took place at the Goethe Institute in Hanoi in January, 2015. Beside each photo of an *ao dai xua* court robe is the story of the person it belonged to: Bao Dai, Vietnam's last Nguyen emperor, who died in Paris in 1997; court gowns of several princesses and concubines of certain Nguyen emperors; beautiful court robes of crimson, golden yellow silk; pale, flowery robes with crimson silk linings, worn by various royal ladies, including the wife of Khai Dinh, Tu Cung, Vietnam's last but one emperor, many heavily embroidered.

One photograph is of the installation mounted for the exhibition in Hanoi, the court robes hung to float freely from the ceiling above a floor covered with bamboo carrying poles, familiar to anyone who has wandered the streets of Vietnam. Even more arresting are the few old photographs of the people who wore these exquisite robes – Vietnam's feudal past that endured into the recent, photograph-able past – ending only in 1945. In one photo, a princess is wearing the immediately identifiable, wide, circular, pleated hat or headdress of the Nguyen court ladies.

'They are called *khan vanh.'* The exhibition was a celebration of Vietnam's forty years of friendly relations with Germany – and also the fiftieth anniversary (1965-2015) of Thai Kim Lan's association with Germany where still, after retiring from a professorship, she spends part of every year, part in her beloved, native Hue.

139

Thai Kim Lan excuses herself and returns with a laptop – to show me a video of the opening of the exhibition, introduced by an English speaker. Then we return to the book where there is a photo of her beautiful sister, wearing one of the *ao dai xuas*. Tragically, she was killed in an car accident in Saigon in 1975.

Thai Kim Lan turns the pages to show me a photograph of her maternal grandfather, an austere looking gentleman under a winged hat, wearing a silk robe, sitting four-square in scroll-toed boots, knees splayed, staring straight at the camera. He was a Nguyen dynasty prince, her ancestors having fought in the incessant wars against the Trinh family of the North – civil wars that lasted from the Nguyen's migration South in 1558 until Nguyen Anh united Vietnam for the first time and crowned himself the first Nguyen emperor, Gia Long, in 1802.

When her military grandfather retired, he became a monk.

It is these traditions, the scholarly, refined manners, the ceremonies and rituals, the memories of a sophisticated imperial court life passed down two generations from grandparents to those still living, that make Hue so special.

SINGING *CA HUE*

His wife first, heaven afterwards
– Vietnamese proverb

Entrance is at the rear of a trendy restaurant, up stairs to the flat above, occupied by Professor Buu Y, his son and daughter. I had first met my friend Buu Y, glancingly, eighteen years ago when I was invited to attend the Sunday afternoon music lessons of my then interpretor, Thao, who was learning to sing *ca Hue.* The music lessons were hosted by Professor Buu Y's wife, Nguyen Thi Loy, who sadly, has since died.

Buu Y's daughter, Meu (Rain), is wearing a short black shift. Like her father before her, Meu teaches French literature at the College of Foreign Languages. She leads me to the sitting room. On a low table rests an ink drawing of Buu Y, as a dashing young intellectual wearing a beret. Sketched by his wife, Thi Loy, I wonder? Opposite hangs a huge painting of the Citadel, painted by his wife, surrounded by several portraits and a photo of my departed friend, playing her sixteen-string zither *(dan tranh).*

Several traditional instruments stand propped against the wall: two *dan tranh* and a lute *(dan ti ba).* A large flat-screen TV rests on silk brocade on a chest, next to a printer on a low table. Beside the television set, a strange, carved root is displayed on a china torchere. As Westerners love driftwood, the Vietnamese find beauty in wildly twisted roots.

Solid, lacquered, traditional armchairs with curled arms line the other three walls of the room. I drop into one of them. Glass-front bookcases cover the wall behind me. Buu Y appears and offers a bowl of *longans* fruits, a cousin of the lychee with thin, leathery peel.

'Do you know what *longan* means?' he asks. 'It's Chinese. Long means dragon, *nhan,* which sounds the same, means eye, so *longan* means eye of the dragon.'

There is a small commotion on the stairway. Minh Man, at ninety-one, a tiny, dark, fragile figure, her grey-black hair drawn back tightly in a ponytail, wearing a flowery two-piece pyjamas suit, has been carried upstairs by her cyclo driver. With a walker, she manages to get from the door to a chair nearby where extra cushions have been placed for her, beneath and for her back. She is skin and bones. I can well imagine that only one thin cushion on the square, hardwood chairs would have been uncomfortable for her bony frame.

I greet her with *xin chao ba* (hello, grandmother or old lady).

She corrects me: *'xin chao me'* – the correct address in Hue for elderly ladies – which I am later told, suggests a certain regality. She is accompanied by her daughter. More fruit is brought in and placed on a mat on a low table in the centre of the room: sliced mangoes, *longans,* green bananas and small packets wrapped in pale violet rice paper. Three young women arrive and remove their sandals – following Buu Y's example, I have kept mine on – and sit on the floor mat around the low table, nibbling delicately at the fruit.

Buu Y explains that all three are singers and that we won't be able to start until some instrumentalists turn up. The three singers are wearing loose blouses and jeans. The days of the traditional, flowing *ao dai* are almost gone. These days, it is only worn in hotels and restaurants catering to tourists or as the high school uniform. One singer has a fringe. Two have pulled their black hair back into ponytails; the third has permed, short hair.

How many instrumentalists are necessary? I ask.

'A maximum of five or six, a minimum of two or three. The *dan tranh* (sixteen-string zither) is the principal instrument.'

After half an hour when no instrumentalist has appeared, Minh Man takes out her wooden knockers and announces that they will start without musicians, with just her wood knockers. The sound of her voice is impossible to describe, the glottal vibrato intact, although slightly lower than I recall. I well remember her voice as a well-projected howl that could easily have been heard across the river. Hue singing was often performed on boats for mandarin, princes and kings, and now, for anyone who pays a fairly modest fee for a musical dinner afloat. The genies of *ca Hue* must have heard the instrument-less singing, for through the door bounds a young man wearing a chartreuse shirt and jeans, carrying a black canvas instrument case, out of which comes a two-string fiddle, the *dan nhi.* It is 5.45 – the session was to have started at five. He seats himself cross-legged on the mat opposite the three singers and stands his fiddle vertically on his thigh. Much chatter and laughter as he tunes the fiddle. Once tuned, he starts playing and the curly-haired woman

142

begins to sing as she taps the wooden stick and block, passed to her by Minh Man. The fiddler keeps the rhythm with his bare toe. The song ended, she passes the wooden stick and block to the next singer and they discuss what to sing. A high fiddle melody begins. I glance at the old singer, wondering what she is thinking.

Minh Man in her time was considered to be the best singer of *ca Hue* in Hue – she became famous, singing on the radio. But she was already old when I first met her in 1997; I calculate that she must have been seventy-three, even then. She sits with her legs crossed at the ankles. Years ago, she sat with her legs crossed yoga-fashion in the chair. I remember asking her then how many *ca Hue* songs she knew to which she replied, 'all of them' – several hundred!

The second singer sings in a slightly higher range. Buu Y whispers that Hue songs are mostly romantic or about the beauty of nature. And now, the third singer also sings in the higher range, an octave above middle C.

Another man has arrived and sits in a chair.

'Not a musician, the cyclo driver,' Buu Y explains. Maybe he is anxious to leave. It has now been over an hour. But the singing has only been going on for quarter of an hour.

Ca Hue songs stop abruptly; one can never anticipate when they will end. There is no predictable resolution to the tonic as one would expect in Western music. The two or three of us, not singing, clap rather hollowly at the end of each song, me sometimes a little belatedly, having been caught unaware by the sudden ending.

Even without understanding the words, *ca Hue* sound melancholy. I couldn't help wondering if some of them might have been composed by the sad, unloved and neglected royal concubines, offered at court by their mandarin fathers, hoping to gain favour.

The curly-haired lady takes another turn to sing. Then all three sing together – 'A folk song', says Buu I, 'about the ten reasons to fall in love with a woman, some rather surprising: pretty, nice eyes, having to wait, but not the woman's form' – he uses the French word for figure – 'but the style of dress she chooses to wear.'

How very Hue, to be concerned about the style of dress. I ask about the singers. 'All manual labourers,' he replies, using the term that would no doubt be used to classify them in a Communist country. 'One is a cleaner in a restaurant, one makes cakes and the other makes flowers from fabric.' The fiddle player is a teacher of music in a primary school.

At 6.15, a young monk in a brown robe arrives with a beaming smile. He takes down one of the 'house' *danh tranh,* a beautiful black lacquered instrument with inlaid mother-of-pearl, sits legs crossed on a corner of the mat, rests the left end of the instrument on the floor and the right end on his lap. He takes plastic pluckers out of a jar, strums a waterfall of strings and starts to tune the instrument. Now Minh Man sings, then stops the music – maybe something has been incorrectly tuned?

Buu Y explains that formerly, monks were not permitted to attend musical evenings. It was forbidden. But now, if a monk is spiritually solid, it is permitted – with authorization – as a diversion.

'This monk is considered brilliant, he has been chosen to travel, he spent nine years in India.'

The monk later tells me that he spent his time in Delhi and Poona. The name he was given as a child was Doan Phuoc Tri; his new name as a monk – the old name is changed when a boy becomes a monk – is Thich Phuoc Nhu.

And now Minh Man sings, tapping the rhythm on her chair arm. 'A Buddhist song – she adapted,' says Buu Y. When she finishes, the monk starts to sing. The fiddle player and the female singers don't know the song. He accompanies himself on the *danh tranh.* Buu Y whispers that it is very rare for a musician to sing and play at the same time. The cake-maker starts a new song with a long, low wail – or calling? The old lady joins in. By the end, Minh Man is sitting at the front of her chair. She pushes her feet into her plastic slippers – a signal – and her cyclo driver tenderly picks her up in his arms and carries her downstairs.

Continuing, the flower-maker sings with the *dan tranh* – the fiddle player has gone down to help the old lady and the cyclo man. The cake-maker slips out.

Ça, c'est la poesie,' (that's poetry), says Buu Y, ecstatically.

A bit of chat and green tea from a thermos, then the two remaining female singers sing what becomes the finale.

My second *ca Hue* evening happened almost by chance. I had gone round to see Professor Buu I to ask him the name of a pagoda and he invited me to a *ca Hue* gathering the following evening. Arriving exactly at five, I am followed up the stairs to his flat above the restaurant by a four-person TV crew. Another surprise in Hue! The doyenne of *ca Hue* singers, Minh Mam has already arrived, this time

144

wearing a turquoise *ao dai* and a pearl necklace. The TV crew busies itself, setting up a lamp and attaching a microphone to Minh Man's *ao dai*. Next to arrive is the *ca Hue* singer with short curly hair wearing a pale green *ao dai*. Clearly, everyone but me knew about the TV crew. Another elderly *ca Hue* singer arrives, Thanh Huong, wearing a purple velour *ao dai* and a pale jade necklace – she is only eighty-six.

In troop three musicians, carrying a *dan bau* (one-string monochord), a *dan tranh* (sixteen-string zither) and a *dan nhi* (two-string fiddle). Three more singers appear, one in a shocking fuchsia *ao dai,* and two more in purple *ao dais,* one a real beauty with long, flowing black hair. They seat themselves on the mat around the low, black tea table, now loaded with plates of lychees and tiny triangular *banh u tro* wrapped in banana leaves.

The two-string fiddle starts. The wood tappers are passed out as other instruments join in, stop, then start again. Checking the tuning perhaps? The curly-haired singer begins to sing – and I suddenly realize that her voice is possibly the most like that of the old singer, Minh Man.

While she is singing, the monk arrives and the circle parts for him to sit down. He is handed one of the 'house' *dan tranh,* and sits with the left end on the floor, the right end resting in his lap. To my surprise, I realize that Thanh Huong, eighty-six years old, is sitting quite happily on the floor – how did she get there, and how will she get up again? At the end of the song and the clapping, the wood knockers are handed to Minh Man. Meanwhile, the camera man has been moving around the circle, zooming here or there across the circle, sometimes closing in on a keyboard or a particular singer.

For the first time ever, I am sitting not a meter from the *dan bau,* my favourite traditional Vietnamese instrument and see that the pitch is determined not only by where the single string is plucked. The curled 'cane' that the left hand vibrates, also alters the pitch as well as the intonation. At this moment, the cameraman is on his knees, focusing the camera on the single string of the *dan bau.*

At last, Minh Man lets fly, the intentional vibrato intact, almost a gurgle, and I cannot help wondering as many others present must be, how many more of these *ca Hue* evenings she will be able to attend? *Ca Hue* singing is definitely an acquired taste, but once the ear has acclimatized to the five-tone scale, it grows on you. It is very intimate, and very, very Hue.

The cameraman climbs onto a chair to get a down-view.

Next to sing is Thanh Huong, the old lady in the purple *ao dai*. She has a low voice, a contralto. Looking at these two lean old ladies, I think back on the times they must have seen, having been born in 1925 and 1929 respectively. They would have witnessed the last years of the Nguyen dynasty, albeit under the French, they would have survived three wars: the Second World War, the French Indo-Chinese War, the Vietnam War. And here they are, still singing. I catch the word Hue – a good many *ca Hue* songs are about Hue.

The beautiful young singer sings next, a jolly song, trembling two tea cups in each hand, tea cups used as a percussion instrument – quite a dexterous skill. Minh Man taps a water glass to add to the jingle. Another singer wearing a purple *ao dai,* who I remember from the first *ca Hue* evening, takes the wooden knockers to sing the next song, the tea cups continue to be trembled by her near neighbour. The other *dan tranh* is passed to the monk – he couldn't get the sixteen-string, 'house' *dan tranh* tuned with the singing going on.

It's the turn of the singer in the fuchsia *ao dai*, as the others begin to nibble at the lychees. There are no wooden knockers this time, perhaps a lament, although Minh Man's left hand rises and falls where the knockers might have been. The fiddle is making a sorrowful whining, the *dan bau* always makes a poignant sound, only the *dan tranh's* metallic waterfall relieves the sombreness.

The singer in the fuchsia *ao dai* sings again, a song that seems to be calling – perhaps to a far away lover. The tempo quickens and what had seemed quite plaintive now seems to turn positive, not unlike a shift to a major key in Western music.

Minh Man takes back the wooden knockers and the camera moves in close on her old hands.

In the next number, the *dan tranh* and the fiddle begin, but the *dan tranh* soon drops off, leaving only the fiddle to accompany the monk's singing, a rather sad song. Holding the wooden knockers, he taps very gently and I notice that the bowing of the fiddle is virtually against the sound box at the bottom.

The monk refits the pluckers to his fingers and takes up the *dan tranh*. It's now the turn of the singer in the pale green *ao dai,* who started the evening, the eighty-six year old singer in the purple *ao dai,* sitting on the floor tapping the wooden knockers.

An evening to remember.

146

ANOTHER *TUONG* ENTHUSIAST

That which belongs to heaven,
will return to earth
– Vietnamese proverb

Early in my stay, the Hue Monuments Conservation Center arranged an interview with the director of the Citadel's royal theatre, Duyet Thi Duong. Arriving at the Conservation Center's address, I find it is a private house. I am sure it is the right address as I have copied it carefully off the printed bag handed out at the Crafts Festival. A very old lady, squatting in the garden of the house, shouts to someone inside. A younger woman appears and tells me in English, 'This is the old address, the new one is a few hundred yards to the right, a gate with three entrances' – which to me, says pagoda.

Seeing my perplexed expression, she says 'wait,' goes back into the house to get a helmet and motions me to get on the back of her motorbike. She drops me in front of the gate, which indeed, was only a hundred yards away. The people of Hue are so kind, I am always bowled over by their friendliness, helpfulness and generosity. Even so, had I arrived at the triple gate alone, I would have taken it for a pagoda, which is what it originally was.

Inside the gate is an entire complex of gardens and buildings. Having learned from experience that it is impossible to pronounce Vietnamese names properly, I show the guard the name of the person I am meant to meet. He motions me to a building towards the back, a low row of what might formerly have been monks' quarters. A person passing indicates which door. Inside I find Nguyen Tan Ton Nu Y Nhi, her second and third 'names' being royal titles

But instead of proceeding to the theatre for the ten o'clock appointment as arranged, inexplicably, she now tells me that the time has been changed – to half past three – which means another hot journey later in the heat of the day. It is already 33C (93F) at 9 a.m. We are to meet inside the Citadel at the theatre director's office.

147

At half past three in the blazing sun of mid-afternoon, I fetch up at Duyet Thi Duong theatre, ask for Phan Bach Hac's office and am directed to a single-story building across a sunny, grassy lawn. Her name is on the door, but I wait outside for the translator, Nguyen Tan Ton Nu Y Nhi, to appear. She has brought a young girl along with her, Che Le Hien. The director of Duyet Thi Duong theatre, Phan Bach Hac, appears, a small, intense, young woman of perhaps forty, wearing a loose, abstract design blouse over grey trousers, her hair pulled back. We sit at a table with leather chairs and the young girl, Che Le Hien, serves tea.

How long have they been giving performances of traditional music and dance in the renovated theatre? I ask. She replies that performances started in 2003 after *nha nhac* court music was declared an Intangible Heritage of Hue by UNESCO. They give two, forty-five minute performances twice a day, at ten and at three. She goes on to answer my questions. Employed at the theatre are 172 people; 135 are artists – dancers, actors and musicians – of which about sixty are musicians. 'How much the various performers earn', she explains, 'is set by the government, not by the theatre manager. It depends upon how long the artists have worked and what educational degrees they have. The range is from about two to six million Vietnamese *dong* per month (US\$93-280, £74-224). They work two days and have one day off, because there are performances every day of the week.'

It is difficult to say how many hours per week they work as it varies so much. They do far more than the two daily performances in the Duyet Thi Duong theatre, often appearing at official ceremonies. I had seen the *nha nhac* musicians at least four times at different functions during Craft Week. And then, of course, there are rehearsals. I ask how often the performances in Duyet Thi Duong theatre change.

'The programme used not to change at all, but recently, there have been changes. Since the first of April, we have added a scene of *tuong,* Vietnam's traditional classical opera' – the scene in which a general is sent to kill the demon who lives in a cave, a scene that demands rapid costume changes by the demon, behind the facade of the cave mid-stage. I tell her how much I enjoyed the scene from *tuong* and how I hope that perhaps Hue might revive its fine tradition of *tuong* by mounting evening performances, perhaps with dinner, as is done for the Tang performances in Xian, or with tea and snacks as they do at the opera in Beijing – earning a fair amount of revenue.

148

Plunging in with a diagram, I explain how the dinner tables are arranged in Xian, lengthwise from the stage, so that everyone can see, looking sideways. Here, the interview goes seriously off track. It isn't often that a translator forgets to translate, but this one starts talking to Tran Bach Hac, and no matter how many times I ask her politely to translate what she herself is saying, and what Tran Bach Hac is replying, the conversation between them carries on.

It turns out that the translator herself had trained in *tuong*, and therefore, feels very strongly about reviving it. So she and Tran Bach Hac discuss why they think my idea is unworkable in Hue. It takes some determined effort and tapping on the shoulder to stop the conversation to find out what they are saying.

The floor of the theatre is flat, not raked, and because it is a historic building, they cannot change it (but you couldn't set up tables on a raked floor anyway). And there is the problem of marketing. The tour operators won't sell the tickets to the performance now, because they don't make enough commission from the ticket sales and it wouldn't be different if the tickets were for *tuong.*

Also, *tuong* uses archaic language (perhaps the equivalent of Shakespearean English), so the words are difficult even for present-day Vietnamese to understand. True enough, young Vietnamese seem to be only interested in whatever is modern. With the arrival of television, the Vietnamese have almost completely lost interest in their traditional theatre, not only *tuong,*, but also a more modern musical theatre, *cai luong.*

I tell them of my experience in taking foreigners to see the 'taster' performances of *tuong* in Hanoi, an experience without exception that they have very much enjoyed: the flamboyantly colourful and extravagant costumes and make-up, the pure exotica of the music and performance, every bit as good as the classical opera in Beijing. And how here, a few days ago, when I took a French friend to see the performance that included one scene from *tuong,* the response was the same, pleasure and enthusiasm for more.

The Vietnamese often underestimate the curiosity of foreigners in regard to their culture, projecting their own feelings that it is old fashioned, and therefore, of no interest or value to anyone else. The two-way conversation swirls on to a point where I begin to be annoyed at being excluded. Finally, I get in another question.

Tran Bach Hac herself did not come from a family of performers, but she herself had trained in *tuong.* Her older sister also performs *tuong.* There used to be training in *tuong* in Hue, but as there was little or no demand, the courses stopped. Herein lies the danger: if the old performers and teachers die without passing on the precious baton of *tuong,* it will be lost forever.

'Instead, there are courses at the College of Culture and Arts for the royal dance, which is near to *tuong.* There will be some different movements, other types . . .' Bach Hac explains lamely, through the translator. But I know, and she knows, *tuong* is *tuong.* Each role must be learned, the sometimes acrobatic dances, the songs. The former director of Hanoi's National Tuong theatre had spent three years learning *tuong* roles at the University of Fine Arts in Hanoi.

'In August there will be a rise in the ticket prices. But again, the tour operators think it is too expensive and the tourists won't come.' Nevertheless, she is raising the ticket fee.

Tran Bach Hac agrees that 'it would be very good for the artists to perform *tuong* and she would be grateful for support.

'There are different types of *tuong,* in the North, in the South, and in Central Vietnam, different styles,' she explains. 'Of Hue's *tuong,* there are four genres: royal, folk, historic and comic.

'The founder of *tuong* in Hue was Tan Hoa Dan Tan – he was very famous in *tuong.'*

Perhaps only a paragraph or two in English and in French, I suggest, on a single sheet of paper, not only for *tuong,* but also for their current performances, what the dances are and when – for what royal occasions or ceremonies they were performed, what instruments are used in *nha nhac,* and a brief summary of the *tuong* scene – a single sheet of paper given out at the door so that people have some explanation and a souvenir to take home, reminding them of what they've seen would be helpful.

The translator disagrees, saying that 'a programme would spoil it' – the surprise? – by telling them what they were about to see? I explain that international audiences are accustomed to having a programme when they go to the theatre, so that they know what they are seeing. And I explain about Western opera librettos, which can be very complicated and usually sung in their original languages – that there is always a summary of the plot in the programme.

Well, at least, I've planted the idea of evening performances of *tuong* . . .

A UNICORN, A LUTE AND A DRUM

Ten girls are not equal to one testicle of a boy
– Vietnamese proverb

Today I met a unicorn, well, a baby unicorn. Or what the Vietnamese call a unicorn – a *kylin*. This particular unicorn appeared in the guise of a lean, wiry young man wearing an open plaid shirt, a heavy silver cross on his chest and tiny silver studs in his ears. His name is La Tuan and he is a fourth generation dancer of the Royal Ballet Company that performs twice daily in Duyet Thi Duong theatre of the Citadel. Both of his paternal and maternal parents were dancers, all of his relatives were dancers, his elder brother and sister both dance, though not professionally. He himself began dancing at six. He grew up dancing. His uncle and his wife dance in the theatre.

'His wife, Vu Ngoc Anh, is very beautiful and a very talented dancer,' the translator volunteers.

La Tuan never studied dance at college, but from his father and grandfather, 'because all of them were masters in the college.'

How many of the old Nguyen court dances do the present troupe know how to perform? 'Over twenty *tuong,*' he tells me to my delighted surprise. 'About nine traditional dances, but I perform in only seven as the others are for only female dancers.'

La Tuan dances the baby unicorn – the most difficult role, as it requires the most sensitivity, the baby quiveringly coming to life on stage. I ask about the Six Offerings Dance in which the dancers carry a lighted candle in a lotus blossom in each hand.

'In the Six Offerings Dance, the person on the top (of the pyramid) has the most difficult role because of climbing up and balancing. It requires a different kind of technique to get down.'

Are the costumes traditional?

'We have to follow tradition, but sometimes we cannot follow tradition one hundred percent because some fabrics we cannot find now, so we have to use replacements.'

How many costumes does he have? To my amazement, he says that individual dancers do not have their own personal costumes.

Rotating dancers, dancing the same roles, have to wear the same costumes. Each week he works three days – one-and-a-half days on and one-and-a-half days off, dancing twice a day in the theatre and also around the Citadel, for other ceremonies, for many extra jobs.

When I ask how much dancers earn, the translator tells me that La Tuan earns three million dong ($140, £112) per month, and that he is forty – an extremely young forty. I would have taken him for his mid-twenties.

La Tuan started early on by studying different kinds of circus, then comedy. At the age of fifteen, he studied *tuong*. In his maternal family, there used to be circus performers, but later they switched to *tuong* and now, his paternal family is very famous in *tuong*. So there are still professional *tuong* performers about in Hue, it's just that they are not performing. His late aunt was director of the royal Duyet Thi Duong theatre. La Tuan has only one child, two years old – so not quite yet a dancer.

On the same day, I am also privileged to meet a fourth generation *nha nhac* court musician, bright-eyed Tran Diep, who is the grandson of a very famous *nha nhac* musician, Tran Kich.

I ask how many instruments he plays.

'Four: the *dan bau* (monochord), the *dan tam* (three-string lute), the *tam am* (set of three small gongs) and a drum.'

Then at last, I find out what the strange wooden sticks are called that are twirled and flourished in performance – *sanh tur*s (coin clappers) – indeed, wooden sticks with coins attached to rattle.

Tran Diep has been a member of the court musicians ensemble for three years. He graduated from the Academy of Music and had been invited to teach there as a lecturer, but something happened . . . the translator does not elaborate and I dare not ask.

How many musicians perform in *nha nhac,* known as Great or Grand Music, as it was, and still is, performed at important 'royal' festive occasions.

'From five to nine musicians, as it is very loud – and is usually performed outdoors. Small Music, as in chamber music for ceremonial occasions, requires nine to eleven players.'

How many uniforms do they have?

'Red and blue and from the first of April, a new uniform that was restored for Small Music, light green, and for Great Music, blue with a hat.

152

'Musicians work two days and have one day off. There are three troupes of musicians. Every morning there are performances, the Changing of the Guard, plus ten shows in the theatre per week and if there are special events, those instruments will be used.'

Three generations of musicians in his family are alive. One grandfather died three years ago. His great-grandfather, Tran Thai, died many years ago. He never knew him. He only knew his grandfather, Tran Kich, who on several occasions performed before Bao Dai – before he abdicated. This is a family that remembers well the last days of feudalism, the last Nguyen imperial court, albeit controlled by the French.

How much do musicians earn?

'Less than two million dong ($92, £73) a month.'

Astounded, I ask if he ever considered doing anything else and get a rather surprising reply.

Sometimes he plays for special Buddhist festivals and on river boats for tourists. He will play in the parade of monks on Buddha's birthday, walking from Dieu De pagoda (near Thai Kim Lan's house) to Tu Dam pagoda on the far side of the river. So a bit of freelancing, supplements his income. Tran Thai, despite being paid a pauper's wage, carries on his family's proud tradition of serving as court musicians. Royal traditions die hard in Hue – even years after the end of the royal regime.

GUARDIAN OF HUE'S HERITAGE

You catch fish with two hands
– Vietnamese proverb

Somewhat surprisingly, his office suggests a breakfast meeting at my hotel on a Saturday morning at 7.45. Clearly, Dr Hai has picked up the awful Western habit of breakfast meetings. At precisely 7.45, I receive a call from his Director of Public Affairs to tell me that he will be late.

By eight, he has not yet arrived. Having already been up for three hours – given the heat, everyone rises early in Hue, in my case at half past five – I am more than a little eager for a cup of coffee. I am still sitting in the lobby at 8.15 when he appears, accompanied by another man. As they rush past, he apologizes and says he will join me at 8.30. Who knows how long he will be in his meeting, so I decide to have breakfast without him. Far better to have mind and pen free for our chat.

At 8.45, having had breakfast, I decide to go down to see if he has finished his meeting. We meet in the lift and return to the third floor for his breakfast with a view overlooking the Perfume river.

The director of Hue Monuments Conservation Center, Dr Phan Thanh Hai, is a quick, energetic man of about forty with a bristle mop of black hair. He is a very busy man. The HMCC employs over seven hundred people, three hundred of whom are graduates or post-graduates, whose purpose is to research, restore, renovate and rebuild Hue's royal heritage, mostly located in the royal Citadel and the Royal Tombs. In addition to his duties at the Conservation Center where he was named director in 2012, Dr Hai has recently been named a member of Vietnam's National Heritage Committee. His doctorate is in History.

Although he himself comes from Hue, his family migrated south from the north three hundred and fifty years ago to settle in Than Hoa Province (150 mi, 240 km) south of Hanoi. He can trace back seventeen generations.

Then he tells me that Viet means running, a word that could aptly apply to Dr Hai's own pace of life. 'The Viets were always running', he explains, 'south, because we have a very powerful enemy to the north. South was the only direction we could run – with the sea to the east, the mountains to the west. Nam means south.

I start by asking what his three to five-year plan is for Hue and the Citadel.

'I hope I can renovate some gardens and reconstruct some important buildings: Can Chanh palace, the working palace of the Nguyen emperors, Kien Trung pavilion, the royal colonial-style residence built by Khai Dinh' – at the top of the steps now leading to nowhere. And he would like to build a proper museum on the site of Thua Tien Hue's provincial museum, opposite the current Hue Museum of Ancient Objects, now housed in Long An pavilion, so that the antiquities might be better safeguarded in a building where the air and temperature can be controlled.

When I ask him about the Emperor Thieu Tri's twenty favourite Hue beauty spots, we get onto the subject of gardens.

'There were thirty royal gardens – inside the Citadel, five. I spent six months in China studying gardens. Da Vien is the name of the garden on Tiger island,' one of the Citadel's guardian islands in the Perfume river.

Dr Hai studied and speaks Chinese fluently. He explains that 'in antiquity, the Viet people first used Chinese ideograms, not having a written language of their own. Then they borrowed the Chinese writing system to express their own, quite different language. Somewhat later, they started modifying the ideograms to better suit their own language and this modified form of ideographs which became known as *chu nom,* was used from the fifteenth to nineteenth centuries for all official government documents', until the Romanized form of writing, *quoc ngu,* was declared the official language by the penultimate emperor, Khai Dinh, under the French in 1918.

Another of Dr Hai's long-term projects is 'moving between six hundred and a thousand families out of the Citadel – to another, better place, so that certain gardens can be restored.' He has a special affinity for gardens, it seems.

'When I have a project, I have to get the money for this project. There are several methods: ask the Government, or by myself from ticket entrance fees. I get seven million US dollars (£5.6 m) per year and I can keep half of it for restoration. I have about half of this one hundred billion Vietnamese *dong* for restoration. Other money could come from help from abroad.'

Then I bring up the subject of *tuong* performances in the evening in Duyet Ti Duong theatre, handing him my research on the ticket prices for performances in Xian and Beijing.

'Can I keep this?'

Of course, it's for you.

And with that, he hurries off to greet the prime minister of Laos at the Citadel!

PART V

HUE CUISINE

COOKING FOR A KING

Throw away the fish hook to eat the fish
– Vietnamese proverb

Several centuries ago, before chefs in the West started presenting their theatrically designed dishes, chefs in Hue's imperial court were competing with the emperor's concubines to tempt the royal palate – visually. The tastes of fresh tropical fruit, vegetables and seafood and the subtle combinations of herbs in delectable sauces, were only a part of it. A royal dish had to be stunningly, extravagantly appealing to the eye, or it didn't merit the first royal bite.

Rather understating the case, historian Mai Khac Ung writes, 'Food (in Hue) has progressed from meeting a basic survival need to becoming an art form.'

And the poet, Ngo Minh has written, 'Gradually with time, delicious dishes have been created, passed down and imbued with a specific, unmistakably distinctive Hue character.'

When I first came to Hue, I was bowled over by the artistic creations of chef, Madame Ton Nu Ha, who carved – sculpted – vegetables into whimsical flowers and the four sacred animals: the turtle, phoenix, *kylin* (unicorn) and the dragon. She is still serving her amazing multi-course royal banquets (book one day ahead) for no more than you might pay for a main course in the West.

Hue cuisine is highly revered by the rest of Vietnam – in Hanoi, and even in spice-loving Ho Chi Minh City.

Food in the Purple Forbidden City was taken very seriously by the Nguyen, starting with the early Nguyen lords long before they became emperors. Lord Nguyen Phuc Nguyen, the second Nguyen lord, set up the Ly Thien department in Le Huan Street of Phuoc Yen village, the street just inside the Citadel walls that runs along the outer, western side of the Imperial City. During his rule, there were up to three hundred fifty cooks employed by this department. Each chef prepared one dish, presumably for each meal. With no refrigeration, food had to be prepared fresh, on the day.

Two centuries later, Emperor Minh Mang added the Thuong Thien department, placed near Duyet Thi Duong theatre inside the Imperial City, which had fifty chefs. One source states that there were these two departments – without explaining quite why. But then, it begins to become apparent when you start to add up the number of people who had to be catered for, three meals a day, plus snacks for tea parties and ceremonies. Adding to the numbers exponentially, were the numerous feasts prepared for mandarin, scholars, and foreign emissaries.

Meals for the emperor and his family of wives, concubines and royal children – were served separately – at half past six in the morning, at eleven and at five in the evening, for a total of more than a hundred people. And then, there were the servants, who lived in the Purple Forbidden City to feed as well.

Huge banquets multiplied the work of the chefs: banquets at *Tet* (the lunar New Year), at the Ploughing Rice Fields ceremony, banquets for royal birthdays, for the newly graduated scholars (who were to become mandarin), and for foreign emissaries. These banquets were extremely elaborate: one tray of fifty dishes, seven trays of forty dishes, twenty-five trays of thirty dishes.

There was also food to be prepared, according to strict regulations laid down in *Ceremonial Rules (Hoi Dien)* for offerings and worship – hundreds of these ceremonies every year: the Sacrificial Nam Giao ceremony; the death anniversaries for each of the deceased emperors, numerous queens and Nguyen lords; the number of dishes for a ceremony dependent upon the rank of the individual being commemorated.

Food for the emperor had to be prepared to the highest degree of hygiene, a tradition of hygiene that remains in Hue.

Truong Thien soldiers were charged with buying food for the emperor, his wives and concubines. Once prepared, the pots were labelled with the name of the dish, each pot tied with a strip of bamboo, placed in baskets *(sieng)*, covered with a red towel and hand-carried under the shade of two parasols.

It must have made quite a procession of food carriers, considering how many people had to be served – the emperor

158

receiving no fewer than thirty-five dishes at each meal. Food for the emperors' wives was divided by their maids.

Once in Can Thanh palace, or later in Kien Trung palace for Emperor Khai Dinh, there were small kitchens to cook the rice to make sure it was hot, another to heat the food, if necessary.

The emperor's rice came from An Cuu rice fields south of Hue, had to be selected grain by grain, whole grains only, and cooked in a small clay pot from Phuoc Tich village. These earthenware pots would have been brought by Truong Thien soldiers from the village and steeped in a large pot of green tea to season them. Having been used once, the pots were destroyed. Water to cook the rice had to be carried from Ham Long well near Bao Quoc pagoda – on the south side of the river – by boat.

Emperors ate with bamboo chopsticks, carved by a skilled craftsman, or chopsticks carved from *kim dao* wood, ivory-white in colour. It is said that if there were poison in the food, these *kim dao* dao chopsticks would change colour to dark grey or black.

The same craftsman carved toothpicks from bamboo that measured about eight inches (20 cms) long, sharp at one end for picking the teeth and broad at the other, the wood finely split into a soft fluff, a royal toothbrush. They were called 'flower' or 'cotton' toothpicks, presumably because the soft end resembled a boll of cotton – or the blossom of a flower. Or perhaps because the Vietnamese word *bong* translates as both cotton and flower.

Most emperors ate 'alone' – with only one guard to fan him and two attendants on duty to keep him company, as well as a musical group to perform court music. Sometimes an emperor might offer a meal to a mandarin attendant; then a guard would prepare a separate tray at another table or on a low wooden bed.

China bowls in the Forbidden Purple City were inscribed with the words Inner City and painted with a five-paw, blue enamel dragon, differentiating them from the four-paw dragons on bowls used by mandarin. These bowls, originally made to order in Giang Tay province of China, were later made by Chinese potters in Hue.

In addition to the thirty-five dishes prepared for the emperor's meal, favoured concubines often offered him special dishes and if he didn't taste them, they were extremely disappointed. To return the favour, he would ask the eunuchs to take them some of his food, to indicate they were in favour. A large tray of deserts always included sweet soup, jams, cakes and fruit, decorated in an artful arrangement.

All of the Nguyen emperors drank wine, most often containing ginseng and herbs, the most infamous of which was that devised by Minh Mang' physician, Le Quoc Chuoc, which became known as the 'sexual intercourse five times a night with five different women wine,' the name, said to have been added to by Minh Mang himself with – 'and four women pregnant.' I have read with amusement that 'it was necessary for Nguyen emperors to drink ginseng wine because apart from court business, an emperor was 'responsible' for having sexual relationships with hundreds of concubines' – a responsibility that many a Westerner might well envy, I suppose. The ingredients for Minh Mang's wine eventually escaped the secrecy of the royal palace and when I first came to Hue, it was sold in tiny blue and white jugs. Of course, I had to taste it: very medicinal and no erotic effects, but then, I'm not an emperor.

Naturally, the emperor did not consume all thirty-five dishes he was served at each meal, so sometimes to show favour, he would give them back to the Truong Thien soldiers, who would place them in red lacquered boxes to be delivered under parasols to the mansions of certain mandarin. When mandarin received these supreme tokens of favour – 'given the emperor's food' – they were required to wear court dress to receive it at their gates and to bow five times to show their gratitude. This custom was adopted later by the mandarin themselves when they offered food to their close friends; it is said that even Ho Chi Minh followed this tradition.

Not all emperors were served thirty-five dishes at each meal. Apparently, the first Nguyen emperor, Gia Long, only took a small bowl of pure rice soup for breakfast and when he was away from the palace, ate rice, meat, fish, vegetables and fruit along with the mandarin in the royal boat – and he did not drink wine.

Dining customs changed with the arrival of the French. Emperor Dong Khanh chose European china, spoons and forks, and chopsticks were rarely used by emperors thereafter.

Emperor Duy Tan, soon after he was crowned, was so dismayed to discover that an emperor's meal cost 'dozens of *quan*' (the unit of currency, now thought to have been worth a few hundred thousand *dong*). If a *quan* was worth, say only 300,000 *dong* – roughly $15 – times 'dozens of *quan*' – you can understand why he became alarmed and declared: 'In the past, I used to have two bowls of rice and some goby (small fish) cooked with salty brine. Just give me that kind of food and it will be enough.' Emperor Duy Tan ate alone, or sometimes invited his teacher, Mai Khac Don, to dine with him to enjoy the court music, eating from a separate tray, of course. When he married, it is said that Duy Tan dined together with his wife like ordinary married couples.

The last emperor, Bao Dai, grew up eating the popular dishes of Hue – *ruoc kho* (fish paste cooked with brine), *mam* (salty fish) and goby soup. However, after he was sent to France to study, his tastes became completely Westernised – French – and he dined with his queen, Nam Phuong, and later with his children. Both he and the Emperor Dong Khanh, drank wine, the latter, partial to Bordeaux – on his French doctor's orders.

Thirty-five specific dishes served to the emperor were only available within his residence, which is not to say that he was confined to only thirty-five dishes. He had a selection from hundreds of dishes. The chefs devised menus depending upon the season, his tastes and his health. Dr Thai Van Kiem describes the most extravagant Vietnamese dishes in his book entitled, The Vietnamese Land in the South *(Dat Viet Troi Nam):*

1) Peacock-shaped fermented pork rolls *(nem cong),* in which the multi-layered, colourful rolls are thinly sliced and placed in a display like the feathers of the peacock's tail, spreading round the plate from the carved peacock's head.
2) Phoenix-shaped meat paste *(cha phuong),* the description of which suggests that the phoenix is a living bird of the high mountains, having feathers of five colours, predominately red.
3) Rhinoceros skin *(da tay ngu),* indicating that only the skin of the poor beasts' armpits makes edible, delicious meat. No wonder the rhinoceros has disappeared from Vietnam.
4) Bear's paw *(ban tay gau),* only the skin of his paw, apparently, is delicious. Poor bears.
5) Tendon of the deer *(gan nai)* was considered to be a tonic for the vital organs.
6) Orangutan's lips *(moi duoi uoi),* but only his lips – and no more orangutans in Vietnam.
7) Meat from the elephant's feet *(thit chan voi),* that is, a layer of soft tendon. Very few elephants are left in Vietnam – none in this area that used to be known as Elephant Forest.
8) Swallows' nests *(yen sao),* still gathered from certain off-shore islands, highly nutritious – now all exported to China.

As these dishes were difficult to obtain, expensive and required elaborate preparation, they were only served to emperors, and rarely, to a few important officials and guests. Feasts were served according to a strict hierarchy of protocol. A first-rank feast consisted of two trays of sixty dishes; a second rank feast had seven trays of forty dishes; a third rank feast, thirty trays of thirty dishes.

One type of first rank feast had twenty-seven main dishes, fifteen kinds of salty and sweet cakes, twelve jams, three fruits, three kinds of sticky rice and sweet soup. The main dishes might include swallows' nests, deer's tendon, abalone and fish fins.

Recipes were not written down. They were handed down from one chef to another. Fortunately in 1915, Mrs Truong Thi Bich wrote a cookbook – in poetry – *Cent recettes de cuisine Annamite (Thuc Pho Bach Thien)* to teach her daughter how to cook. It included one hundred recipes, a few from the Nguyen court – peacock-shaped, fermented meat rolls and swallows' nests; as well as more common food such as rabbit, salted field cabbage, salted lemon grass and meat.

After the abdication of Emperor Bao Dai, the Ly Thien and Thuong Thien cooking departments were disbanded. Chefs returned to ordinary life, a few opened restaurants and they taught their daughters to cook. Cooking also was taught in the old Dong Khanh High School for Girls (now called Hai Ba Trung), where the cookery teacher, Ms Hoang Thi Kim Cuc used her lesson plans to write *Cooking in the Hue Manner (Mon an nau loi hue).* Its six hundred recipes concentrate on popular dishes rather than delicacies. It includes one hundred twenty-five vegetarian recipes – as Mahayana Buddhist monks in Hue are vegetarian – and one hundred seventy-five sweet soups. Following the book, a Hue cook could serve guests one hundred meals of six dishes each without ever repeating a dish.

More than elsewhere in Vietnam, girls in Hue are taught that the four virtues of a woman – one writer says subjections – apart from being beautiful and speaking softly, are 'cooking delicious food for a full stomach and wearing smart clothes that last a long time.' As I think of the elegant Hue women with whom I am acquainted, every one of them, despite their many other accomplishments, are mindful of their appearance at all times and without exception, are excellent cooks. I'd never make it as a Hue lady.

TO A COOKERY CLASS AND BEYOND

A man without education is an uncut gem
– Vietnamese proverb

It has been written that there is a total repertoire of 1,300 Hue dishes. With that wide a field to survey, I ask myself quite where to begin – perhaps with a deep draught of Minh Mang's wine. But then, as it had so little effect the last time, perhaps not. I decide to start with a cookery class at Hai Ba Trung High School for Girls to see what they are teaching young Hue girls these days and suggest it to my translator, Thanh Thanh. She obligingly sets up an interview with a cookery class teacher, not at Hai Ba Trung, but at Hue Star School, which takes pupils from primary through high school.

Inside the walls, a watchman on guard at the gate, Hue Star School is a complex of ultra-modern buildings surrounding a vast, paved courtyard, a row of meeting rooms to the right. We are asked to wait in what feels very like a boardroom, leather executive chairs around an open, rectangular table, leather inserts at each place around the table. I am amazed at the luxury of state schools, only to learn that this is, indeed, a private boarding school and a very expensive one at that, the only one in Hue to have golf on the course curriculum. A pro comes from Singapore to teach the students. So not quite the traditional Hue high school that I had in mind, nevertheless . . .

His Monday morning meeting concluded at 8.0 a.m., we are greeted by the principal, Ve Van Lam, a man who clearly likes his food, wearing a white shirt and spectacles. I am introduced to his team of six earnest looking gentlemen as well as the young female cookery teacher, who is wearing a vivid orange *ao dai*. I ask the principal about school fees.

At Hue Star School, for high school day students tuition costs 1.2 million *dong* ($55, £44) per month; 4.5 million *dong* ($208, £166) per month for boarders; for junior high students, 1.8 million *dong* ($83, £66) per month; for primary students, 1.6 million *dong* ($74, £59) per month, 'because we take care of them all day.' It's a ten-month term from August to May.

163

'Under state education, children start kindergarten at six and it is free. But they must buy uniforms and text books. For university, students' parents have to pay 4 million *dong* ($185, £148) per term), it varies a lot, unless they go to teacher college, where they pay nothing because they have scholarships to support them.

'There are three private schools in Hue. In the past, there were no private schools. The first opened only about twenty years ago. Star Hue School opened in 2009, with the first students attending classes in 2010. In the kindergarten we have three hundred pupils, in the primary school one hundred fifty pupils, in the secondary school one hundred fifty pupils, and in the high school one hundred fifty pupils.'

Ve Van Lam tells me that parents are very determined for their children to go to school. 'Very often when they meet, the greeting is, "Are your children still going to school?" And it is especially respected when children go on to university.'

A meeting with the cookery teacher, Miss Trang, has been arranged. The principal departs and we are led by Miss Trang into a lesser meeting room with a light-wood table. Beneath the windows, a steel rack holds drums and red Vietnamese flags. Female teachers, she explains, only wear the *ao dai* uniform on Mondays and Fridays, because it's so hot and uncomfortable. Why Mondays and Fridays remains a mystery.

As we are talking and tiny cups of green tea are being poured, a group of young adolescent students file in and seat themselves round the table, along with the English literature teacher, Miss Ngo. The school uniform is grey skirts for girls, grey trousers for boys, white blouses and shirts with a fine red thread running through in squares, and the ubiquitous red scarf indicating young Ho Chi Minh Pioneers. There are three boys and four girls. I am slightly surprised to see boys in a cookery class and wonder if it is compulsory.

After introducing myself as Carol – sometimes maddeningly, nearly everyone in Hue refers to themselves only by their given name – one of the three boys, a strapping lad, slightly taller than the other two, repeats 'carrot' . . .

'No, not carrot – Carol,' and we all laugh. I'm surprised they speak enough English to get the joke. Discussing with Thanh Thanh, whether both boys and girls learn to cook at home, the cheeky 'carrot' lad volunteers, 'My parents work, so I have to cook for myself.'

Through Thanh Thanh, I ask the cookery teacher what she teaches the students in their first ever cookery class?

164

'First, theory, what ingredients to buy and the various cooking processes: frying, grilling, steaming, boiling. There are alternate classes, one class of theory and one class of practice.'

What do they cook in the very first class?

'Rau luoc' (boiled vegetables), but boiled in such a way as to keep their crispness and colour – *'and rau chien'* (battered, crispy fried vegetables). What they cook in the classes to follow is optional. They bring the ingredients to the class and they decide what to cook.'

So everyone in the class may be cooking something different – not an easily-managed proposition for a cookery teacher, I would have thought. There are only two cookery classes a week and classes range from only three or four students to as many as twenty. The classes are only forty-five minutes long.

'Yes', Miss Trang admits, 'it has to be something simple.'

The students must be at least twelve before they can choose to take cookery.

'Everybody likes cooking, all the students want to take cookery classes,' says the cookery teacher. 'Because we like to eat – the teacher, too,' quips the cheeky lad.

However, they are only allowed to take cookery classes for one year. Cookery, obviously, is a very popular, fun subject.

Then I go round the circle to ask their names and ages. All of them are twelve: the cheeky lad who calls himself Tony (alias Hoang), Phung, Phuc, Ngoc, Quyen, Nhi, Tran and Trinh.

The cheeky lad volunteers that both his father and brother are chefs in Hanoi, so he eats 'lots of good food – noodles.'

As we are about to leave, the principal invites Thanh Thanh and me 'to an event at my mother's home on Thursday. I want you to taste good Hue food.'

How very kind of him. As it happens, this was the first invitation of many into private Hue homes.

In the taxi back, Thanh Thanh tells me that as it is his mother's death anniversary, we should take a cake. I suggest a bakery across from the hotel, but she has a better idea, a bakery on the way to the principal's mother's home – we can buy it en route, no need to order in advance.

A few days later, a taxi takes us through rural lanes to the village of Chuon. As we thought the invitation was to the headmaster's mother's house for her death anniversary party, I am surprised to be introduced to his *mother.* So I assume that it must be his grandmother's death anniversary, but then, I am introduced to *her* – she is eighty-six. It is sometime before the truth tumbles out – this is the annual death anniversary celebration for the headmaster's *great* grandmother – no longer with us. It is a grand family event, members of the family having travelled for miles to come together for this special family reunion. One member from each of the distant families will have been nominated to attend and represent their family.

We remove our shoes on the terrace.

Two aged gentlemen wearing royal blue silk, long traditional gowns and round circular hats – court dress – are elderly neighbours with relatives in this family.

We are seated at a table with a red lace tablecloth under glass beneath a staggeringly complicated, three dimensional creation hanging on the wall – one could hardly call it a picture – more a sculpture: mandarin crossing over a bridge, the path winding up through a complicated landscape. It demands far closer examination than I am able to give it. Above white tiled floors and white walls, colourful tableaux form a cornice to divide the two rooms. Outside later, I see that this is only half the house, beside a two-story section.

A middle-aged chap approaches and asks in English, 'Can you speak Vietnamese?'

When I cravenly answer, no, his response is a blustering, 'Why not?'

'What I need is a Vietnamese mother to teach me' – I reply and everyone laughs.

Sitting next to me is a young, female English teacher. I am introduced to a shy young girl, who is studying English. Her first question is 'How old are you?' – to which I explain that in the West, it is not a question that one asks ladies as they do not like to tell their age. I normally say that I am a hundred, which after a pause, usually gets a laugh. The young girl's name is Anh and she is twelve.

The baby in the English teacher's arms is named Sen, which means Lotus Flower. Four generations, over twenty people, have come to the celebration, some from as far as eighty-four miles (140 km) away. Those coming from a great distance have travelled by motorbike. The headmaster's son, Linh, tells me that Vietnam has GPS on smart phones. But then, I'm a techno-ignoramous and GPS would be absolutely necessary, for once off the few main numbered highways, there are no road signs – none at all.

166

Attending this birthday party are several teachers, the headmaster tells me proudly: a physics teacher; his son, Linh, who teaches engineering at the Agricultural University near the Citadel. There are at least two English teachers, the English teacher beside me, the father and headmaster, of course, whose daughter teaches English – she has been in the kitchen working all morning. And there's also a primary school teacher – how many is that? Six teachers in the immediate family. The headmaster himself was born near Ho Chi Minh City (HCMC), but his grandmother was from Hue. She has two daughters in Melbourne, one a nurse, the other retired. He himself has relatives in California and hopes that his grand-daughter will be able to study there.

We sit in the front room at a table with the grannies. His granny is wearing a violet pyjamas suit, her teeth black from betal chewing, what few she has left. Young wives sit with babies in their laps, while their mothers prepare the food at the back of the second room, children playing under their feet. There are shouts from the little ones and the clanging of a tin drum.

We sip cool water and chat until dinner is served – for me and seven others, outside on the terrace at a round table, choked with platters and plates of food and small bowls of sauces. Chilled Huda beer is served. Salad is heaped in the centre of a large round plate over thinly-sliced meat; slices of pork *nem* and *paté (da)* line another platter. A huge *mu* fish, smothered under grated vegetables and herbs, curves to fit another large plate. A mountain of chopped, boiled chicken fills a bowl. Another plate is piled high with shrimps to be dipped in a red sauce – mild, to my relief.

Mounds of something that looks like wax paper is identified as *kinh,* a special Hue fish 'pancake' made of sticky rice. A bowl of sticky rice has been cooked in coconut milk. And a tureen holds noodle soup should anyone still feel hungry at the end of this feast. The food is all extremely delicious, eaten with gusto and obvious pleasure by those around the table. But eating and asking questions about the food simultaneously, simply doesn't work, everyone is eating so fast.

We move inside for tea and one of Hue's famous sweet soups – soup only because it is liquid. This one is called *ngu* – bean soup – rather like white lima beans in a sweetish juice.

'It is only served at birthday celebrations.' What a privilege and what a special treat.

167

HUE SALADS AND SPECIALITIES

When you eat, check the pots and pans;
When you sit, check the direction
– Vietnamese proverb

Nearly every restaurant in Hue offers at least half a dozen special Hue dishes, and certain small family restaurants specialize in one or another of them with finite variations. Even so, with temperatures in the high thirties, my culinary curiosity shrank to the pleasant restaurants in the near neighbourhood of streets lined with interesting, small restaurants.

Just two doors from the hotel in Le Loi Street was Grain. The poster at one end of the terrace pictured the five or six specialities of Hue offered by most restaurants. After settling on the terrace and a waitress having set up a fan to blow directly at me, I would decide what to try. The first was *banh khoai,* a fairly large, crisp rice pancake stuffed with bean sprouts, shrimp, beef and who knows what herbs. It was delicious, but served hot, so better eaten in cooler weather.

'The Vietnamese eat them in the winter,' the waitress volunteered afterwards.

One day I ordered *banh lui,* which to the uninitiated look like kebabs: ground lean pork mixed with fish sauce, powdered grilled rice and a dozen other ingredients, mixed into a paste, shaped round the stalks of lemon grass and grilled. The uninitiated (me), might nibble them off the stalk, but the proper Vietnamese diner gently eases the grilled meat off the lemon grass stalk with a piece of lettuce and rolls it in a piece of rice paper with the lettuce and herbs to dip into a special thick sauce. Really delicious.

Next I ordered fresh spring rolls *(banh cuon):* soft rice paper wrapped around bits of ground pork, bean sprouts and unidentifiable herbs. Again, delicious, dunked in a tiny saucer of *nuoc mam,* an excellent, cool dish for lunch. Not a speciality of Hue, but very good, nonetheless. In the interest of not gaining weight, one day I ordered a green papaya salad – how refreshing. Another day I ordered a green

168

mango salad, then a banana flower salad. Soon I fell into such a salad habit at lunch time that the Grain waitress would simply ask, 'Papaya, mango or banana flower?' Not unique to Hue, but these salads are irresistible in a hot climate, all served with sliced shrimp, peanuts and sesame seeds sprinkled on top. A huge plate of salad was just right for a working lunch.

One day fairly early on, I was astonished when the waitress plopped a small transparent envelope on my table with the words, 'For you, from the manager.' Inside was a pearl necklace. I am still open-mouthed at the spontaneous generosity. Pity was probably mixed in with generosity – poor lady, no family, no friends to have lunch with. Being alone in Vietnam is to be pitied as the Vietnamese are constantly surrounded by their extended families and friends. Privacy is almost unknown and less understood.

Yet it was some time before I summoned the courage to ask if I could watch the salads being prepared in the kitchen. Highly amused, they said yes. The kitchen was quite small and to a Westerner, immaculate though quite rudimentary, but had everything necessary for good, quick Vietnamese cooking. The girls all crowded round to watch me, watching the salad making.

First, the green mango came out of the fridge. The cook skinned half the mango with a huge wide-bladed scraper – a very sharp potato peeler might do as well, leaving half the mango un-skinned in order to have something to hold onto as she grated the flesh of the skinned half into a large aluminium bowl. Next came a cucumber, which she half skinned, then grated the white flesh into long strings, avoiding the seeds in the centre. Next came a carrot, again grating long strands from the pointed end.

Donning a plastic glove – Hue's tradition of hygiene – she mixed by hand the grated fruit and vegetables and added the sauce, chopped peanuts and sesame seeds, then she hand-mixed it all again. The mixture was then arranged prettily on a plate, more sesame seeds and chopped peanuts sprinkled on top with sliced shrimps arranged in an attractive circle, garnished with a few leaves of a fresh green herb.

Getting the sauce just right is more delicate: one spoonful of fish sauce *(nuoc mam)*, three spoons of water, half a spoon of lime juice or white vinegar – 'very little' finely chopped red pepper (for me, two or three thin slices chopped finely without the fiery seeds) and a pinch of sugar. Mix well. The restaurant, I noticed, kept a jar of the sauce already mixed; it probably matures well as it stands.

169

Another day, I asked to watch as the banana flower salad was being made. I had never seen a banana flower, apart from hanging on a tree, never in a market – the bud, actually – so I was interested to see that when used in cooking, it looks like a fat ear of un-husked corn. The outer husks are removed and the cook started by slicing the pointed end with the wide-bladed peeler, rather like a grater. The rest of the banana flower salad was identical to the green mango salad.

One morning early, I strolled along the causeway beside the hotel and watched a fisher woman washing mussels *(hen)* in loosely-woven baskets in the river. Then she tossed them through the air – *en masse* – to another woman, who caught them in another basket and emptied them into plastic sacks. They were sold nearby in a roadside stand under a parasol beside the boat from which they had been caught. I had been hearing about *com hen,* this renowned Hue mussel dish since I had first visited Hue, but never quite had the nerve to risk my liver. The tiny mussels, the size of the end of a chopstick, are named after the island, Con Hen, in the river opposite, where the mussels come from *(com* means food, *con* means island). When *com* appears on a sign, it simply means food, indicating a restaurant.

So famous is *com hen,* that there is even a well-known Vietnamese jingle about it:

'Whoever wants to come to Hue can come,
When seeing *com hen,* must stop to eat.'

Golden Rice Restaurant, around the corner at 40 Pham Ngu Lao Street, became my favourite restaurant in the evenings, a restaurant that serves *only* a wide variety of delicious Vietnamese food. As the evenings passed, I ticked off the various *banh* (cakes) on the menu, based on rice, cassava or manioc flour, where I knew they would be well prepared.

Banh beo, three-inch wide 'pancakes', are made of rice powder and water, stirred to a paste and steamed in tiny, shallow saucers with chopped, dried shrimp on top. Eaten with a small spoon, a few drops of *nuoc mam* adds piquancy to an otherwise bland dish. Oddly, the Vietnamese think they resemble fern leaves, hence the name. Another night I ordered *banh cuon,* the soft, fresh rice paper, spring rolls around a shrimp or two and bits of pork and salad, dipped in sesame sauce. To follow each of these starters or snacks, I ordered sliced, grilled egg plant, long and narrow egg plants cooked with finely chopped, caramelized onion on top in a soy and lemon grass sauce – utterly irresistible.

Slowly working my way through the menu, favourites included shrimps in tamarind sauce, chicken and herbs cooked in half a bamboo stalk, the tofu and mushroom hot pot, the fresh tuna hot pot, the hot green fig salad – and the taro ice cream.

Nguyen Huang, the charming waiter, became a familiar and friendly face at the end of many a hot day. One evening he asked how my work was going and I told him that I needed to try *com hen*. I had been hearing about this special Hue mussel dish, but had never seen it on a menu. I asked Huang if he could suggest a good *com hen* restaurant and he said, 'Yes, I can help me.' He asked me to come to the restaurant the following evening an hour before he started work and he would take me to a *com hen* restaurant on his motorbike. Can you imagine that happening in Europe?

As it happened, when I arrived the following evening, the Golden Rice was already quite busy, so Huang asked one of the waitresses, who was not busy, to take me instead.

With me on the back of her motorbike, Nguyen Thi My Duyen puttered across the causeway at the east end of Le Loi and turned right. A strip of restaurants here specialise in *com hen*. When I started to write down the name on the sign, Duyen laughed and told me that 'the restaurants along here have no names – they go by their addresses. This one is 17 Han Mac Tu.'

It was a big, open-front restaurant with low metal tables and child-sized plastic chairs. The kitchen was a couple of stainless steel tables with surrounding protective glass. I was mildly surprised to see that the two cooks were wearing plastic gloves – again, Hue's tradition of strict hygiene. We were surrounded by noisy families, tucking in and waitresses scurrying to and from the kitchen.

The tiny river mussels – Duyen called them clams in English – were fingertip-sized, served already shelled, too tiny to see dropped on rice in a cereal bowl, topped with crispy bits of pork rind, peanuts and bean sprouts. Another cereal bowl of clam broth is served separately, not to pour over as I assumed, but to sip spoonfuls of as you eat. Duyen took charge like a mother and mixed everything in my bowl. She also ordered two large mugs of *che bao* to drink, one of Hue's sweet soups, this one made of sweet corn, coconut milk and chopped ice – very refreshing. I had assumed that Hue sweet soups

171

were deserts, but no, they can be consumed simultaneously with a meal. Huang had told me that there are several kinds of *com hen:* with rice *(com hen),* with rice noodles *(com bun);* or with egg noodles *(com my).* We had the one with rice. And it was good, not the spicy confection that I had half expected.

The biggest surprise of all was the bill – oh yes, I had to try the noodles as well as the rice. So for three bowls and two cups of *che bao,* the bill came to a staggering 35,000 dong (US$1.62, £1.29).

Another evening, I asked Huang where to go for various Hue specialities – not on his restaurant's menu – and he suggested taking me to another restaurant. So off we went the following evening to a restaurant only a few blocks away (Hanh Restaurant, 11 Pho Due Chinh), another wide-open-front place with metal tables and low plastic chairs, as noisy as an inferno and full of happy Vietnamese.

Three small, colourful altar houses stood side by side at the entrance, holding tiny white horses and a yellow dragon. Across the road, a vendor was grinding sugar cane 'to get sugar water.'

The menu was on a blackboard, but eventually a waiter appeared with a written menu. We decided on *banh loc* – jellied tapioca paste around a shrimp and a bit of pork, and *banh nam* – jellied rice paste around a bit of pork and lemon grass, both steamed in banana leaves.

Fortunately, they are served with a spoon as cutting the sticky paste with chopsticks would have been nigh on impossible for a Westerner, maybe even for a Vietnamese. I noticed that Hoang used the spoon.

Did I like them? Well, they were different in texture from anything I had ever eaten in the West and otherwise, fairly innocuous, no strong tastes, no hot pepper. And although they were individually quite thin, having split a serving of each with Huang – a serving is perhaps a dozen banana-leaf packets of each – afterwards, I was not at all hungry.

One day I was invited for a duck lunch at Golden Rice Restaurant as 'Vietnamese people eat duck on the fifth of the fifth lunar month, it's a tradition,' said Hoang. But nobody at the lunch seemed to know why or where the tradition derived from. One Vietnamese I questioned later told me that it was the day that his village always went to the mountains to collect medicinal herbs.

172

The entire staff of Golden Grain was seated at a long table over large tureens piled high with chopped chunks of duck. Another long platter of duck blood was garnished with herbs on top, which I managed to ignore, and there was a heaped plate of salad with banana flower shavings. Everyone served themselves with chopsticks, and happily, ate the duck with their fingers. Holding an awkwardly chopped chunk of duck with chopsticks to gnaw off the bone would have been farcical. The newborn baby of the owner of the restaurant, Giang, and her husband were there, but she soon rushed off to her other restaurant (Elegance) around the corner, presumably to treat the staff there to a duck lunch.

The following morning I received an explanation from Professor Buu I, as to why everyone eats duck on the fifth of the fifth lunar month in Hue.

'A long, long time ago there was a Chinese Confucian poet named Khuat Nguyen. He was the author of *Ly Tao* – one of the six greatest Chinese works of poetry of all time. He counselled the king not to go to war. But the king did not take his advice – and died a year later. The poet was so distraught, he felt that he no longer had a place in life, so he drowned himself. The people were very sad. So since that time, he has been commemorated on this day, the fifth of the fifth month, by eating cold food – duck – and the little, triangular rice cakes, which are almost insipid, called *u tro*. They are only eaten in Central and South Vietnam, not in the North.'

(Note: In China, Khuat Nguyen is known as Binh Qu Yuan (340-278 BC), who lived during the period of the Warring States and the proper name of the Fifth of the Fifth Festival in Vietnam is *Tet Doan Ngo.)*

HUE'S CHEF'S CHEF

Qualities of the wife are shown by her cooking
– Vietnamese proverb

The one-storey house nestles beside the An Cuu river – actually a canal that Emperor Minh Mang had dug to supply water to the southern part of the city where the French built their villas. Hoang Thi Nhu Huy is standing, waiting and smiling, outside her front gate in a Hue purple *ao dai,* a slim woman of a certain age, her hair pulled back, waving to the taxi driver. She leads me up the central, tiled walk beneath a cooling canopy of trees – monkey trees, bamboo – providing an oasis of shade in Hue's blazing summer.

Once inside, she motions me to the corner tea nook where dark, inlaid mother-of-pearl chairs stand four-square opposite a matching tea table. On it is a floral arrangement seemingly made of tiny rose apples, each on a stalk surrounded by leaves. How fitting for a chef, I think. The dark, glass-front cabinets that line the room are full of an assortment of blue and white rice bowls, stacks of small and larger plates, tea sets, all manner of pretty dishes – the tableware a chef would require to serve Vietnamese food, elegantly.

She disappears for a moment and reappears with two white, heart-shaped sweets in dainty saucers, garnished with two artfully placed blades of grass, served with tiny two-pronged forks. 'Made of fava bean paste.' Next comes a black ceramic teapot, the tea poured into liqueur-sized, black ceramic tea cups, placed on ebony coasters.

The style of presentation and the subtlety that has gone into the preparation is clearly several levels above the very pleasant restaurants I have been frequenting.

I feel somewhat overcome by humility. As practically a non-cook, albeit one who appreciates the effort and creativity that goes into producing not just tasty food, but food that appeals to the eye, well, what does one ask a chef's chef? I ask first about her family.

'All teachers,' which means that Hoang Thi Nhu Huy has not been descended from a grand family. Both of her parents were teachers, which means that they were not highly paid. There were ten

174

children, five boys and five girls. She was number five. Her father taught French and education; her mother taught in a primary school. In fact, Hoang Thi Nhu Huy trained to become a teacher of literature, but life's path led elsewhere.

'Ten members of my family are teachers,' I think she means her generation. 'Me, too. My brother and sister are famous. My brother teaches history at university and is president – director – of the Hue Sien University. My sister is a teacher at Hue College of Education.' Thi Nhu Huy has three sons.

'No, they don't like cooking, they only like eating,' she smiles wryly. 'The first son studied about seafood' – marine biology. The second is a mechanical engineer. The third is a designer. He studied architecture at university.' They are thirty-nine, thirty-seven and twenty-one. She has two granddaughters and one grandson.

Her husband died four years ago after having been bedridden for nearly ten years, following a stroke. In 2007, in recognition of her determination and energy in carrying on with a busy schedule of teaching, writing and working with international organizations (UNIDO, NAV, JICA), the Vietnamese Government gave her the Award of Vietnam for Overcoming Difficulties. Apart from teaching, she had developed programmes to teach poor women to improve food processing, and how to provide a nutritious diet for HIV patients.

I had read that she had won two gold medals in a cooking contest sponsored by the Vietnam Office of Tourism. She has been a TV chef, both in Hue and Hanoi, and she has appeared in two films: *Food for the Hunter,* and *Madame Huy's Perfume Wine: Hue Traditional Food.*

'I started to cook with my mother and with many other Vietnamese ladies around me. Whenever I meet Vietnamese ladies, I always ask them for recipes.'

After her teaching degree from the Hue University of Education, in 1988 she received a scholarship from Germany's Schmidt Foundation to study cookery at the Viet Nam Women's Union, following which she became a trainer at the same institution – until 2000 – so she became a teacher of cookery instead of literature. She now trains chefs as head of department at Thua Tien Hue's Professional College of Tourism.

In 1998, she received a grant to attend a three-month cookery course in France. While there, she entered a *Toques Blanches* competition, cooking European dishes alongside European chefs.

Hoang Thi Nhu Huy was one of five medal winners – the other four were Europeans. This award made her an Honorary Member of France's prestigious National Academy of Cuisine.

Back in Vietnam, she has acted as consultant chef to numerous prestigious hotels and restaurants, training their staff: in Hue, at the five-star Saigon Morin hotel, at the five-star Ancient Hue restaurant, at the Duy Tan Hotel and at the Nam Chau Hoi Quan restaurant; in Hanoi at the Hanoi Opera Hilton hotel; in Saigon at the Majestic hotel and in Nha Trang at the Anna Mandara.

Furthermore, she has taught professional chefs both in France and Belgium to cook Vietnamese food and chefs from many countries beat a path to her door in Hue. Framed colour photographs of Hoang Thi Nhu Huy with international chefs from all over, hang from the dark wooden beams, chefs she has taught to cook Vietnamese – and Hue cuisine.

Yet perhaps the culmination of all of her prizes was in 2008 when she was named A Living Human Treasure of Vietnam.

The prizes didn't stop. In 2010, she received a prize for her writing. There had been two famous cookbooks written by Hue women chefs, one written – in poetry – years ago in the old Chinese *chu nom* script, one later, in French. Following this tradition, Hoang Thi Nhu Huy's cookery book has one hundred five recipe poems in Vietnamese. She also has written numerous magazine articles.

She then tells me that she may receive an award from the Vietnamese Government in September as a Vietnamese Meritorious Culinary Artisan.

'There will only be three: one from Hanoi, one from Hue and one from Ho Chi Minh City.

'I am preparing my profile,' by which I understand, her application for government recognition, sometimes a matter of competing against others who may apply.

Then it takes me a moment to comprehend what she says: 'There are 10,000 persons on my blog,' by which I think she means that there are 10,000 followers!

Having exhausted family, awards and honours, I plunge into Hue cooking with some trepidation. I have been more than a little baffled by what goes into Hue's famous, five or six 'cakes' – not cakes at all in the Western sense of the word, but there is nothing in the English lexicon that quite describes these semi-transparent, glutinous savouries, *banh*. What are they made of?

'Cassava, cassava powder and root, rice and sticky rice, also tarot root.' Still not much the wiser, I ask what influence she thinks the Chams and the nearby hill tribes have had on Hue cuisine.

'Figs and wild vegetables, the banana flower, fish paste sauce, sweet potato leaves – boiled. For fermented shrimp paste *(tom chua)*, you have to wait fifteen days before testing. There are restaurants at Dong Ba market, there is a woman there, she is very famous, she has a big shop in Dong Ba market.'

I ask about *com hen,* the Hue dish of cold rice and tiny shelled mussels the size of a small fingernail from the Perfume River. Is it a breakfast dish? 'For *com hen,* there are many small restaurants, eat any time,' morning and all day.'

I ask about Hue's famous sweet soups, which rarely appear on menus, telling her that I found one restaurant that serves lotus seeds in a clear, sweet syrup.

'No *longans?* she asks in astonishment.

'No, no *longans',* which I adore. *Longans* are large, grape-sized fruit that grow on trees in clusters rather like cherries, related to lychees. Beneath their thin, leathery skin is a transparent pulp, which is what you eat, surrounding a single round, brown seed. I am trying to grow a *longan* tree in a pot at home.

Without a word, she disappears and returns with a small bowl of three *longans,* each stuffed with a lotus seed for me to try.

'You are lucky, I made these last night.'

Having tasted the delicious *longan* soup, the conversation drifts to markets. Several times I have gone through Vietnamese markets accompanied by a Vietnamese friend, but never with anyone who knew the English names for most of what I was looking at.

Perhaps seeing my hesitation – I am well out of my depth, she asks, 'Are you free?'

I gather that we are going to the market, but as she has said that her motorbike will not carry two people, I suggest that I pay for a taxi to Dong Ba market on the far side of the river. Before we go, she hands me one of the tiny rose apples that I thought were part of the table decoration, which they are – it is not a fruit at all – but another sweet Hue confection. She disappears and returns with two conical hats, one for her, one for me. As we leave, she points to the altar she has set up to honour her dead husband and as we depart through a side door, she shows me her kitchen along the side of the house – an aluminium table, more photographs of international chefs ...

She leads me along the pavement of the street outside her house, past vendors who have laid out their morning offerings of fruit, vegetables, fish and seafood along the pavement, en route to her local market. We stroll among the motorbike browsers and other shoppers. This is a very special treat as Hoang Thi Nhu Huy is able to tell me the English names of the herbs, fruits and vegetables.

Slabs of 'tofu and soy milk' – in plastic bags.

'Guava, amaranth (leaves), pennywort (curly), wild vegetables, banana flower (a large bud), lotuses, jasmine buds – for a vegetable soup with beef, pumpkin flowers (and stalks), bamboo shoots, loofah (looks like a blistered cucumber), passion fruit (round and slightly pink), mung berries (look like limes).'

White 'cherries' turn out to be tiny white aubergines, snuggling in a basket beside slightly larger, recognizable purple aubergines. 'Winter melons' look like fat cucumbers. 'Sliced bamboo shoots. Prunes (plums), avocados, frogs, snails.'

A flopping fish in a shallow basin is a 'snake egg fish' – caviar? Mussels of various shapes and sizes; 'krill' – infinitesimally tiny shrimp; more fish that look like sardines; 'jelly fish, raw,' sliced and floating in a basin. I decline her invitation to taste it.

'Taro' (stalks), crabs bound in red cords. I ask about another sort of stalks – 'a kind of mustard.'

Black catfish look more like shortened eels. Then she points to a jar of round white balls floating in liquid: 'lemons in brine, it changes the taste.

'Goby,' small fish about five inches long, basins of shrimps of varying sizes.

'Young jack fruit, cook like a vegetable. Bamboo and bean sprouts. Star leaf' (green).

Nubbly 'bitter melons, lemon grass (stalks), ginger, water morning glory greens' – Vietnam's ubiquitous green, spinach-like vegetable that winds around your teeth like the tendrils of a jungle. Long, thin, twirled shells – 'black snails.'

Then the egg stall: 'duck eggs, chicken eggs, goose eggs' and small, speckled 'quail eggs.' The black eggs? 'Keep for a long time.'

By now we have arrived at the door of the market proper where a meat stall has been set up. 'Chicken and pork meat, killed early in the morning. We buy only fresh food.

'Bamboo shoots (sliced), seaweed jelly, good for the neck – iodine,' looks like half moons floating in a basin.

178

'Custard apples, dragon fruit (bright pink), turmeric.'

I never knew that turmeric was a root – it looks a bit like ginger. 'Good for stomach and lungs. Lotus seeds,' shelled in plastic bags. All kinds of beans and rice in open bags ready to be measured out. 'Different, dependent on quality.'

Then she leads me to a vegetarian stall with food ready-made to purchase from basins that look for all the world like meat casseroles – 'made of wheat flour.' Some even look like salami. The next stall has noodles: 'cassava, wheat and rice flour noodles.' More pork and beef on the butcher's block opposite. 'Fresh green tea', beside 'betal nuts, lime powder and green areca palm leaves to wrap it in, for betal chewing.' She then points to the red, spicy shrimp sauce *(tom chua),* packaged by her friend in Dang Ba market, the brand on the package is Bo Ri. Suddenly I remember that I have never known quite what galangal is, often called for when I am reading oriental recipes. She finds it for me. It's a stalk, rather like lemon grass.

I point to some long cylinders wrapped in banana leaves.

'Banh Tet, like *banh chung'* – of which I have embarrassed memories of battling ineffectually with chopsticks – steamed, sticky rice cakes with pork and onions inside.

Then she shows me what the delicious heart-shaped sweet that she served me was made of – 'fava beans,' then yellow 'mung beans.' Small black beans are 'roasted doleque' (cowpeas).

Red chilli powder is stacked in plastic bags, 'Very hot.'

While she is buying some 'rock sugar,' I ask a stall holder about the crisp rice paper covered in sesame seeds, hoping for a Vietnamese name. 'Rice paper' – he tells me in English. Well, yes. His stall has mounds of vermicelli noodles and a barrel-sized plastic bag of dried mushrooms, opposite a stall selling joss sticks and fake money to burn for prosperity and good luck.

On our way out, I point to a new fruit. 'Figs' – but these are green, not purple and look slightly squashed like certain kinds of squat, flattened Italian tomatoes and peaches. As I love figs, now I remember ordering a fig salad and being surprised that it was served hot and that the figs tasted more like a vegetable.

Purple mangosteens, at least I recognize. We pass a round, open crate of live chickens and the last large nubbly fruit I query her about at her gate turns out to be a ripe jack fruit.

Brain swirling with new names, I thank Hoang Thi Nhu Huy profusely for the short course in Hue 'market-ology.'

179

A CHEF OF ROYAL BANQUETS

Affairs of State take precedence
over those of the family
– Vietnamese proverb

When I first came to Hue, almost on arrival I heard about Madame Ton Nu Ha's Garden of Tranquillity Restaurant (Tinh Gia Vien), and that reservations must be made a day in advance.

At twilight when the riverboats had become silhouettes, another guest from the hotel and I took cyclos over the bridge, through the thick wall of the Citadel and into the leafy lanes of the old royal city, some of it now practically rural. One of the great pleasures of Vietnam is to take a cyclo on a still evening.

Tinh Gia Vien Restaurant is in Madame Ton Nu Ha's villa up a narrow lane. The cyclos dropped us just inside the gates. This would be intimate dining, only half a dozen lantern lit tables on the balustrade railed terrace. Flowering orchids hung from the arches; potted bonsai and cacti crowded the railings. One of Madame Ton Nu Ha's pretty daughters, Ton Gian Hien (Gian Hien means tender), wearing a purple *ao dai,* seated us and presented a handwritten menu. On the table, the bouquet of orange and white flowers had been artfully sculpted – from carrots and green papaya, standing on stalks of spring onions!

The first platter to appear was a ravishing Dancing Phoenix, its feathers thin swirls of *paté* and ham. The phoenix cocked an imperious peppercorn eye from its carved carrot head before disappearing as an *hors d'oeuvre.*

A perforated pineapple, hollowed out like a jack-o-lantern with a candle inside, carried in dramatically on a tray, became an aromatic lamp giving off the sweet scent of burnt sugar, as well as serving as a vehicle for the spikes holding bites of chicken.

The delicious soup that followed was thick with vegetables, mostly unknown. Two huge shrimps under chopped garlic appeared, rapidly followed by half a plump river fish smothered under a mildly spicy tomato sauce on a bed of 'seaweed' – shredded green papaya.

180

The Fantasy Chicken had the rounded rice paper body of a sitting hen with feathered carrot wings, a sprightly onion tail, a round white turnip head and a pert, red pepper beak.

The next creature to appear was a Swimming Turtle, one of the four sacred animals, its head and feet of carved carrots, the Cantonese rice of its body under a latticework of omelette to resemble a turtle shell.

The creative presentation of the food revealed a playful, innocent whimsy. Moreover, it tasted very good. Having given up more than pecking two courses back, we were looking forward to *Fruit Tropique Déguisé,* only to bite into – something like marzipan!

By the end of the meal I was determined to meet Madame Ton Nu Ha, the *chef extraordinarie* behind these creations.

'Please come tomorrow at half past seven,' she said, explaining that Vietnam-TV would be making a film and that there would be beautiful food to photograph. She meant half past seven in the morning.

My cyclo rolled through the gates just before half past seven, into the sun-drenched garden, unlike any garden I had ever seen. A bronze sculpture of two young lovers, lost in one another, the young man tenderly touching the arm of his beloved, stood to one side of the entrance. White china elephants bearing pot plants guarded the steps to the terrace. More than two hundred bonsai pots lined the paths past a two-storey tea house cage holding gerbils in the penthouse, a squirrel on the ground floor.

Low trees made a leafy tapestry: grapefruit, apple, palm, cedar and a tropical weeping tree with needle-like red blossoms at the tips of the branches. In every direction the eye fell upon a different contrived scene: artfully arranged standing stones, a miniature fig tree – with figs, the white statue of a young Vietnamese girl holding a candle-shaped lamp.

Madame Ton Nu Ha had been preparing food since five and I was just in time to see the last two platters being completed. She worked at a folding table on the terrace beside a goldfish bowl from the top of which sprouted the tiny leaves of a bonsai. A huge plastic basket acted as the palette for her edible collages: red peppers and tomatoes, orange carrots, yellow bamboo, pale green *chou chou,* green and white cucumbers. A meat platter offered more shades: salamis in tones of pink, red and beige; white chicken and brown cooked meat. Bright green gherkins and mayonnaise awaited the call for a flourish of green or cream.

A sinuously undulating dragon was taking shape on one platter, his scales individually cut from tiny round slices of *paté* and salami. Two girls cut, chopped and notched vegetables. A thin man like a Giacometti statue himself, was sculpting a head from a potato. Two months earlier Madame Ton Nu Ha had fallen in a climbing accident and broken four bones in her left elbow – and she is left-handed. A month later, her elbow was still hugely swollen and the doctor had operated. Two months after the accident, it was still giving her pain and slowing her work.

I felt like a sorcerer's apprentice, watching as she lined the edges of an oval serving bowl with thin slices of ham and *paté,* then filled the centre with thinly sliced omelette and fried rice. She placed a platter on top of the bowl and tipped it upside down – the bowl had acted as a mould.

Soon, four carrot reptilian feet, a curled tail and a head joined the oval body, its carrot head held upright in the same position of curiosity as the heads of the stone turtles that support the stelae in the Temple of Literature in Hanoi. At a jaunty angle in his mouth, the turtle brandished a spring onion, a reference to the legend of the sacred turtle in Hanoi's Lake of the Restored Sword.

Cutting carefully around carrot templates, the girls were making the turtle shell from lean brown meat. The thin man introduced himself as Phan The Binh, a sculptor and professor of sculpture at Hue College of Art. It was he who had created the statues of the young lovers in the garden. Despite very little English he managed to convey the plight of creative artists throughout the world: 'With this money', he motioned to the food platters, 'I can sculpt.'

The television crew arrived. Two pretty girls in red and purple *ao dais* arranged a vase of red gladiolas and strolled through the garden for the benefit of the TV cameraman. From upstairs came the sounds of pounding and the cries of a baby. The little white dog, Lucky, settled down for a snooze beneath the stairs. It had already been a long day by nine.

Madame Ton Nu Ha disappeared and reappeared wearing a purple velvet *ao dai,* splashed with silver bead-work and a sparkling necklace round the high-necked collar. The effect was – imperial. Four platters about to be filmed were placed on a purple tablecloth, the four sacred animals: phoenix, turtle, *kylin* or unicorn, dragon.

Then Madame Ton Nu Ha explained that the TV producer would like for *me* to wear an *ao dai* so that she could teach me on camera how to carve a flower. Oh, dear. Reluctantly, but to show willing, I slipped into one of hers and the girls tactfully tried to arrange a round crown of purple over my fluffy fringe and loose hair. Vietnamese women traditionally wore their hair sleeked back in a bun beneath these crowns.

The young daughter of one of the kitchen staff exploded in a fit of giggles and I searched out a mirror. Always trust the honesty of a child. It looked positively witch-like. I refused to wear the crown and we were all happier. The TV cameraman politely shot a few minutes of Madame Ton Nu Ha demonstrating how she works and then to my relief, one of her pretty daughters took my place and the chef showed her how to sculpt a flower from a green papaya. A much prettier scene. I have yet to see a Western woman, who looks anything but ridiculous in an *ao dai*. Madame Ton Nu Ha's husband, a slim man in shirt sleeves, returned carrying a briefcase like a businessman coming home from the office and the TV crew insisted upon his saying a few words to camera.

Next morning I had Madame Ton Nu Ha to myself. The Ton in her name indicated royalty. Seven generations of her family had served at court as mandarin in the days when to become a mandarin meant passing stiff examinations.

'My great-grandfather acted as an emissary to China and received many gifts from the last empress dowager of China. But they were all burned, destroyed during the bombings of Hue (1968). When Bao Dai abdicated in 1945, life became very hard for my family. We were very poor.' Out of necessity, Madame Ton Nu Ha developed her numerous talents. At the beginning, she had trained as a nurse and her first job in 1963 was in Quang Tri, a nearby province where already in her youth there was war and much poverty. She became head nurse in emergency, then after another examination, a teacher of nursing. In 1965 she went to Saigon to study nutrition under the Americans and cooking at a French school, then returned to Quang Tri. In 1967, she moved back to Hue and married. In 1968, she received the highest medal attainable for nursing, one of only three to be awarded in the entire country.

She met her husband-to-be while she was studying at nursing college. He was already teaching traditional Vietnamese music at Hue College of Art.

'He plays five instruments,' she told me with pride.

Madame Ton Nu Ha had passed the age for coy modesty.

'Many persons loved me, but I was afraid,' by which I think she meant that she had many suitors. When she first caught sight of the man who was to become her husband, she wanted to meet him, but felt too shy.

'The first time I met him I could see that he was a very kind person, his eyes, he had very kind eyes. With him, I knew my heart would be safe.

'He makes me feel very tiny before him, he is very serious. I always feel he is higher, he always supports me. It is because of him that I am successful. It is for him I always try to do things a little bit better. I always say, it is because of you.'

I empathized with Madame Ton Nu Ha's attraction to her husband's gentle, idealistic spirit. They were in love for three years before they married, she at twenty-three, he at twenty-eight.

'We had only been married for five months when he went off to the mountains to fight for liberation' (Vietnam War 1965-1975).

Neither knew that she was pregnant. For seven years they were separated without a word of communication. She had no idea if he were dead or alive; he had no idea of her whereabouts or welfare, nor that he had a son.

'Those times were terrible. My house was bombed, my mother's house was bombed. But we were both spared.'

Madame Ton Nu Ha was immensely proud of her husband.

'There are only three things: party, government and motherland. Politics come first, higher than family. He is very important in the party.'

Her husband was a member of the Central Committee of Hue.

After her husband's return from the war in 1975, Madame Ton Nu Ha continued nursing and nutrition management at the University Hospital. Three daughters were born, in their twenties when we first met. The name of the youngest, Tinh Hai, means Sea of Tranquillity and one might have thought that at last with the French and Vietnam Wars past, the family could settle down to a quiet life. But 1989 brought change.

'My government wanted oil from Iraq. So I helped my government.' Vietnam sent two hundred Vietnamese nurses to Iraq in exchange for oil. Madame Ton Nu Ha was one of them. Once again, she was separated from her husband and this time, her children.

For two years she lived and worked in a war zone; her husband looked after the children.

The nurses were paid very little, only just enough to eat. Arriving towards the end of the Iran-Iraq War, there was peace for less than a year before war broke out again, this time with Kuwait. Madame Ton Nu Ha remembered watching for four or five days from her fourth storey hospital window as a constant thread of cars carrying whole families poured into Baghdad from Kuwait.

'The post office was bombed and we lost our electricity. In a hospital, that meant death to those patients who were on life-support machines. There were dead patients in the refrigerators and after five days, the odour was so overpowering that we had to bury the bodies without waiting for the families to collect them.'

For six months food was scarce. While they were working in the hospital they were given sugar and a bit of meat, which in turn the nurses shared with their ambassador, who had no food at all.

'The Iraqi police were very' – she searches for a word – 'uncharitable. They were very strange. When we worked, our salary was petrol, we had very little money, we did not have enough money to eat. So in our spare time, we made hats. It would take one day for two people to make one hundred hats and we earned about 15,000 *dong* (then $1.50, £1.20) for the lot. I had to go to the market to sell them. If the police caught me, because foreigners were not allowed to sell, they would put me in prison.

'In Iraq, we were afraid. In the market, the political police would come and stamp on the merchandise and put people in a car and take them to prison. Sometimes they had sticks. Sometimes we didn't know why we had lost a friend. Then the ambassador would go round and find that the person was in prison. Then that person would be sent home in disgrace. For the sake of only $1.50, maybe prison.'

The market was so dangerous that Madame Ton Nu Ha struck upon another moneymaking idea, making portraits of Saddam Hussain. 'Every officer's room had to have his picture. Because I am a woman, my paintings were soft. That's how I had the money to open the restaurant.

'There were many bombs in Baghdad, like Hue in 1968. My ambassador was afraid. Everybody was leaving Baghdad. Only soldiers, security and government stayed. Others deserted the city. But I was not afraid. God gives us life or death' – this, from a staunch Communist.

185

Eventually, to get out of Iraq they drove for nine hours to the border, the highway littered with burnt-out cars, many still smoking, and bodies.

'Lots of bodies. On the way at night, it was very cold.'

At the border they were not allowed to cross, so they had to turn back and return along the same road to Baghdad. Finally the Vietnamese government asked the UN to assist in their release, and nine days later, once again, they attempted the journey to the border. This time they were allowed to cross into Jordan to a refugee camp. Madame Ton Nu Ha had brought her pastels and pens for drawing portraits, thinking, 'If we are suffering, I can use my pens to get enough food for many friends.' While they were waiting in the camp, she wanted to go out and see something of the country, but the officials refused. It was only after she had made a portrait of King Hussein that they lent her a car for a bit of sightseeing.

'I was so glad to return to my country. I love my land, I cannot explain how we love our country. It is in the blood.'

The returning Vietnamese nurses managed to reach Hanoi on 16 January 1991 – not quite in time to get home to Hue for *Tet,* the all-important annual New Year festival. Madame Ton Nu Ha paused, remembering those times.

'We have to be very strong. Many friends say a big knife can cut tiny or big pieces. A small knife can only cut small pieces. Many things I can do.'

And indeed, apart from making hats and painting portraits, at various times she has made and sold concrete flower pots and administered injections to earn money. In 1973, she received a certificate for proficiency in English from the Vietnam-American Association and in 1975, she obtained a bachelor's degree in law (earned during the last years of the Vietnam War).

'Four years of study, as well as working at the hospital. After the revolution, it was of no use for work, but it has been very useful in life. People of high rank didn't work with their hands, didn't sell in the market. But after the revolution, labour was considered to be good, so I sold things to make money.'

She planted flowers and bonsai and sold them in the market.

'Anyone will tell you, I am a trader,' she says, seemingly oblivious to the contradiction of a born marketeer being married to a high-ranking Communist official. But then, times in Vietnam were changing, towards a market economy.

186

The 1943-vintage villa in which she lives once belonged to a former princess. 'During the war it was broken in half.' Madame Ton Nu Ha bought it from a descendant, added the terraces and the garden. A few years ago, she opened the restaurant.

'I love my cooking. I have always cooked, my cooking is from my childhood. In the hospital every day I cooked for 1,200 patients, three times a day. I have cooked for the President of Thailand, the Prime Minister of Vietnam and many ministers and officials.' One year, all the government officials of the party met in Hue and she cooked for three hundred. Once she did a wedding for five hundred. She has even been televised cooking for four hundred people in the throne room of the Citadel. She gave up her job at the hospital only a few years ago. Until then, it was the hospital early in the morning, the restaurant at night.

'I loved my patients, I could not leave my patients. But the restaurant became very busy and I had worked for the patients for a long time, thirty-two years.'

Rarely for a Vietnamese, she has ticked off travelling to both extremities of her country, although she seldom travels with her husband. He is too busy. The North, she managed when she was given five days off from the hospital for an appendectomy. She rested for two days after the operation, then set off on a day-and-a-half train journey to Lang Son bordering China, where she hoped to add a purple flowering variety of the *hoa dong tien* flower to her collection of twenty-one. On arrival she collapsed and never succeeded in finding the plant. More recently, she had visited the southern extremity of the Mekong Delta.

It appeared that whatever Madame Ton Nu Ha does, she does with passionate fervour. 'I cook with my heart, I am an artist, I like to please my clients.'

Asked how she saw the future, for a moment Madame Ton Nu Ha looked completely nonplussed, as if she had never looked beyond today. Then after a moment, she said vehemently: 'I like to learn. Every day, if I have the time, I go to a big bookshop. I am always reading. If I see something I want to do, I learn to do it and always try to do it well.' Apart from her extraordinary talents as a chef and restaurateur, Madame Ton Nu Ha is a truly inspiring, phoenix-like survivor, a resilient and elegant Hue woman for all seasons and political climes. What she has lived through in triumph made me feel quite humble. What soft lives we lead in the West.

PART VI

ARTS AND CRAFTS

HUE ARTISTS

If you sharpen the steel,
it will turn to needles
– Vietnamese proverb

In Hue, it is especially difficult to decide where crafts stop and where fine arts begin. Since as far back as the Nguyen lords, the aesthetic people of Hue have been highly discerning in the design and decoration of their royal palaces and tombs, their temples and pagodas, their homes and gardens. All have been crafted by highly skilled artisans.

Emperor Thieu Tri even ordered paintings of his favourite Hue beauty spots on glass and had his own poems commemorating these beauty spots attached. Hue artists have painted on lacquer, drawn the designs for embroidered 'pictures' and of course, painters and sculptors have produced their work for royal tombs, pagodas and private homes for well over four hundred years.

Today, Hue streets in the tourist areas are lined with galleries hung with paintings and carving shops selling sculpture, large and small. Every night I meet a man carrying a pile of watercolour paintings on silk and every day at lunch time I see a woman with a foot-high stack of watercolour paintings tied to the back of her motorbike. When I first came to Hue, I bought a dozen of these delicately painted watercolours on silk – unique to Hue – for five dollars each, paintings of wispy bamboo, of slim boats on the river, of people ploughing, fishing, and carrying their baskets dangling from poles along dykes. At Ngo Mon (gate) of the Citadel, little girls used to sell fine watercolours on silk, mounted as greetings cards.

Seeking Hue's Fine Arts Museum, as often happens, I am directed somewhere else – to two galleries dedicated to two Hue artists of international repute. In fact, there is *no* Hue Fine Arts

Museum, but as Vietnamese people are reluctant to say the rude word, *no,* I am sent to the next best destinations.

La Ba Dang Art Foundation (15 Le Loi Street), named after the artist, is a museum dedicated to a contemporary 'revolutionary artist'. The Foundation occupies a white, French colonial villa on the south bank of the Perfume river, which only slightly more than half a century ago, served as the office of the French Ministry of Finance.

In the first room, a mural entitled *Giao Chi Feet,* which included Hue, must refer to the footsteps of those who lived here long ago in what was then the southern-most Chinese-dominated trading territory, Giao Chi, as early as the pre-Christian era. A revolution in 192 AD resulted in the establishment of a new, independent kingdom, which the Chinese referred to in their records as Linyi, its boundaries still unknown to this day.

Nearby, thick slices of wood have been cut by the aritist, La Ba Dang, into the perforated shapes of men and women, life-sized wooden silhouettes. A hallway is lined with ink drawings entitled Dien Bien Phu: ranks of soldiers, barbed wire, soldiers shouting and women bringing trays of food to the soldiers.

Upstairs, hallways and one room hold abstract paintings on pressed paper; another room is full of blue Buddhas – echoes of Picasso? Numerous abstract paintings fill another large room, seemingly angry splashes of black, each with a thin red streak – the blood spilled on the Ho Chi Ming Trail, the labels explains.

The series entitled *Aftermath of War* portrays several grieving mothers with their children. Another room holds paintings, each screaming the words: *Armée des Intellectuals pour le Vietnam (Army of Intellectuals for Vietnam).*

A work on another theme, *To Be Or Not To Be,* I find rather baffling inasmuch as it is a barren tree hung with perforated, coloured, paint-splashed, pieces of metal – shrapnel from bombs?

My heart lifts when I read the title *Cats,* but fail in the half dozen or so paintings to detect anything more than several curved lines. In the back room, opening to a small balcony overlooking the Perfume river, are more blue meditating monks. The French finance man must have chosen this pleasant room for his office.

A hollowed-out stone basin, balanced on a tree stump as an altar, has been placed in front of a meditating monk. Two roses float in the shallow stone basin – tender, subtle, understated. Instinctively going to the balcony to view the Perfume river, I am almost struck in

189

the face by a stunning flamboyant tree, its flame-orange blossoms bursting in exuberance.

On leaving, I pick up the artist's biography. He was born in Quang Tri, just north of Hue. I am surprised, considering his anti-French, nationalistic Vietnamese subject matter, to read that he left Vietnam for France in 1939 and graduated from the University of Fine Arts in Toulouse. He has had numerous international exhibitions, received several prestigious awards and in 2005, the title of 'Vietnam Land Glory' was conferred upon him by the Government of Vietnam.

From here, I take myself to the gallery (corner of Nguyen Hue and Ngo Quyen Streets) of another famous, local artist who made her name in France, the sculptress, Diem Phung Thi – a rare woman to be listed in France's Larousse Dictionary. Moreover, she was admitted to the French Academy – Arts Europe in 1991. Diem Phung Thi first trained as a dentist and then 'surrendered to her passion for sculpting.' Apparently, no fewer than thirty-six of her large, clunky sculptures are dotted around France.

Once again, staring at her rounded, heavy-shouldered figures, vaguely reminiscent of Henry Moore, the artist's intentions are not clear. On the other hand, her realistic sculptured heads are very fine portraits. Male and female figures kneeling with a baby, the baby's chubby, sculpted legs wound tightly round one another, are far more appealing. A strange queue of carved *Soldiers to the Battle Front,* the first soldier in the queue, oddly, carrying his wife on his shoulder, is more puzzling. But my heart is won by two life-sized, standing figures, one male, one female, entitled *Having a Conversation.* They could have walked in off the street.

Diem Phung Thi died in 2002 after returning to Hue to retire, donating her life's work to her city and spending her last years, teaching others to sculpt.

ANTIQUE JEWELLERY

One often abandons the old for the new,
One often abandons the lamp for the moon
    – Vietnamese proverb

Summer events start early in Hue, as from May to September temperatures soar to the high 30s C (90s F). The starting time for the Antique Jewellery Exhibition at the Hue Museum of Ancient Objects, therefore, is 8 a.m. The exhibition, part of Hue's Golden Crafts Week, has been organized jointly by Vietnam's National Museum of History in Hanoi and the Hue Monuments Conservation Center. All of the exhibits are normally held either by the former in Hanoi or by Hue's Museum of Ancient Objects, although they are not always on display in either place.

In the courtyard in front of Long An, the royal palace housing the Museum of Ancient Objects in Le Truc Street, rows of cloth-covered chairs have been set up. Many Vietnamese consider Long An to be the most beautiful traditional building in Hue. Unusually for a royal pavilion, it has no lacquer nor gilt. The interior is a forest of dark brown, hard wood pillars, supporting the heavy, two-tier, yellow tiled roofs, above floors of smooth, dark hardwood. The effect is of a restful mellowness.

Long An palace was built in 1845, not here but in Tay Loc ward by the third Nguyen emperor, Thieu Tri – who also built the tower at Thien Mu – for 'his rest and refreshment when visiting local farmers.' He used it as a quiet retreat for reflection, writing poetry and entertaining. Thirty-five of his texts and poems have been engraved on the wooden surfaces of the palace.

China chip mosaics line the ridge line of the building, an angry dragon face in the centre, wavy rays emanating out from what might be a sun above his head. Enamelled tableaux in pastel colours form a cornice just beneath the mosaic ridge line, where flowers alternate with Emperor Thieu Tri's poems. A turtle and a phoenix cling to the ridge lines sloping down to the eaves.

Long An pavilion was seized by the French in 1885 when they burnt the Citadel, to use as their headquarters. Later in 1909, Emperor Duy Tan had the pavilion dismantled and rebuilt in Le Truc Street. It became first a library, then offices of *The Bulletin of the Friends of the Old Capital,* where a collection of valuable books was stored. In 1923, it was renamed the Khai Dinh Museum after the penultimate emperor. Now, after many changes, its official name is the Hue Museum of Ancient Objects.

An official disturbs my musings and suggests that I go inside for a look at the exhibition – before the speeches.

This exhibition of antique jewellery includes many ancient artefacts, such as a 5,000-year-old mollusc shell necklace from Quang Binh province – round disks with holes drilled through the centre. It would have been much too heavy to wear as a necklace; the shells are thought to have been used as money by people of the Bau Tro culture. Many centuries after this shell money was made, this area in what is now Quang Binh Province, the second province north of Hue, became the northern-most region of Champa, an area heavily fought over by the Die Viet nation in the North and Champa in the South. Smoothly rounded nephrite bracelets 4,000 years old make one wonder what manner of life the craftsmen of their time lived. What did they use to grind so evenly these surfaces to such convex perfection?

A couple of millennia later, the bronze bracelets of the northern Dong Song culture from 2,500 and 2,000 years ago, bear intricate patterns, like grains of rice, curled around the edges of the bracelets. Other Dong Son bronze bracelets are highly perforated. How very sophisticated they were in working with bronze.

The heavy Dong Son bronze 'wrist covers' have such narrow openings that one can but wonder how they were placed on the wrist. But the show-stopper is a transparent quartz Dong Son earring, a thick circle with a thin opening to squeeze onto the ear. It must have been extremely heavy – how did the wearer keep it from falling off?

I come to the familiar three-pointed nephrite earrings from the Sa Huynh culture – the pre-historic culture around Hue and further south, to east of Ho Chi Minh City – dated 2,500 to 2,000 years old. The dating is news. The earliest Sa Huynh artefacts to have been discovered in Vietnam by 2010, when I was researching a book on Hoi An, was 300 BC. And at that time, the very earliest Sa Huyn artefacts of this wide-ranging, sea-borne, trading people ever to have been found anywhere were in the Philippines, dating from 500 BC.

192

Perhaps now, more recent discoveries have pushed the earliest date of Sa Huynh finds in Vietnam back to 500 BC. Archaeology in Vietnam is an ever-shifting scene, new discoveries revising earlier findings, an exciting, on-going detective story.

Sa Huynh two-headed nephrite earrings are unique. A central bar connects the two heads of an antelope or an oryx in profile, nose down, the curved horns pointing upwards; a loop or hook attached them to the ear. These animals were unknown to modern science until they were 'discovered' as recently as 1992 in Vietnam's highlands and identified as a hoofed animal that looks rather like a mountain goat, now classified as *pseudoryx nehetinenis*.

The displays conjure up shadowy peoples, long gone, people who were adept craftsmen: intricate bronze hair ornaments, a puzzlingly intricate bronze belt buckle, nephrite and glass bangle bracelets, a multi-faceted agate bead necklace made by the Sa Huynh that might have been made yesterday, their four-pointed jadeite earrings, a necklace made of ground, precious stones made by the Dong Ngai people south of Hue, gold beads and a ring from Oc Eo in the Mekong Delta, the former Funan.

And then I come to the exquisite heirlooms of the Nguyen dynasty: a gold hairpin of extraordinarily intricate design – a phoenix holding a loosely-dangling lantern; gold bracelets set with precious stones for extremely thin wrists; a gold name plaque set with precious stones; several carved jade 'belt plaques' framed in gold, inset with precious stones; long, carved jade, dragon-shaped belt hooks; and an astounding gold filigree 'forehead cover' – a crown? Who wore it, and for what occasions, one wonders?

There are numerous elongated, gold ornamental hairpins. During the Nguyen dynasty, by royal edict, the empress and the concubines of all ranks received one gold hairpin. Those of the second rank received ten flower-like brooches. As it is thought that the second emperor, Minh Mang, had several hundred concubines, no wonder there are so many.

Then there is the silver: a silver filigree 'neck-let'; a heavy, deeply engraved silver bracelet; a thin, silver cord necklace with dangling ornaments – like charms. And the jade: white jade amulets, flower earrings, peach-shaped pendants, snail and fish pendants, a mandarin duck, a white jade pendant, and a stunning red jade pendant carved in the shape of a bat. Oh, to have seen the ladies who wore these beautiful objects!

193

A small silver hand mirror would have been the ritual object held by the emperor on the throne, and here is a silver jewel box with compartments. Whose was it?

I am lost in wonder when suddenly, I hear 'the band' – the *nha nhac* ensemble – and I rush past a large wooden gilt sphere, carved in the form of nine dragons, supported by three dragons rearing up to form legs. The band is starting to play.

The *nha nhac* ensemble is clad in blue and red silk brocade tunics, wearing black caps with knobs on top, rather like misplaced buns. Standing beside them is a line of girls wearing red and white *au dais* and red velvet, moon-shaped crowns *(khan vanh).*

Following the officials' speeches, the girls in red *ao dais* file in front of the audience, carrying their long, red silk streamer hiding the framed certificates, and await the officials to snip the silk between each girl. The people of Hue revere these ceremonies, these traditions. And these echoes, these remnants of royal rituals are one of the characteristics that serve to distinguish the people of Hue from other Vietnamese.

From the Hue Museum of Ancient Objects, back across the river to the Hue Buddhist Centre in Le Loi Street to the opening of an exhibition of inlaid mother-of-pearl *(nacre),* the private collection of Tran Dinh Son. Display cases hold inlaid plates and boxes, all manner of exquisitely crafted objects.

Then in late afternoon while the sun is still blistering, back to the Citadel where several rows of meter-high, pressed bamboo paper creations *(truc chi)* hang from easels in the courtyard behind the Palace of Supreme Harmony. It may be uncomfortably hot, but the timing is perfect; the low afternoon sun glows through the bamboo paper art to advantage. Created by artist-painter, Hai Bang, he has adapted designs from the early period of the Nguyen lords – pre-Nguyen dynasty – and pressed the designs into paper, sometimes adding a few brush strokes of paint. Perhaps because of the thick, rough paper, they are slightly reminiscent of rubbings taken of Khmer bas reliefs in Cambodia.

This time everyone is standing as it is a space open to visitors. Following the speeches, Nguyen Phuoc Hai Trung, a calligrapher in both *chu nha* (Han Chinese) and *chu nom* (Chinese ideograms representing Vietnamese words and concepts), brushes his calligraphic contribution onto one of the paper art works.

194

Professor Buu I tells me that Nguyen Phuoc Hai Trung has written a book on the symbols of the Nguyen lords.

The *nha ngac* band has been standing to attention, waiting at last to play, nine musicians wearing black caps with topknots and blue and red brocade tunics over white trousers. Their ensemble is made up of moon-shaped and pear-shaped lutes, a two-string violin, a small rectangular lute, a flute, two wooden tappers and an oboe.

Six girls in red *ao dais,* stand holding their red silk streamer, hiding the certificates. Five officials rise to the occasion to snip the silk. And now, we can all get out of the sun.

HUE GLASS PAINTINGS COLLECTOR

Pay first and then get what you have paid for
– Vietnamese proverb

On a street just inside the western wall of the Citadel, up a central garden path from the covered verandah, I am greeted by Nguyen Xuan Hoa, a gentleman of a certain age and his daughter-in-law, Thu. The first thing that strikes the eye on entering the house – apart from several antique display cabinets holding blue and white ceramics and the lacquer and mother-of-pearl poetic parallel sentences hanging from a series of pillars – is a four-part glass screen standing on an upright piano at the far end of the L-shaped room.

We are seated in square, black, wooden armchairs with red silk brocade cushions around a low tea table. A lacquer, fan-shaped tableau *(hoanh phi)* hangs over the family altar in a nearby alcove, the altar holding bronze cranes and braziers. This villa serves as the family home, although in the garden there are more traditional houses that serve as dining rooms, as this garden house has become the Nguyen Xuan Hoa restaurant.

'My parents have passed away, I live here with my sons and daughter-in-law and two grandchildren, Nguyen Xuan Hoa tells me, through his daughter-in-law, Thu, translating.

When I explain that I am searching for the reasons why Hue is distinctive amongst Vietnamese cities, he replies, 'As many rank Boston as the spiritual soul of America, Hue is the spiritual soul of Vietnam. We can change the word Boston for Hue and have the same meaning, and it would be particularly true in art. Hue is a place where you can find many precious and valuable Vietnamese paintings. You can find very nice glass paintings in the Hue Museum of Ancient Objects, or in the Citadel, or in the royal tombs, but also kept in families of the local people here.

'The glass paintings appeared during the Nguyen era from the seventeenth century,' so from as far back as the Nguyen lords before they became kings.

'When Nguyen Hoang's son came to Phu Xuan (Hue) from Quang Tri in 1626, they found the artists. At the beginning, the Nguyen lords invited the artists from China and after they came, they stayed in Hue and made it their home and their children continued in this art. Because of the wars, those original glass paintings are very rare. Glass paintings are mostly from the Nguyen kings, not the lords. The king asked the ministry to have buildings painted on paper and then they sent the pictures to China to order the paintings on glass. So the style of these two kinds of paintings is a little different. The traditional ones from China, and the Vietnamese style of the Chinese, who left China and lived in Hue. They are in the style of the Chinese, but different in the organization (composition) of the picture.

'So all of these paintings you may find in Hue are Vietnamese. The colour is more colourful and the technique is more complicated. Normally, this kind of picture is a painting of the landscape and the architecture of Hue, and if they were ordered by the Emperor Thieu Tri, with a poem above.'

At this point he disappears and returns with two books: one, of Thieu Tri's Twenty Poems on Hue Beauty Spots, which I have been searching for in vain, but disappointingly in Vietnamese; and another, an art book with illustrations of both the ink drawings made by the Vietnamese artists to be copied by the Chinese artists on glass – beside illustrations of the actual paintings on glass – which are a revelation. Sometimes the artist painting on glass took huge liberties with the original composition he was supposed to be copying, for instance, reducing the size of a lake pavilion to a tiny, distant image when in the ink drawing it was far more prominent.

'Thieu Tri was the only one to commission paintings with poems on glass, mostly just the kings (commissioned glass paintings). All of Thieu Tri's glass paintings were placed in gilt frames with a poem above. This one was painted for the ministry,' he says, showing me illustrations of the ink drawing and the painting of one that still hangs in the Citadel in the queen mother's tea palace (Cung Dien Tho). Then he shows me the drawing for a painting of the Perfume river, showing the boat pavilion in front of the Citadel walls and the guardian islands in the river – a glass painting most probably lost.

'So the picture is Vietnamese, but the style is Chinese. Most of the pictures are in the family.' He means the royal family. Then Nguyen Xuan Hoa shows me round his own collection. First is a painting of 'about twenty-four children, who do good things for their

197

parents,' then a portrait of what looks very like a Chinese court lady, the only portrait on glass that I have seen. But then, the Nguyen modelled their court after the Confucian Chinese court, perhaps right down to court ladies' fashions.

'It is the portrait of a princess,' explains Nguyen Xuan Hoa, he doesn't know which one, 'painted for an ancestral altar to be worshipped' after her death.

The entire collection, perhaps twenty glass paintings in the house, he has collected personally, not his father, nor his grandfather. The first was the four-part, gilt-framed screen' – and then finally, we get to the stunning screen on the piano at the far end of the room. 'In each of the four paintings, two court ladies are doing the things that court ladies enjoy: music, chess, writing poems, painting pictures.'

How he happened to buy the screen is a singular Hue story.

'At the time, the museum wanted to buy the screen and the seller really needed the money, so they found me to buy it, because at that time it was the museum in Hanoi, and it would have been a long time to get the money. The seller sold for a low price instead to get the money quickly. That was around 1995.'

Beside the screen on either side of a door, hang two more vertical glass paintings, 'part of a set of four, but the other two got damaged.' These paintings are wildly imaginative, surreal. In the first, a figure is riding a flying peacock while below him, another man is riding a tiger! In the second, what looks like a kind of angel is riding a peacock, while below, a man is holding some sort of line that winds up above his head, while riding a turtle beside a pink stream.

Nguyen Xuan Hoa explains that he is holding a wine jug in his hand, and that the wine – which I took for a line – is drifting skyward. Both paintings are extravagantly colourful, but somehow just escape being kitsch. Perhaps displayed elsewhere than in a traditional Hue home, they might be. Here, they look absolutely magnificent. As Hue is grey and sepia for much of the year under monsoon rains, these colourful paintings would have brought a welcome mini-world of colour into a rather gloomy atmosphere.

Nguyen Xuan Hoa then begins to explain further about the Chinese and Vietnamese types of paintings on glass – that the Chinese ones are colourful and that the Vietnamese ones are black and white, which seems to contradict what he has said earlier. Indeed, the glass paintings that I have seen in royal palaces of the Citadel and the royal tombs are extremely colourful, whether Chinese or Chinese-

Vietnamese. He then shows me a black and white 'painting', explaining that the white is, in fact, shells, mother-of-pearl – but glued – not into a carved wooden surface, but instead onto glass.

'These are very, very Vietnamese.'

He leads me to what could be a huge European landscape painting, a river scene and a walled gate to an estate or a pagoda.

'The first generation of Vietnamese painters in Hue learned the style of Western painting and they painted landscapes, a different river view, but on glass. When I collected this painting, this picture had a newspaper attached to the back of it dated 1925. The seller kept the newspaper, because it was a very rare newspaper – it mentioned the funeral of Emperor Khai Dinh. The artist of the river landscape was Luong Quang Duyet.

'People from Hue feel very strongly about Hue. This landscape belonged to a family who worked for the government in the South and this family was being settled in the US and they didn't want to leave the painting in their home here. They were afraid that the younger generation would not appreciate it and sell it out of Hue. So he found me to sell it to at a good price in order to keep it in Hue.'

I ask about the fretted, gilt, spade-shaped carvings resting in carved, wooden half-vases attached to the wall on either side of a display cabinet.

'They appeared during Khai Dinh's time. At that time, art from Western countries had been imported to Hue.' These elaborate carvings were, in fact, 'flower vases with carved wooden flowers. They would have been owned by a high-ranking family.'

And then, Nguyen Xuan Hoa tells me the Vietnamese name for the red lacquer and gilt that appears ubiquitously throughout the royal palaces and tombs – *son thep vang.*

I ask how he managed to acquire so many glass paintings.

'People knew that I loved glass paintings, they knew that I already had a collection of blue and white porcelain. Many people knew about it.' Only a small part of the blue and white ceramics came down through his family from his grandfather, who was not a member of the royal family.

'He was a mandarin, just a small mandarin.'

The family fled Hue during the French Indo-Chinese War.

'We stayed five kilometres (3 mi) from the centre of the city, but moved back to Hue in 1956, about a kilometre from here. And then in 1976, we bought this house and moved here.'

199

The family's Nguyen Xuan Hoa restaurant opened in 2000. He and Thu then lead me over rustic stone paths to the two old houses that serve as dining rooms in the gardens – past a wandering stream with a miniature bridge, flowering trees, trees whose slender stems seem to have been trained to twirl around a post no longer there, a truly enchanting garden. The dining rooms, antique wooden chairs and tables laid with white tablecloths, are in traditional wooden houses that the family bought, moved and had reconstructed here, their arched crab shell ceilings similar to those in royal palaces.

So the artistic spirit of Hue lives on, beyond the walls and gates and gardens, in the homes of the people of Hue.

SECRETS OF ENAMEL AND LACQUER

Don't celebrate until you are sure of success
— Vietnamese proverb

About a city block from Dong Ba market, the white metal gates of Phap Lam Hue are closed and the taxi driver shouts through. Out comes a young Vietnamese artist, as it turns out, who leads me into the two-storey display area, huge lacquer paintings of orange fish stacked along one wall, an equally huge lacquer painting of Ngo Mon (gate) reflected in the moat along another wall, beneath smaller, framed lacquer and enamel paintings. Do Huu Triet, a man in his forties, greets me and I ask him to show me through his workshops.

Behind glass to protect their work from dust sit five artists at work, painting with infinitesimally tiny brushes, intricate flowers on small enamel cups, bowls and plates. Do Huu Triet picks up a large, nearly round white 'vase', black lines marking the lotus petals. Pointing to the white vase, Do Huu Tuit identifies it as, 'an enamel vase for the Citadel, white with black design.'

In the next room, three young men sit sanding a pile of shallow wooden boxes – lacquer boxes for tissues. 'Souvenirs for tourists. They are painting an early layer of lacquer, ten layers for an ordinary box, for something special, maybe more, up to seventeen.'

Beside the lacquer box makers stands a huge oven.

'Very high heat, higher for enamel than lacquer.'

He leads me on to a workshop room where wooden drawers stand open, full of the odds and ends and tools used in their work. A smaller oven stands in one corner, a huge filing machine on one side of the room with all manner of attachments to suit the task at hand. A rack holds small cloth bags – of what? He opens one and shows me a very small, intricately moulded filigree brass, designed to be affixed to a copper surface. These bags hold various of these moulded bits.

'Enamel is fixed to copper, always copper, it's cheaper than gold! For an enamel painting, it is either tapped out or moulded.'

In another room stand huge, approximately six foot by eight foot (2 m x 2.5 m) black canvases. These are boards made of ground wood, then covered with two layers of black fabric on which large lacquer paintings will be painted. Baking the lacquer yet not burning the fabric and the wood must be a delicate business.

'I do many sizes, I can show you a picture – very large.'

We pass a small altar on a pedestal between the workshop and the showroom in front. Do Huu Triet has around twenty artists working for him, plus another ten people selling. We pass a huge lacquer painting, the graceful back of a woman with flowing hair sitting amongst lotus blossoms. 'Traditional lacquer – we keep the traditional technique, also enamel,' he tells me.

'Lacquer goes onto wood, enamel always onto copper,' he explains. 'Lacquer has only a few colours: red, brown, black, green and blue – basic lacquer is brown. We use a technique with ash', he says, pointing to small white places that look like crackled ceramic, 'because we have no white. In the traditional method we cannot do white flowers, because we have no white.'

So they do white enamel lotuses first, bake them, and then apply the lacquer around them on the rest of the painting.

'Four times in the oven,' for a small enamel bowl with pale pink chrysanthemum flowers.

Back in the workshop where the enamel is being painted, he shows me the dented remnants of a damaged lotus bud, which I suddenly recognise as the tip of one of the bronze poles of the inner gates of the Imperial City. The black lines delineating lotus petals that I had seen being painted earlier was *not* a white vase, but replacement lotus buds for the tips of the gate posts. They will be enamelled with several colours to replace the damaged lotus buds.

'With enamel you can do any colour.'

Outside again in the showroom, I point to a large six-sided lacquer screen. 'It took three months to finish.

'The oil paintings of fish are for a hotel,' also a large painting of the lake pavilion at Tu Duc's Tomb.

'Lacquer came originally from sap, but it took a long time to work with, maybe one year. Now we use a new material, we buy it. This new material has been available for only about twenty years.

'Enamel, only in Hue, the old method of making enamel had been lost for a long time, it was a long time before we found this technique – about ten years ago.'

But what is enamel, what is it made of?

'Enamel is a glaze made of glass, that holds to metal.'

He has been in the enamel and lacquer business for about twenty years. Unlike many Vietnamese, he did not follow in his father's footsteps.

'No, my family was not in this business. My father was a teacher and so is my wife. At first I was a restoration person.'

He started at twenty-four, working for the Hue Monuments Conservation Center, where he learned the enamel technique.

'I was with the Center for fifteen years, then left to start my own business. This was one of the ways to restore (the enamel) for conservation. I saw that we must change, I had to understand this technique in order to do it.'

But if the traditional technique of making enamel had been lost, how did he do it?

'I researched into the traditional method – at university, I got my Masters here in Hue.'

We finish over tea in the showroom. Although Do Huu Triet's showroom is not much more than a city block from Dong Ba market, it is not the sort of place a tourist would stumble upon. Although there is a big sign reading Phap Lam Hue, the locked gates would not be welcoming. So how do his customers find him?

'I sell to tourists in some hotels – *Indochine, La Residence* – and some people who want decoration for their big houses. And I sell to the Conservation Center.'

Sometimes he makes things on spec, other times people order what they want. So all those restored tableaux of poems and flowers lining the roof ridges and the cornices inside the royal palaces of the Citadel, when replaced, were most probably replaced by Do Huu Triet or his workshop. I ask how long it takes to learn how to make lacquer and enamel, but he explains that he starts with artists who can already do it.

But how do they get the delicate shading on the petal of a lotus flower in the lacquer?

'Lacquer is done in many layers and the picture is revealed by polishing off the excess layer – or layers of colour(s) to get the right shading. With enamel, paint shading is done the first time.'

How do you know when you are finished – with the lacquer?

'The feeling of the artist.'

CRAFTS GALORE

Girls look for talent,
boys for beauty
– Vietnamese proverb

Historically, Hue was surrounded by craft villages that served the imperial court. Many of those craft villages survive and continue to produce their high quality wares.

Hue's Golden Crafts Week celebrates these remaining, highly skilled craftsman of Thua Thien Hue, crafts handed down, often through generations, skills that without nurturing, could easily vanish in a country fast-moving towards industrialisation. The bi-annual Crafts Festival (every odd year) draws together the skilled local craftsmen and women from outlying villages, placing their wares on display in a central location before an ever-increasing crowd of travelling Vietnamese as well as foreign visitors. While many of their crafts are sold in Hue shops, without this support, some others are threatened with extinction and might well disappear.

At 8.0 a.m. it is not yet too hot. Crafts stalls line the promenade along the south bank of the Perfume river. Accompanied by Nguyen Thanh Thanh and Tran Linh, two recent graduates from the College of Foreign Languages, who kindly volunteered to translate, at the first stall a young man taps away at a huge round, wooden ball, at least a meter in diameter. He has hollowed out the interior; he is now carving a design on the exterior. This extraordinary hollow object is a *mo,* tapped in pagodas as monks chant their prayers. I have seen many a *mo* in the past, but never one remotely this big. The shelves of the stall are lined with finished, carved, lacquered and waxed *mo* of varying sizes, from fist-sized to teapot-sized, to nearly a meter in diameter, but none is as big as the one the young man is finishing.

Le Thanh Liem is the third generation of his Hue family to carve *mo* – and much else as well. His father taught him to carve, starting when he was eighteen; he is now forty-seven – the Vietnamese always look much younger than they are. He is teaching his son and daughter to carve, as well as eight students.

'It takes about three years, depending upon the ability and talent, for a student to become a craft person.'

The tool for gouging out the interior of the giant *mo*, is a long metal rod with a very sharp, curved end, not much more than half an inch (3 cm) in diameter, rather like a sharp-ended shoe horn. It must take a very long time.

'It can take three months to carve out the inside, only a month to carve the outside. Little ones, only three days. Others paint the designs on the *mo,* if there is a painted design. Or we carve the decoration on the exterior.'

I try to imagine, sitting with a sharp instrument for three months gouging out the inside of a wooden ball – and my imagination will simply not stretch beyond ten minutes.

The wood used for carving a *mo* is jack fruit, a hard wood that comes from the hills and mountains around Hue.

In the adjoining stall hang long, narrow, lacquer and gilt poem panels, parallel sentences called *lieng.* Most often, they are hung in pagodas and temples, sometimes in wealthy private homes.

Overhead hang arched panels called *hoanh phi,* measuring perhaps a meter high by a couple of meters wide. They look a bit like carved banners and often carry the name of a pagoda, or a family name in private homes, where they might be placed above the ancestral altar. Long, lacquered poles stand erect in a lacquered stand. Ceremonial weapons?

'No, they welcome people to a pagoda.' Strange welcome.

To one side, a giant, carved, bumpy-skinned toad, easily the size of a large tree stump just under a metre in diameter, sits with a carved coin in his mouth. The coin has a hollowed-out square in the centre, so an antique coin. He is a good luck charm, a money toad, which traditionally sits on a pile of gold to help a family or a business to prosper. His bumpy skin has been made by retaining the bark. Were you to buy him to adorn your entrance hall, he would cost around US$1,600 (£1,300).

Beside the toad crouches the figure of an old, bearded man, glaring from beneath heavy eyebrows, clenching his fists.

'Dat Ma, *kung fu.'*

Ask a Vietnamese who Dat Ma is and you get very vague answers, which oddly, however, doesn't seem to diminish their reverence. According to varying legends, it was Dat Ma who brought Zen Buddhism from India to China, sometime between the third and

205

fifth centuries. He is also somehow connected with *kung fu*, though you would never guess it from his dumpy, carved physique.

Liem stands with a small, yet unpolished *mo* in his hands, absent-mindedly pushing the wooden mallet that will be used by a monk to tap it during prayers, in and out of the small holes on either side, the small holes through which it would have been hollowed out.

Behind him, a black, unpolished, life-sized adult crocodile leers at us. The crocodile, it seems, is a symbol of the force and fury of primal energies, the power to survive, which the poor Vietnamese have been much in need of during the wars of the past century. Crocodiles are also the keepers of ancient wisdom.

Behind him is a Chinese general, Hoanh Phi.

The Vietnamese often have different names for historic Chinese personages, and vice versa. Hoanh Phi (Vietnam) is Quan Cong, a Chinese general of ancient times, much revered by the Vietnamese for his loyalty and sense of justice. Traditionally, when a Vietnamese made an agreement, instead of signing a contract, the two parties would go to a temple and swear their agreement before a statue of Quan Cong.

Near him, a regal-looking figure sits holding a fan, wearing a crown-like headdress: 'Ngo Dung from China, a strategist.'

At the back of the stall hangs a mirror in a highly desirable fretted and carved, lacquer frame – for sale at around $350 (£280). Along another wall, as though attending a conference, sit a row of round-bellied, happy Buddhas of the future, Maitreya, each waiting to preside over an altar. Sharing this display space is Dai Nghia, an artist of three-dimensional metal pictures, which he produces by tapping: metal flowers, calligraphy, the face of Buddha, and – a rooster.

Yet the most staggering piece, even after the huge *mo*, is a set of rustic table and chairs, so heavy and rough-hewn that they look as though they might have grown straight out of the earth, which indeed, they did, having been carved from the roots of the *huong* (aloe) tree. Trees grow to immense size in this tropical monsoon climate and no part of the tree's wood is wasted, not even the roots.

Moving along towards the river, Le Thi Le is the third generation of her Hue family to work in inlaid mother-of-pearl *(nacre)*, but she is not yet teaching her children. She has been a crafts person for thirty years, having started at the age of eighteen. Years ago I was told that freshly inlaid mother-of-pearl is always white and only starts to take on colour with age. Le Thi Le tells me that it takes two to three years to begin to develop the opalescent spectrum of peach, pink, indigo and deep green tones.

The process starts with carving the wooden plate, tray or box – to cut the cavities into which the tiny chips of mother-of-pearl will be placed. Then the craftsmen washes the shells and uses a very small, sharp knife to cut the shells into the infinitesimally small chips to fit the shapes they want and glue them to the surface. The black surface is obtained by waxing.

'Old things cost more.' A plate with intricately inlaid, multi-coloured mother-of-pearl, over twenty years old, sells for a bit more than $100 (£80).

A tray with raised edges on a carved stand that could be used as a side table would also cost a bit more than $100; a black inlaid box, also on a carved stand, just over $200.

'And the parallel sentence panels?' – intricately inlaid with birds and flowers. 'If they are old, they would sell for between $1,800 and $2,400 (£1,440-1,920); if they are new, between $900 and $1,400 (£720-1,120).' So if you buy new, they will become more and more beautiful as they age.

Overhead hangs an inlaid, arched *hoanh phi,* a carved scroll to hang in a pagoda or over a family's ancestral altar. At the back of the stall, an inlaid cabinet, roughly two meters high by two meters wide, 'took one year to make with many people working on it. It is sold' – for over $2,000 (£1,600). Le Thi Le has had a good two days. Her products have sold well this week. The inlaid table and benches in the centre of the room sold for $1,500 (£1,200).

At the far end of her stall stands a display cabinet with open shelves and glass-front compartments at different levels, one holding the inevitable bust of Ho Chi Minh. Mercifully, he has not been inlaid with mother-of-pearl. She pulls out a round box with a lid ($375, £300). The compartments, Thanh suggests gently – no hard sell here – could be used to serve jams or for jewellery.

Twenty people work in her company: three members of her family are employed, both she and her husband, and many more.

Unhappily, the owner of the lantern stall is out, lanterns of every shade and hue: painted silk lanterns, silk lotus bud lanterns just beginning to open, hexagonal silk lanterns, box-shaped and diamond-shaped paper lanterns . . .

Seated at a bamboo table, Nguyen Dinh Hung, who works in bamboo, is something of a local celebrity, having appeared on television. His sacred canon made of bamboo with dragons along each side, brought him third prize in a competition. More importantly, at forty-two he is the second youngest Crafts Person in Hue, a distinction for which he had to apply, his work considered and judged.

'As well as the quality of workmanship', he explains, 'what is important is what you have done for the community, and how many exhibitions you have shown your work in.'

Nguyen Dinh Hung has taught deaf and dumb people to work with bamboo. He has ten people working for him; six of whom are blind and deaf. He entered the Hanoi One Thousand Competition in 2010, the year Hanoi celebrated the one thousandth anniversary of the founding of the city as the capital.

Nguyen Dinh Hung knew how dexterous and talented handicapped people could be, as previously, he had taught at a disability school. He has now been working in bamboo for ten years. Before that, he made kites.

He roots around in an old tin box and brings out an astonishingly life-like variety of splinter-limbed, bamboo insects: a dragonfly, a grasshopper, beetles, butterflies, a bee. The insects, a favourite with children, only cost $3 (£2.50).

Bamboo napkin rings are dead easy to make, he says. But on the table is a teapot, carved from one piece of bamboo. He then shows me his intricate table lamps made of split bamboo, split so thinly that they could almost be matchsticks and he lifts the shade to show me how easy it is to change a bulb. The small lamps are very tempting for under $19 (£15).

There are vases carved of bamboo, tiny tea cups, 'made from near the root of bamboo.'

While we have been talking, from a distance I have been eyeing a four-rigger sail boat, its sails made of toothpick-thin, split bamboo. 'The ship was made by a student, as a hobby.' Hours and hours of loving skill.

Nguyen Dinh Hung says that he wants his products to be useful in life, to enhance people's life styles. Then he shows me those that are precisely not exactly useful! Here is a one-meter-tall replica of the tower at Thien Mu pagoda, also a two-meter-tall tower. And he plans to make a four-meter-tower, 'maybe even a seventy or eighty-meter tower that can be lowered and folded into itself to pack' – like a collapsing silk lantern. He likes to make products that are easy and small to take home, he says.

Propped at the back of the stall is a framed, bamboo mosaic portrait of the Madonna and Child, making me wonder if he might be Catholic, or merely appealing to prospective Catholic buyers.

'Many other companies try to imitate my products.'

The hanging, perforated bamboo tube lamps would be particularly appealing for cafes and restaurants – or my terrace.

At the next stall hangs a framed Artisan for Tea, Chung Nhan Certificate, but the stall is so busy selling tea that it would be unkind and extremely unprofitable to tear Nguyen Thi Mai away from her customers. The crafts fair is filling up with Vietnamese visitors, who have a week's holiday at the beginning of May to celebrate 'independence from the US invaders.'

Nearby, hill tribe women sit weaving, looms resting on their out-stretched legs. They are from the Ta Oi tribe, forty-two miles (70 km) inland from Hue. Others are weaving straw hats, mats and tightly-woven, open baskets to carry on the back. Some have tightly fitting lids – beautiful, intricately woven baskets, works of art. A bamboo flute *(khiem)* costs around $70 (£56).

A little farther away, six women sit on mats making *non la* conical hats from palm leaves. Sewn onto split, round bamboo frames, some hats are plain, some have embroidery. The hat makers are from Van The village, Thuy Thanh ward. Only in Hue do they make 'poetry' hats. The poem is cut into the middle layer of the straw, so that when the sun shines through, a shy lass can flash a flirtatious message to her prospective lover.

Near the hat makers is a woman sitting barefoot, intently drawing a cross-and-square design onto a long scroll of paper. Behind her a man is spinning by alternately pumping as one would a bicycle, a wooden bar that somehow turns a wheel. Another woman is weaving on a hanging loom. They are all members of the Muong tribe from Ha Giang province near Hanoi.

Luong Thanh Hien has been making pottery since 2006. Formerly, there were many families in the village of Phuoc Tich making pottery. There had to be, as unglazed pots from this village were made by the

209

hundreds to serve rice to the Nguyen emperors, pots that could be used only once and then thrown away. So the entire village was busy making pots. Sadly now, Luong Thanh Hien is the only person left making Phuoc Tich pottery. At forty-three, he remains unmarried, but he plans to open a class to teach young people to be potters.

Phuoc Tich pottery is a special kind of pottery, unglazed on the outside, glazed inside. It is only made in the village after which it is named. Luong Thanh Hien's father and grandfather were both potters – three generations of potters – a craft on the brink of vanishing. The clay comes from near the village. These days, Luong Thanh Hien sells his pots mostly to local customers, rarely further afield. If the pots are decorated with painted designs, he also does the painting, but he is teaching young people to do the painting.

How long does he bake the pottery?

If baked traditionally, it takes three days, and they have to wait two to three weeks to finish the products. Now, thanks to technology, it takes only fifteen to eighteen hours to finish the entire product, baked in a gas oven.

He puts the glaze on first and then bakes it. 'The colours never change. Every step is difficult. The percentage of breakage depends upon the person who makes it, how careful he is.'

Pretty hanging bells cost only $2.50 (£2), a teapot in the shape of a peach *(dao)* – you put the water in from the bottom – a masterpiece – costs under $10 (£8), a three-hole bud vase resembling tubular candle holders ($8.50, £6.80), a tiny tea set of six cups ($9.50, £7.50), a two-cup tea set ($7, £5.60), a bud vase with a long neck ($5, £4), lamps ($7, £5.60), a parrot figurine ($6, £4.80). To the Westerner, accustomed to paying dearly for designer objects, the prices are staggeringly low. His pots and lamps hang in numerous Hue restaurants. One can only hope that wider marketing and the training of young potters, will preserve this fine, local craft for posterity

Tran Nam Long has been working in enamel *(fap lam)* and lacquer *(son mai)* for ten years. A pretty girl in an *au dai* introduces him. An enormous lacquer painting hangs at the back of his stall: gorgeous white lotuses on a slightly incongruous red pond, perhaps five feet by more than six feet (1.5 m x 2 m). The smooth, gleaming patina of lacquer is breathtakingly exquisite.

How long does it take to bake the lacquer? 'The panel took six months to make and it was baked at a high temperature. You draw it first and then bake it for about two hours. It took two days to draw the design. The raised lotus blossoms were enamelled first, then the lacquer was added to the leaves and the background – it was baked two times.' For a lacquer of this size, the oven must have been huge. The wood they use is called *go ghep,* thin slices of wood, glued together to make one long, wide, panel of wood, rather like plywood or hardboard. The panel is priced at $2,800 (£2,250).

From a shallow box, I pick up a tiny, enamelled, spidery dragon. A wall-hanging?

'No, they are decorations for designer dresses.'

A ten-inch-square lacquer plum blossom, framed, costs only $33 (£26), a little dragon screen that might stand on your desk or a bookcase ($70, £56). Then I spy the jewellery, both enamel and lacquer: lacquer bangle bracelets ($8.50, £7), earrings ($3.50, £2.80), pendants ($6, £4.80).

I should have tucked my notebook away and bought a horde.

Le Van Xanh also works in wood as has his family for many generations – six generations, he counts them. Yet a more different style of carving from the carver of *mo* would be difficult to find.

Small statuettes of Buddhist dignitaries; solid wooden vases with curved, fluted lips ($60, £48); a twelve-inch Buddha ($38, £30); long, thin chopstick boxes ($9, £7).

Neither painted nor lacquered, they are oiled. He is the brother-in-law of the owner of the business, aged fifty-six, and was only fourteen when he started carving.

At the next stall entitled Thai Vinh, astonishing, galloping horses reminiscent of St Paul's in Rome, leap out of a piece of wood nearly two meters wide! They took six months to carve. An incredible, similarly large pair of horses rear on their hind legs in a *tour de force* of balance from another piece of sculpture standing beside it – that took only one month to sculpt.

Unfortunately, I miss the two artisans, Nguyen Vinh and Hu Thai, but an assistant tells me that either of these sculptures – masterpieces – would sell for just over $2,000 (£1,600). A much smaller, very round Buddha, Maitreya, Di Lac in Vietnamese, to place on your altar, would only set you back $70 (£56). But a more ambitious, life-sized, set of three statues of Buddha, Quan Am and a mysterious third, would cost a bit over $2,000 (£1,600) for all three.

211

Than Van Huy and his family have been making paper flowers for three generations. He proudly shows me the small, brightly-coloured flowers *(hoa giay tho tung)* that have been made traditionally to place on ancestral altars and explains that they are now in danger of disappearing again. They all but disappeared about fifty years ago – he re-introduced them in 2008.

'People these days want modern.' They far prefer the lotus buds – yellow, pink, white, pale green and blue – that he also produces. Two people at the front of the stall sit making paper lotuses, gluing pleated petal by pleated petal.

'It's very easy, even children can do it.'

He could do it when he was only four, he tells me. His entire family makes paper flowers together. He has nine children and they all make flowers, a total of thirteen people. The whole village of Thanh Tien makes paper flowers, about sixty per cent of the people, eighty people in total.

The paper comes from another village near Hue.

How much for the bright, traditional flowers? Only fifty cents US for a stem of several flowers – then the stems are stuck to a branch to make a bouquet of as many as you like. The huge, pleated lotus buds cost $6 (£4.80) each, smaller ones $1-1.50, big open blossoms just under $5 (£4) each.

The head of the family at the next stall is not there, but his daughter tells us about the family business in bamboo furniture. Her father, Than Loi, is head of the business. She is still in college. The entire village of Thuy Lap, roughly eighteen miles (30 km) from Hue, over five hundred families, work in making bamboo furniture.

This is sumptuous, mature, wide-diameter bamboo. There are also carved boxes and split bamboo tables. Some of the furniture has been stained dark brown, some left its natural, pale yellow colour. The double bed, its split-bamboo surface allowing air to filter through as you move, looks quite comfortable and extremely well-suited to Hue's muggy climate ($130, £104). A rather charming, open-weave, swinging cradle only costs $30 (£24), a hexagonal lamp $24 (£19), a carved bamboo vase $3. There is also a table and matching, straight-backed benches.

If only I had a private plane!

212

As we are leaving, I spy the kite stall and inquire if perhaps this is the same family of the man I interviewed years ago, living east of the Citadel. With a moustache, Nguyen Van Hoang, aged fifty-one, assures me that he is, indeed, the son of the man I had interviewed. The stall is afloat and hung with beautiful kites, large and small, the largest more than a meter wide with long, long tails: a colourful orange and yellow phoenix, blue fish, birds, butterflies.

Nguyen Van Hoang is the fourth generation kite maker in his family and during this past year alone, his famiy has competed or flown kites in France, Malaysia, Thailand and India as well as attending an international workshop. His father, now ninety, is no longer making kites. He has retired, but he is well remembered. Whenever Nguyen Van Hoang goes abroad, he tells me, he is always referred to as 'the son of Be.'

He himself has one daughter and one son. The son is studying at the College of Economics and has learned to make kites. His daughter is getting ready to take college examinations and yes, she also makes kites.

The kites are made of fabric, *vai khuya,* the same as that used to make umbrellas.

How long does it take to make the big kites?

'Five days.'

The long dragon, stretching across the stall diagonally would sell for $2,800 (£2,240). Yet quite large kites can sell for $47 (£37), the big butterflies for $23.50 (£19), smaller fish and phoenix kites for $5 (£4), and tiny kites for toddlers for under $1. A gorgeous peacock, and behind it a mobile that turns out not to be a mobile, but a small kite, sells for under $5.

It makes you want to get out your running shoes to fly them.

Finally, we sit down for an avocado smoothie with Nguyen Hai Thien from the Thua Thien Hue newspaper, the poor girl having trailed around with us the entire morning, me refusing to stop to chat until we had finished the interviews with craftsmen, hoping to beat the crowds and not deter the craftsmen from making sales.

Although the Crafts Fair pulls in the craftsmen from outlying villages, many of their beautiful products can be viewed anytime in the large shop adjoining the Book Cafe in Le Loi Street.

(Note: Contacts for above craftsmen, see Historic Appendix)

BIRD SINGING COMPETITION

The old spiced hen is worth
as much as the young chicken
– Vietnamese proverb

One of the last events of Hue's Golden Craft Week is a Bird Singing Competition, although I am a little uncertain as to why bird singing is classified as a craft. Nor have I ever been to a bird singing competition, so I am more than a little curious as to how song birds can be judged in a bird singing competition. At 7.30 a.m., I decant myself from a taxi at Hi Ba Trung School for Girls.

Birds and their owners start arriving by motorbike just after 7.30. Some owners appear carrying two cages. How do they manage to hold two cages and drive a motorbike? The owners, all men, are in their thirties and forties. For some reason, I had expected it to be a hobby of elderly men as I have often seen several elderly gentlemen with their bird cages, sitting in cafes drinking tea. Then two little girls, the first females I have seen, arrive with their father.

Steel hanging frames have been erected the length of the straight, paved walkway a hundred meters long through the grounds to the entrance of the school. Obviously, this is a serious event. Already, several cages under their covers have been placed in neat lines on the pavement beneath the steel frames, sections numbered 250-300, 300-350 etc. Each bird has a proper place. Each square cage under a navy or burgundy cover, imprinted with FESTIVAL HUE, has a number tag.

The birds are chirping under their covers. I count more than fifty cages by 7.45. Owners of birds perch on metal stools on the lawn. The leaves of the tall phoenix trees filter the sunlight, providing welcome, dappled shade.

More cages keep arriving. A loud speaker at the far end of the pavement makes announcements, perhaps instructions. A round cage passes – an individual. Up to now, all of the cages have been square.

More non-conformist individuals begin to appear, one with a pretty oriental design cover, another with a checked cover, another with a red silk cover.

Every ten meters or so a metal table, two bottles of water and a chair, have been set up for the judge as he moves progressively along the line a hundred meters long.

I am approached by a young girl who tells me in English that she is a volunteer, working at the Festival. But before I can question her about the competition, she wanders off again. Looking down the growing ranks, there are now cages in red, green, even pink covers as well as the official navy and burgundy covers.

A red and white tape is now strung a few feet behind the metal tables to keep the bird owners and spectators a short distance away from the birds. Two very little boys stroll past with their father. The birds keep up a lively, chirping chorus. At last, I see three other women, two young ones and a granny. Bird competitions are clearly a male hobby.

At 8.0 a.m., from the loud speaker comes a different tone – it sounds like a formal speech. Birds are still arriving. At 8.05, officials wearing black T-shirts, printed HUE FESTIVAL, start to remove the covers and carefully hang the cages on hooks from the steel frames above. There must be several hundred birds by now. Most of the cages are made of bamboo, both round and square. The birds have black faces and backs, pointed black topknots and white breasts. By 8.15, all of the birds have had their covers carefully removed and the cages hung up, each cage and cover numbered. Very well organised.

The sun is already blazing through the tall trees. The cages are now three and four ranks deep, which brings me to wonder how on earth a judge can differentiate the song of any individual bird – even in the row nearest him? A judge arrives in a white T-shirt and sits at the table with the bottles of water. Judging a song bird competition can be a hot business. The birds continue singing. Over the loud speaker, the judge is introduced. He stands and waves a hand to take a small bow in acknowledgement.

I watch the judge, watching the birds. He writes something. What? Surely, he can only see and hear the two or three birds hung on the outer row nearest to him? The judge stares intently, looking, listening. Perhaps the canny bird owner arrives late so that his bird is hung on the outer rank of birds?

Later, a bright young man in Hue Tourist Office identifies the species as *chich mieu* in Vietnamese, which translates as red-whiskered bulbul in English, and he informs me that their singing is judged by how *long* the birds sing – that they are timed. So the bird that sings longest – and presumably loudest – wins.

PART VII

HUE LITERATURE

EARLY HUE LITERATURE

Summer is present in all the four seasons
Just one rain brings about winter
– Emperor Tu Duc

To state the blindingly obvious, all literature has to start with a
written language. When the Chinese first conquered the Viet tribes
north of Hanoi in 179 BC, the Viets had a rich oral tradition, hence
the many historic legends still told to Vietnamese children, but they
had no written language. Therefore, although Vietnamese is a
completely different language from Chinese – they only seem to have
tonality in common – when they were conquered by the Chinese, the
Viets were forced to adopt the Chinese system of writing: calligraphy.
All official government documents and scholarly literature in the
North, Central and South of Vietnam, were written in Han Chinese
known as *chu Han* or *chu nha*.

The Viets in the North threw off Chinese domination in 938
and sometime between the tenth and thirteenth centuries, Vietnamese
scholars devised a new-old system of writing, still using Chinese
calligraphy – ideograms – but this time using Chinese ideograms to
express Vietnamese words and meanings, as well as modifying and
adding new ideograms to express particular Vietnamese words or
concepts. This Sino-Vietnamese form of writing became known as
chu nom. To be sure, after a thousand years of Chinese domination,
the Viets had borrowed – adopted – many Chinese words, but their
own language remained intact.

When Catholic missionaries arrived in Hoi An, eighty-seven
miles (139 km) south of Hue in the early years of the seventeenth
century, they soon realized that if they were to succeed in
proselytizing, they would have to learn Vietnamese. The Jesuit priests

217

made use of their experience in transcribing Chinese and Japanese into a Romanised script and over the years, devised a Romanized version of Vietnamese.

It was not an easy task. One French priest, Alexandre de Rhodes, recounted how once when he asked his cook to buy fish, *ca* in Vietnamese, the cook returned laden with a basket of aubergines – the difference in pronunciation being only in the tones. He also recalled ordering his men to cut down some bamboo, *chem tre* in Vietnamese – and all the children ran away. In his mispronunciation, the missionary had ordered the men to 'kill the children!'

This Romanized script, which was not adopted as the official language until 1919 – by order of the French – is known as *quoc ngu* and somewhat modified, is the national language used today.

So literature in Vietnam has had a rather rough ride, first borrowing a foreign written language, adapting that foreign written language to its own use, and finally, creating a whole new system of writing – and by doing so, dramatically cutting off Vietnamese society and culture from its earlier literary roots. Only scholars today can read *chu nha* or *chu nom*.

'Literature is the historic voice of a country, its people and their lives; it is the expression and description of life by means of a language system,' as Sino-Vietnamese scholar, Ngo Thoi Don, has so eloquently put it.

Following the Chinese tradition, writing poetry is deeply embedded in the Vietnamese psyche. Long before Hue became capital, one part of the triennial four-part doctoral examinations in Hanoi to become a mandarin required the candidate to compose two different genres of poems to strict form – in *chu nha*. So writing poetry was a vital part of a young man's education.

The development of literature in Hue travelled with the Viet migrations from the North to the South over several centuries. In the Early Le dynasty, tenth century, the Viets began to move southwards – to Thanh Hoa (105 mi, 168 km) and to Nghe An provinces (141 mi, 225 km) south of Hanoi. In the fourteenth century under the Tran dynasty, there was tentative migration further south into the O and Ly Provinces of Champa, following the Mongol invasions of the thirteenth century. However, it was not really until the mid-sixteenth century under the leadership of Nguyen Hoang, that the drive southwards followed into Quang Binh, Quang Tri (just north of Hue), and to Thuan Tien Hue – the old O and Ly Provinces of Champa –

and later, Quang Nam, a bit further south. And it was not until the nineteenth century (1802) that Nguyen Anh triumphed, uniting the country from the Chinese border to the Mekong Delta.

Hue scholars admit that under the early Nguyen lords, during the Tran dynasty in Hanoi, Hue's literature reflected Sino-Vietnamese literature in northern Dai Viet. The Chams did, indeed, have their own language, but the Cham rulers and many of the Cham people, those who had not been killed in battle, had fled south to around Phan Rang and into the Mekong Delta following the decisive Viet victory of 1471. With the passage of time, the language and culture of the more numerous Viets came to dominate central Vietnam, certainly from the mid-sixteenth century, following the arrival of Nguyen Hoang.

Moreover, Hue scholars explain that the new Viet migrants, as people settling a new geographical territory, developed a close tie to the land. Yet reflecting their Confucian culture of the North, conversation within the family remained formal, respect shown by younger members of the family to their elders. Even when Hue became the capital of the nation, this formal Confucian tradition blended with the rustic language spoken by the rural pioneers, contributing to the formation of a particularly regional literature.

Hue's early authors were Confucian intellectuals, mandarin and members of the royal family, writing mostly in Han Chinese, *chu nha*. Sino-Vietnamese scholar, Ngo Thoi Don, writes that Hue poetry reflected the conventions of Chinese poetry – 'the ambling habits of Chinese poets when travelling to Dong Dinh Lake in Ho Nam (China), employing long respected Chinese form and style.'

Early poetry written in Hue primarily celebrated the hills and mountains, the forests and rice paddies, the rivers and the sea, the houses and villages of the arrivals' new homeland in Thua Tien.

For instance, the poet, Cao Ba Quat (1809-1855), became a mandarin in the Nguyen court of Hue at thirty-two, though after only six years, he was sacked and later worked at court in a lowly position. A lover of nature, his poems describe the scenery of Hue – *Huong River Boat Trip, A Morning on the Huong River* – but also the sufferings of the poor.

> *Ranges of mountains embracing green fields,*
> *A long river as a sword in the middle of the sky,*
> *Fishing boats singing endlessly the song of rowing,*
> *A couple of birds standing sleeping peacefully.*

Below is one of the Emperor Thieu Tri's twenty poems extolling the beauty of Hue.

> *Rowing the boat on the Huong river in the morning*
> *Running deeply and softly as a cradle of the citadel,*
> *Running a pure and fresh flow of water,*
> *Both the water and the waves are as mild*
> *as they are born to be.*
> *The boat takes the chance to delight and move quickly,*
> *The wine has not been finished.*
> *The flowers are still in love with the scene,*
> *When does this scene vanish, oh dear,*
> *It is so peaceful, this land.*

The mandarin, Tran Tien Thanh, also loved the sea and the scholar, Ngo Thoi Don, considers that in the sea poetry of what he calls the medieval period, the poem below was unique in its idealized imagery of a fisherman.

> *Working on the shore is cheerful,*
> *A boat alone to go in freedom,*
> *Seagulls live in peace,*
> *Rowing the boat to enjoy the moon.*

The Emperor Tu Duc, who along with the Emperor Thieu Tri, considered one of the two finest emperor poets, also loved the sea.

> *The beach is full of summer wind,*
> *Full of the moon kissing the sand,*
> *For those who have no relations,*
> *A glass of wine makes nothing more than a joy.*

Although quoted earlier, one of Emperor Tu Duc's poems that I find quite touching, was written in grief at the death of one of his favourite concubines, composed perhaps at the picturesque lake pavilion of his tomb . . .

I want to break the mirror that held her face,
I want to touch her clothes to keep her scent.

Tung Thien Vuong (1819-1870) was the tenth son of the
Emperor Minh Mang, much lauded for his nature poems, particularly
his poems of the sea. His pen-name was Mien Tham. His poem below
has been called *The Love Poem of Thuan An*, the village where the
Perfume river meets the South China Sea.

My personality is as sparkling as the white waves,
As strong as where it can go.
My heart is as straight as a pole,
It never sinks in the rain.
Beyond the ocean is the immense water,
The sand dune is as high as the mountain.
Though the sea could be covered,
My heart is still loyal to you.

Flowers Along the Road

Beautiful flowers are in bloom along the spring road,
Beautiful flowers go along with you to your home,
Watching beautiful flowers fading and fading,
Going home alone to feel alone.

A flower falls as in a dream, to sadden the willow,
The spring wind stays alone.

But in case you were deluded by the seeming simplicity of
these poems, Mien Tham railed that 'writing poetry is as hard as
ploughing the clouds and fishing the moon' – and that if a poem were
no good, it only reaped derision: 'Laughing at a royal man ploughing
the stone field.'

Although he was a royal prince, Mien Tham was highly
sensitive to the plight of the poor. His poems often express empathy
with the misery of the peasants and labourers, the misery often caused
by the very Nguyen royal court of which he was a prince. His
Collection of Poems on the Mountain (Thuong Son thi tapo) is

considered to be not only his greatest collection of poems, but Vietnam's greatest collection of poetry written in Han (Chinese).

Some of the titles from this collection indicate his sympathy and compassion: *Drought, A Poor Family, Song of an Undershot Water Wheel, Calling for Pulling Wood, The Moan of a Gold Washer, The Moan of a Nomad, Selling Joss-Paper Things.* Here are a few brief excerpts:

> *The sun is so strong this year,*
> *Farmers get exhausted.*

> *Termites that destroy are guilty,*
> *But not as guilty as those who betray the nation.*

> *Vegetables are to replace rice in hunger,*
> *Flame is to replace clothes in cold.*

> *One sad singer is accompanied by nine others,*
> *They all take turns to step on the water-wheel*
> *with heavy hearts.*

> *The family cannot have lunch till late noon,*
> *The debt chaser keeps on chasing.*

> *It was painful when the hand was half broken,*
> *It's still a fortune even when the tax*
> *had been reduced by half.*

> *Passing the border to get to the capital in twenty days,*
> *Clothes get ragged and bodies get sick,*
> *Those who died stayed in the bush,*
> *Those who still live keep crying.*

Mien Tham's younger brother, Prince Tuy Ly Vuong, Minh Mang's eleventh son, was also a highly esteemed poet and a mandarin. Both he and his elder brother, Mien Tham, rose to become two of Vietnam's greatest poets.

Sino-Vietnamese literature scholar, Ngo Thoi Don, explains that in the mediaeval period, Hue poetry written in Han *(chu nha)*, moved from the classical Chinese forms and imagery to more realistic literature. He refers to the language of earlier poetry as having been a blend of real and public in function and form. In both imagery and form, mediaeval Hue poetry in its descriptive and emotive language, developed into a more lively and passionate reflection of life.

Poets using formal literary language began to adopt what Ngo Thoi Don calls 'real-life language' – local vernacular idioms and aphorisms, however, still carefully crafted, arranged and polished, a poem still subject to strict rules of versification, metrical and rhythmical composition – alas, all lost in translation. Despite the strict rules of form, the craftsmanship of the poet retained its sense of naturalness, combined with eloquence, symmetry and erudition.

In *The Story of a Middle-Classed Person,* an important Nguyen dynasty mandarin, Ly Van Phuc, realistically managed to describe Vietnamese family life – in three short lines:

> *Clothes get old and faded,*
> *young children crowded and old mum,*
> *luxury is far away and exotic.*

Scholar Ngo Thoi Don writes: 'Hue writers are appreciated by the community because their language is both stylistic and close to the common language. That is the merit and simplicity of poetry, and the poet's talent integrates the community's language, polishes it and passes it on as part of a nation's culture.'

He goes on to explain how people who live close to the earth, farmers, use language that is direct and transparent. Their lives 'teach them lessons about the soil, the life cycle of rice plants, the germination of seeds, enabling them to be "in love" with their lives, more than city folk. They can fall in love with young *mud,* young banana trees, young rice, the young sun, the wind, tree buds and young birds – all newborn animals and plants – resulting in a language link between young and new – to pretty. All of life feeds the creative process, Nothing in real life is not beautiful.'

When the poem, *Carrying the Clouds Home,* by Ngo Van Phu became a folk ballad in the 1860s, debate among intellectuals ensued over the unclear distinctions between folk and scholarly literature.

> *In the sky, the clouds are as white as the cotton,*
> *In the middle of the fields,*
> *the cotton is as white as the clouds,*

223

A girl with pink cheeks, carrying cotton home,
She looks as if she is bringing home the clouds.

Nguyen Dieu, perhaps Vietnam's most famous and beloved poet, author of *The Tale of Kieu,* wrote most of his work while serving as a mandarin in the Nguyen court.

Young grass is green to the horizon
A peach flower tree is in light blossom
 — Nguyen Du from *The Tale of Kieu*

It was he, more than any other, who lent respectability to and brought the use of *chu nom* (Sino-Vietnamese) into literary use. The titles of his shorter poems describe his feelings of isolation and melancholy: *Seeing You Off, Autumn Coming, Random Writing on a Public Wall, Viewing Thien Thai.*

Within the span of a hundred years of human existence,
what a bitter struggle is waged between genius and destiny!
How many harrowing events have occurred
while mulberries cover the conquered sea!
Rich in beauty, unlucky in life!
Strange indeed, but little wonder, since casting
hatred upon rosy cheeks is a habit of the Blue Sky.
 — the first six lines of Nguyen Du's *The Tale of Kieu*

Scholar Ngo Thoi Don goes on to say that Hue's Sino-Vietnamese mediaeval poetry, developed over seven centuries, in its early period influenced by and redolent of Eastern cultures, notably Chinese literature, but later in Hue, 'a new phase developed which must be described as the reality of the Viet people's lives against a backdrop of nature.'

Lyrical mediaeval Sino-Vietnamese literature expressed the poet's innermost feelings through a passionate and dramatic style, and satirical mediaeval literature, through unforeseen situations and laughter, raised people's awareness and helped to make unfortunate happenings bearable.

'Laughter then becomes part of the art of living and the struggle for a beautiful life.'

LATER HUE LITERATURE

The educated man precedes the farmer,
But when the rice begins to run short,
it's the farmer who comes first.
    – Vietnamese poem

Hue's written literature switched from *chu nom* to the Romanized script, *quoc ngu*, as recently as the 1930s, although certain writers started writing in *quoc ngu* soon after the turn of the century, according to Tran Dai Vinh, writer, scholar and senior lecturer of Sino-Vietnamese literature in the University of Hue's College of Education. The first magazine published in *quoc ngu* was appropriately called *Nam Phung*, named after Emperor Khai Dinh's Catholic empress, the girl he had met on board ship. The first issue appeared in 1917.

It is thought that the first Hue writer to use *quoc ngu* was the poetess, Dam Phuong (1881-1947), writes Tran Dai Vinh. Born into the royal family and married to a mandarin, she wrote for *Nam Phung* and *New Literature (Trung Bac)* magazines, and interestingly, seems to have had early feminist ideas, calling for equality between men and women and a more progressive society. Like earlier Hue poetry, her subjects were often the landscapes of Hue.

Missing the Mountain

Rain water has dried out on the sluggish hedge,
The birds' rhythmical songs are blown in the wind,
Summer sunlight is fading on the lotus lake,
Is there any snow on the daisy in the autumn forest?

Named national poet and playwright, Ung Binh Thuc Da Thi (1877-1961) chaired the Huong Binh Literary Society, an elite Hue poets' circle, according to scholar Tran Dai Vinh. His daughter, Ton

Nu Hy Khuong, was also a poet of note. Another poet of the same vintage, Thao Am Nguyen Khoa Vi (1881-1968), wrote poems often in the form of Hue folk songs.

A poet named Phan Quoc Quang (1889-1960) wrote the poem below, expressing the grief of one of the wives of the Emperor Thanh Thai (Bao Hien's grandfather), who had been exiled to Reunion.

A Wife's Complaint

Dear children, I am broken hearted,
My life is full of ups and downs,
Withered are the trees on the Ngu Binh Mountain,
Tearful is the water in the Huong river,
In a remote land you will live and die,
The debt to our homeland you cannot pay,
I hope the final day comes soon,
So that we can be together again.

Tran Dai Vinh goes on to explain that a whole new generation of Hue poets writing in *quoc ngu* formed a New Literature movement *(Tho moi)* in the 1930s, amongst them Le Thanh. Below is an emotional excerpt from one of his poems composed in the form of a Tang (dynasty) poem.

Sad Feelings in Autumn

Too embarrassed to say a word,
How tragic autumn love is!
Hastily the swallows fly away,
Gentle the wind blows now and then,
More sleep cannot bring about pleasant dreams,
More songs sung to get rid of the sadness,
Green willows in the distance,
The winter is coming and I feel so sad.

Even a list of the titles of Hue poems gives some idea of the grief and longings, of gentle, nostalgic feelings and the melancholy style of Hue poetry: *Countryside Girl, Sorrowful, The Golden Days, The Scent of Colours.* To one who has experienced Hue in its chilly winter, *Dreaming Moon,* by Thuc Te (1916-1947), is evocative.

226

Dreaming Moon

One cold night so dim was the mirror,
The water sighed along the Huong river,
The sad waves tapped the reeds,
Some boats were bobbing on the river,
Grey clouds gathered into a wall on the North Mountain,
Gentle music mingled with the soft mist,
The dim moon dozed off dreaming,
And lying gracefully on the tender willow,
Some ghosts on the White Tiger Bridge,
Disappeared on hearing the morning cock crow,
The moon stopped dreaming and woke up reluctantly,
The willows moved with misty tear,
The moon was full of emotion, shedding tears,
The river filled with light,
The moonlight mixed with the wet mist,
Echoing the spring love song.

More titles of poems – *The Hatred of Battle* (1937), *Mother's Village* (1941), *Sister and Brother* (1942), *The Difficulty of Searching for Aloe Wood* (1943) – poems composed by Thanh Tinh (1911-1988), evoke the heart and gentle soul of Hue.

Tran Dai Vinh writes of another poet, Nguyen Phuc Buu Dinh (1898-1931), who protested against the corruption of the last two Nguyen dynasty emperors. The poet was imprisoned, first in Lao Bao and later on the island of Con Dao where he wrote the novels, *Uncle Tam Lo* and *Autumn Moon,* as well as a volume of poetry, *A Tear for Friends.* Sadly, trying to escape from Con Dao island across the South China Sea in 1931, his boat was hit by a storm and he went missing, presumed drowned.

Also in the 1930s, a new band of revolutionary poets appeared, waging a literary war against materialism and demanding art – not for art's sake – but art for the good of humanity. A whole new generation of writers and poets grew to maturity during the French Indo-Chinese War (1946-1954), many of whom joined the resistance against the French.

Phung Quan (1932-1995) joined the resistance as a teenager and his poems reflect his intense passion: *Escaping from Con Dao* (1954), *The Epic of Vo Thi Sau* (1955). He also wrote an epic trilogy:

A Violent Childhood (1983), but he is best known for his poem, *Mother's Advice,* which admonishes a young man to fight for truth.

Thanh Hai (1930-1980) was another of these resistance poets, who later fought against the Americans in the Vietnam War. His poems were published in *The Loyal Comrades* (1962). He continued to write poems such as *The Mark of the Hammock in Truong Son* (1977) and *Spring in This Nation* (1982) until shortly before he died.

Another, Quang Long, even while a student in the Literature Department of the College of Education, became a noted figure in this anti-American movement. Quang Long's contributions included *Dear Mother, My Heart,* making a desperate plea for the liberation of the country. A band of scholars from Hue University (established 1957), became a campaigning voice during the Vietnam War for national liberation, which resonated through the consciousness of students and intellectuals alike. The year 1964 saw an explosion of patriotic and revolutionary literature from these young intellectuals.

But with peace in mind, from this same generation, the Buddhist monk, Thich Nhat Hanh, wrote short stories, *Love Among People,* and the novella, *The Way Back of Thought,* as well as a volume of poems, *Praying for the Appearance of the White Dove.*

Many writers and poets, who returned from the North after what the Vietnamese call the American War, are still writing: Hoang Phu Ngoc Tuong, Nguyen Khac Phe, Hong Nhu, To Nhuan Vy, Nguyen Khoa Diem and Tran Vang Sao.

A teacher of literature and philosophy, much respected in Hue, Hoang Phu Ngoc Tuong, who fought in the Vietnam War, produced many volumes of poetry: *Footprints in the City* (1976), *Flower Picker* (1995), but he was most famous for his chronicles: *Lots of Firelight, Who Gave the Name to the River* and *Flowers and Fruit Around Me.* 'Tuong uncovers the soul of the Hue people, shown in a simple but accurate relationship between nature, inner emotions and a spiritual tendency,' writes Le Thi Huong.

Also a contemporary writer, Nguyen Khac Phe's works include chronicles, commentary and several acclaimed novels: *The Way by Ha Village* (1976), *The Way Next to the Battle* (1976), *The Position of the Engineer* (1980), *The Call of the Remote Area* (1985), *The Open Doors* (1986) and *If I Could Die For You* (1989).

Writing in 1990 in *Faces of Modern Writers (Nghe Tinh)* about *The Road Bordering the Battle,* Pham Phu Phong says that Nguyen Khac Phe's strength as a writer lies 'in how he reveals the reality of social problems at the end of the war, not just the fierce attacks of the enemy on the main roads. He describes equally the important struggles against bureaucracy, inconsistency, ignorance and the sycophants who are promoted through their social relationships with high ranking officers. His work also recognizes the serious disease plaguing current society – that of opportunism.'

Another prolific contemporary writer, Hong Nhu (born 1932), joined the army in 1948 (against the French) and started writing short stories in 1955 and poetry in 1985. Again, the titles reflect the pastoral subjects of his poems: *The Immeasurably High Pine Forest* (1969), *Autumn Thoughts* (1971), *Voice of the Flower Picker* (1976), *The Quiet Night* (1976), *Wind on the Hill* (1978), *The White Spirited Tree* (1984), *The Boat in Sudden and Brief Shower* (1995), *Rain and Wind All Over* (1999). He also wrote *Inspiration in the Late Afternoon* (1988), *Men's Tear* (1992) *The Boat of Areca* (1995) and *Moss on the Stone* (1998).

Commenting on Hong Nhu's writing in Vietnam's *Sunday People* newspaper, Ngo Vinh Binh wrote: 'Through reading his story, *Wild Purple Ducks Are Arriving*, we can see the whole life of this river region.'

The next generation of Hue poets grew up during the Vietnam War. Nguyen Khoa Diem (former Minister of Culture), whose father was the philosopher, Hai Trieu Khoa Van, and his great grandmother the poetess, Dam Phuong, graduated from the Literature Department of Hanoi College of Education, went straight to war and became responsible for propaganda and training. His *Epic of the Road and the Desire*, although a work of historical fiction, encouraged commitment and participation in the conflict.

Tran Vang Sao, the pen name of Nguyen Dinh, became known for *The Poem of the National Patriot*,, his poems frequently appearing in *Huong River Magazine*. His poem, *The Forty-Three Year Old Man Tells His Own Story*, is full of the sadness and desperation of poverty – a grey picture of life in the Bao Cap years (1975-1986) – a story that has not changed much for many poor people in Hue.

Several women writers reached maturity after 1975, Tran Thuy Mai (born 1954), a graduate of Dong Khanh High School for Girls, who became a lecturer on folk literature, as well as editor of the Thuan Hoa Publishing House. Her poems – *The Sea Poem* (1983), *Grass's Song* (1984), *The Town of Wild, Yellow Sunflowers* (1994),

229

and the short story, *Forbidden Game* (1998) were published in *Letters and Arts Magazine*.

The critic, Ho The Ha, acknowledges that the poetry of the first ten years after 1975, written by those growing up during the Vietnam-American War, tends to be more introspective, focusing more on the individual, expressing insights into the inner being through lyrical poetry.

'The poetry is now calmer, which is necessary so that poetry can sink into one's emotions and mind,' he continues. But these young writers, lacking real-life experience, he feels are not as good as that generation of poets and writers who lived through the agonies of war and described their experiences. However, 'Their purpose is clear: "Be true to yourself – exhaust yourself until all your weaknesses, strengths, beauty and vanities are exposed. And regard others in the same way. Poetry is a mirror that reflects one's heart."'

A PRINCE AND A POET

He who laughs at others today,
will be laughed at by others tomorrow
– Vietnamese proverb

Soon after I arrived in Hue, when I first called on my friend, Professor Buu I, he told me that he was about to be awarded the *Plume d'Or,* one of the French Government's highest accolades, in recognition of his life's work dedicated to the French language. The French ambassador would be coming down from Hanoi to present him with the award. Professor Buu I had not only taught French in Hue, Nha Trang and Ho Chi Minh City, but also in Paris. He is also a writer and translator. His works include translations of *The Journal of Anna Frank, Isabelle* by André Gide, *Les rois des aulnes* by Michel Tournier, also a biography, *Trinh Cong Son – A Genius Musician.*

Professor Buu I was always my first port of call whenever I had questions about Hue, and invariably, he knew the answers.

Reeling back in time, years ago I recalled seeing a large portrait of undoubtedly a Vietnamese grandee, propped up in the sitting room of Buu I and his wife, Thi Loi. At the time, I asked who was portrayed in the portrait and Thi Loi told me that he was a prince, a relative, that it was the anniversary of his death, and that the portrait would be donated to a temple. At the time, I left it at that.

Now, remembering the painting, I asked Buu I who had been portrayed in the portrait and without a word, he disappeared for what felt like a very long time. I began to wonder, as one does in inexplicable Vietnamese situations, if this were a signal that it was time for me to leave. Just as I was about to depart, he reappeared with a slim book in his hand.

The gentleman in the portrait was a prince, Tuy Ly Vuong, he explained, the eleventh son of the second emperor, Minh Mang, the younger brother of the poet, Tung Thien Vuong, whose pen-name was Mien Tham, much lauded for his nature poems, particularly his poems of the sea.

231

The younger prince, Tuy Ly Vuong, was one of Buu I's ancestors. The portrait painted in 1997, had been to commemorate the one hundredth anniversary of his death. The slim book Buu I then handed me was a selection of a few of his shorter poems, translated from the early *chu nha* – into French. It also held a brief biography of Prince Tuy Ly Vuong's turbulent life in troubled times as the French tightened their colonial grip on the royal court of Hue – and Vietnam.

This younger brother, Prince Tuy Ly Vuong's major work, *Essays and Poems in Vi Da (Vi Da hoop tap),* had even been recognised as a masterpiece of literature by no less a personage than the director of the Imperial College of Beijing at the time, Dr Vuon Tien Khiem, who saluted the prince as both a sage and a great poet. The two princely brothers, Tung Thien Vuong and Tuy Ly Vuong, rose to become two of Vietnam's greatest poets.

From the age of thirteen, the younger prince, Tuy Ly Vuong was known in the royal court as the poet prince. He was also respected for his piety towards his mother, a trait highly esteemed by Emperor Tu Duc, who greatly revered his own mother, Tu Du, filial piety being one of the most fundamental moral strictures of Confucianism. Like his elder brother, Prince Tuy Ly Vuong lived a simple, frugal lifestyle. He abhorred the luxuries enjoyed by royal princes and mandarin while the people suffered in poverty. For this, he became known as the prince in cotton.

At the age of thirty, Prince Tuy Ly Vuong was appointed director of the school, Ton Hoc, the school reserved for the princes and sons of members of the royal family and in 1854, he received the title, Tuy Ly Con. In 1865, he entered the Council of the Imperial Family with the title, Huu Ton Nhon.

When his mother died, out of grief and filial piety, he retreated from public life for two years to grieve. Following his two-year absence, in 1878 he took up his post again in the Council of the Imperial Family. Near the end of Emperor Tu Duc's life, the emperor conferred upon Prince Tuy Ly Vuong, management of the affairs of the court. But Prince Tuy Ly Vuong's power was usurped by the two regicidal mandarin, Nguyen Van Tuong and Ton That Thuyet, who during this frightful period of a few months in 1883, dethroned and put to death successively, three young emperors: Duc Duc, Hiep Hoa and Kien Phuc.

As a result of Prince Tuy Ly Vuong's vehement protests against the regicides, the two mandarin decided to have him

232

assassinated, as they had done with the first minister, Tran Thien Thanh. Fortunately, one of the appointed assassins, out of empathy with the prince, instead of stabbing him, warned him of the plot.

Isolated, without power, without the strength of an army to protect himself, the prince sought refuge from the French navy that lay at anchor in the port of Thuan An. But the French, for once, did not wish to interfere in the affairs of the royal court in Hue and refused their protection.

The two mandarin had a free hand to imprison Prince Tuy Ly Vuong, then to exile him to the province of Quang Ngai as well as members of his family, who were scattered about the provinces of central Vietnam. He was unable to return to Hue until the later reign of Emperor Dong Khanh. One of Prince Tuy Ly Vuong's short poems translated into English from the French . . .

Poem on a winter's night

The rain falls heavily all night,
The rice paddies are black as ink.
The lamp glows dimly,
The glow-worms flutter.
The damp blanket, heavy with moisture,
Provides no protection against the cold.
Putting aside my book, I rise, moved,
My soul lost in dreams of love.
                    (tr. Irmeli Pyysalo)

Poème d'une nuit d'hiver

La pluie tombe à verse toute la nuit.
Les rizières sont noires comme de l'encre.
La lampe n'éclaire pas bien,
Les vers luisants voltigent.
La couverture comme mouillée d'eau,
ne protège pas contre le froid.
Laissant de côté le livre, je me lève, ému.
l'âme perdue dans les songeries amoureuses.

The story of Professor Buu I's princely ancestor once more justified my belief that in a country that worships its ancestors, in Hue I would still be able to find people who remembered the stories told to them by their grandparents, who had served in the Nguyen Court. The Nguyen dynasty may have ended in 1945, but Hue's imperial past lives on in the tender memories of its descendants.

A LADY NOVELIST

Thirty years old,
springtime for the boy,
autumn for the girl
– Vietnamese proverb

Hue is still an intensely literary town. It boasts countless poetry and literary societies. In the space of one commemorative ceremony at a pagoda, I met half a dozen published authors: a historian; the author of a book on the Nguyen; the biographer of two princesses; another who had written about the marshal arts; a noted poet and a translator. But when I found the names of a couple of Hue women writers in my research, I was keen to meet at least one of them.

Ha Khanh Linh lives in a narrow lane on the right bank of the An Cuu river to the south-east. She greets us, my translator Thanh Thanh and me, in the lane and leads us into her courtyard past two life-size female statues. 'The one with the rosary is Tran Huyen, the princess who married the Cham king. She is holding the rosary because after she escaped death at the hands of the Chams, following her husband's death, she became a nun in a pagoda near Hanoi. The sculptor was Ma Van.' Traditionally, Cham queens were forced to follow their husbands in death. The Viet princess who became the Cham queen had been rescued from this cruel fate by her fellow Die Viet countrymen from the North. 'The second statue' wearing a moon-shaped, royal court hat *(mu rong vanh)* 'is the Princess Le Ngoc Han. She married Nguyen Hue,' one of the Tay Son brothers, who mounted a rebellion against the Nguyen lords of Hue, who later crowned himself Emperor Quang Trung and married the daughter of the defeated Le king in Hanoi.

'She wrote a famous poem,' an elegy when her husband died after only four years of marriage, leaving her a widow at only twenty.' The statue is holding a stone notebook; the poem is entitled *Lament of Loneliness (Ai Tu Van)*, quoted earlier. Beside the front door hangs a colourful, painted screen with the author's pen-name, Ha Khanh Linh, placed in the centre of a sunburst, painted perhaps by her artist friend, Do Thi La Vang, who drops in later.

Motioning us to sit down at a table where books and a book proof have been pushed to one side, Ha Khanh Linh places a teapot and tiny tea cups between us, along with a plate heaped with biscuits and another holding thinly-sliced, candied ginger.

'Do you like ginger? I made it myself. In the shops, they don't slice it so thinly, not as good as home-made.' She is wearing an embroidered, white satin blouse, her reddish, lightly-tinted hair pulled up in a neat bun. Several antique rings choke the fingers of her left hand; she wears a single white jade bangle bracelet on one wrist. Warm brown eyes stare directly through burgundy-frame glasses.

It is not particularly easy to interview a writer whose work you are unable to read – and one whose work you have been unable to glean much about, other than that 'her books reflect the quiet strength of Hue women.' Probably recognizing the problem, Ha Khanh Linh virtually interviews herself. Only later do I discover that she was a journalist.

Ha Khanh Linh comes from a Hue family. She lives 'alone, very simply,' in a small, L-shaped house, her dining table serving as her work table. 'My house was opposite, but I sold it because it was really too large.' She had a husband and has a daughter in Hanoi, working for the government as an international lawyer. She proudly shows me a photo of her daughter on her mobile phone and tells me that in 1991, her daughter was runner-up in a beauty contest sponsored by a fashion magazine, 'but that's not important.' When I remark that the daughter resembles her mother, she says, 'No, she resembles her father, who was very handsome. My daughter has just come back from Russia and now must go to Singapore, which makes her husband very sad.'

Ha Khanh Linh's son lives in Dak Lak where he is a film director. She met her husband during the war when he, too, was a journalist. After the war, he became a TV director in Hue.

Ha Khanh Linh was the fifth child of seven, a child of the second wife – her father had two wives. 'There was no difference between the first and the second wife,' by which I think she means that it was a very amicable arrangement. 'But the first one was not able to have many children. My father worked at the royal court. My family was very close to the king.'

It is then that she told me that she had been a journalist during what the Vietnamese call the American War, for radio and for newspapers. When she was young, she studied at Saigon University,

236

but before she finished her degree, she left to become a war correspondent, attached to the military.

'It was very difficult to become a journalist, very few people were allowed to become journalists' – and no doubt, fewer women. 'I tried many times, I was good in many fields, otherwise I would not have succeeded. Also, I was accepted because I had a good character. My brother became a political adviser in the South – he was killed in the war. My younger sister became a politician – I was the only writer. I earned little money. Other people are rich, but not me,' she says with irony but no rancour.

Her real name, Nguyen Khoa Nhu Y – Ha Khanh Linh is her pen-name – had been chosen for her by the first wife. 'The name means "very pleasant". As she could not have many children, I was very much loved by the first wife. When I went into battle, the first wife cried – much more than the second wife,' her natural mother.

Ha Khanh Linh tells me that she experienced the results of Agent Orange and has written about it in several of her books.

'Many of my characters come from the war. And I worked with several American journalists.' One of them, Kevin Bowen, now at MIT, had come back to Vietnam recently to see her. She shows me his card. I had read that she had published three novels. Fortunately, I ask her how many novels she has written.

'Twenty-five' – as she reaches for the loose cover of the latest, *Historical Change 1882010 (Bien co 182010 Tieu Thuyet),* proofs of which she is now editing. Several have been translated into foreign languages, at least one into Russian.

She volunteers that she writes about characters and events from the past, about the early period of the Nguyen dynasty, but also about more recent times. Her publisher, Nha Xuat Ban Van Hoc, is in Hanoi. She picks up a book lying among the book proofs and other copies of her books, *My House in Hoi An (Trai tim toi Hoi An).* I tell her that my last book was about Hoi An and she insists upon presenting me with her book on Hoi An – in Vietnamese.

She had started to write novels in 1965, while she was still working as a journalist in Saigon, 'while hiding in a cave.' After the War she went back to university, this time to study Russian. Before, she had studied mathematics.

Thinking that being a journalist in the South might not have been such a healthy function to have had after 1975, I ask if she had any difficulties after the War.

'Oh yes, I was hungry all the time. I thought I would die. I didn't know why I had lived, as so many of my co-workers had died.' She picks up another book. 'I talk about it in this novel, *That Day in Truong Son (Ngay Ay Truong Saon)*. It is very autobiographical.' She pages through the book to find a photograph of herself as a slim young woman in a white *ao dai* and a *non la* conical hat.

So writing for her at first had served as an escape valve, an escape from and a record of the horrors of war, and later, perhaps, it provided some relief from post-traumatic stress, and survivors' guilt.

'Whenever I heard the bombs, my heart' – her eyes grow round with the memory of her fear, she touches her heart to show how terrified she was. 'Many times when I went out, I was lucky – many others died. Once I left a cave to let other people come into the cave – and the cave was bombed – and I was safe, while many other people died. Other times, I was very lucky, too. Many, many stories. My life is in my books.'

I ask where she was in 1968 – during the Tet Offensive in Hue. 'In the Truong Son mountains, a hundred kilometres (60 mi) from Hue, near the Laos border in the South . . . the most difficult time in the War.'

It was during the war that she met her journalist husband. At the end of the War in 1975, he became a TV director, she became deputy editor of *Huong River Magazine.*

I ask about writing in Vietnam. She receives no advances for her books. She is paid after she has finished the book – even after the printing. If the government accepts her book, the printing is paid for. If the government does not accept her book, she has to pay for the printing. Then she voices the lament of writers in the West when she says that now she earns much less than earlier in her career, 'because fewer books are sold, fewer people are buying books. People watch TV and other activities.'

Her good friend, Do Thi La Vang, the French-speaking painter, arrives, carrying a bouquet of yellow chrysanthemums.

'She is Catholic and one chapter in my book, *People Put Flowers in the Church,* is about her.

Having exchanged pleasantries, Do Thi La Vang excuses herself to take the flowers upstairs to arrange, presumably on Ha Khanh Linh's Buddhist altar. Today happens to be Buddha's birthday.

Then I am completely thrown into perplexed confusion when Ha Khanh Linh hands me a yellow plastic beaded religious token –

and a pink one for Thanh Thanh – with a small printed card reading: *'Phap Luan Dai Phap (hao)',* and in English, 'Falun Gong is good.' The back side of the card has the words: 'Truthfulness, Compassion, Forbearance' – in English. Then I am not quite sure what she is saying – nor, clearly, is Thanh Thanh.

' – in 1999, eighty-four ways to meditation . . . then he was invited to go to America in 1996, but he refused, until 1999, he accepted the invitation to the US – the monk went. Seeing our confusion, Ha Khanh Linh starts at the beginning of the story . . .

'A boy was born in China to a normal family. At four years old a very old monk came from the forest and knelt near the boy and the boy didn't understand. Nor did his parents. His family was really afraid of the government. The government didn't like the monk, so they hid the monk. Before the boy was born, the monk had said that the boy was a teacher and now the monk had found him.'

It began to sound like the story of the Dalai Lama.

'When the boy was somewhere between seven and ten years old, he became talented. From grade four he became an infant prodigy.' There was a somewhat confused sequence about the boy forgetting his notebook and returning to his classroom to retrieve it . . . 'When he was eleven, he could save people in the water' – presumably from drowning. And when he was older, he became a soldier. Everybody loved him. In 1992, he became a Buddhist and went around China to give lectures and many other countries in the world. He had a hundred million followers. Also to America. In 1996, he and his family, at the invitation of the US government, emigrated to New York. His name is Ly Hong Chi. On the 13th of May (2015), there was a festival held at the Eiffel Tower in France and many people came.'

Later, looking him up, I find that Ly Hong Chi (in Chinese, Li Hongzhi) was the founder of Falun Gong, his birthday is the 13th of May and he was nominated for the Nobel Peace Prize twice, in 2000 and again in 20001.

Finally, through Thanh Thanh, I say that we must go. Then to my deep embarrassment, Ha Khanh Linh tells me again that because of her feelings of one writer for another, she wants to give me an *ao dai*. Although I had gently refused earlier, now Thanh Thanh whispers to me insistently, that it would be very impolite to refuse.

Ha Khanh Linh brings out a pale violet *ao dai* and tells me that her friend, the artist, Do Thi La Vang, has painted the crimson flowers cascading down the front and back panels, down each sleeve and each of the trouser legs. I explain through Thanh Thanh that I am overwhelmed by her generosity, deeply embarrassed, and feel terrible that I have nothing to offer her in return.

Would I like to try it on? I demure on the grounds that it is so hot, and she carefully packs it away in a plastic bag and tells me to wash it only in cool water, never in a washing machine. Then she signs her book on Hoi An for me.

At the gate, she asks Thanh Thanh to take a photograph of us together on her mobile phone, and we part, with embraces and warm handshakes.

A WRITER AND A THINKER

It's better to eat salty foods and speak the truth
Than to eat vegetarian and tell lies
– Vietnamese proverb

To Nguan Vy has a high, intellectual forehead and doesn't look his seventy-four years. While we are waiting for the student translator, who is late, as it is National Journalists Day and he is to be interviewed later on television, he has brought along a few old souvenirs. He shows me his war-time articles on yellowed newsprint, riddled with insect holes and a few photos encased in plastic – taken of him during the Vietnam War when he was a journalist, always in the Hue area. One of the photos is of him with his left hand and forearm bandaged. He shows me the scar in the palm of his hand.

'Americans.' What can I say?

He was born in Mai Vinh village in Vinh Xuan Commune of Phu Vang District and still lives there, three miles (5 km) from the centre of Hue.

His first novel, *The Tranquil River,* written under fire during the Vietnam War, which the Vietnamese call the American War, was two thousand pages long and divided into three volumes, just possibly, Vietnam's *War and Peace.* His later novels, *The Suburb,* and *The Horizon Is Over There,* were shorter. His most recent novel, he says, he has been working on for ten years and he is still writing.

He is interested in 'the long history of Hue, the region.'

When he wrote the first novel, he did not think about which level of people he was writing about, just wrote from his heart – two thousand pages. 'Too long for young people to read. A number of young people still love the country, but are not interested in reading two thousand pages.'

How are people from Hue different? 'There is no other place like Hue. I cannot explain the reason, the ways, but some typical features: This is a place that has a blending of cultures from Champa and Viet, the whole region, this place contained two cultural regions.'

241

Recalling the times of the Vietnam War, 'It was very difficult for Hue people after the War.' Referring to the Tet Offensive of 1968 in Hue, he explains that 'the Lunar New Year creates many difficulties for Hue people, even now. *Tet* is a special day for everyone. At *Tet* the government always supports with a lot of money the families who died in the war, wanting to imply that a special debt is due to them by commemorating them.

'I always respect the people who were in the war to protect our country and therefore, it is about the cost that they paid in the war. In the world, people always suffer from the American military. No other peoples have suffered from the war like Hue until now' – except perhaps the Japanese and the Germans.

During the war did he move with the army as a journalist or was he always in Hue? 'I was only in Hue. As a writer, I am different from other writers – I was writing the novels during the war. My novel was long and no other writers wrote that long. I wrote a bit about the people who had to suffer, but the long history of Hue is described in my novels. In those novels I was concerned about the difficulties of the people here. Everyone had to be concerned about the people – any writer must do that. After that, I wrote other novels about their difficulties.'

He now writes shorter novels, limiting the pages because, echoing the words of Ha Khanh Linh, not everyone has the time to read novels, because of so many new distractions – television, mobile phones, the internet. Nonetheless, his trilogy of novels – two thousand pages – has been re-published again in Hanoi.

'But few people are going to complete reading my novel because it is so long.'

How early in history does he write about?

'The life around me in the twentieth century. There are many more modern writers. They are interested in these present moments, but nothing happens in modern times. So many complex things were happening here in the old days, because those were complex times. So many publish happenings now, who don't have the ability to publish such stories.'

Do modern writers have trouble writing the truth about what is happening?

'I have written a lot of true things that the government always encourages, but there are some publishers who do not dare to publish them. In fact, there are so many writers who have a passion to describe the true things in life. Some writers now use the internet. I recognize the development of technology – they write on the internet because that way you spread information all over the world, not just to people in Vietnam and I encourage that.'

What is his most recent novel about?

'What happened in the old days. For example, I still want to describe the difficulties of the Hue people in the novels – in remote places, not in the centre. My last novel, *The Deep Area*, took ten years (published 2012). Vietnam, after the war – how to reconcile the people after the war, is the main problem in our country, and we make every effort to do that. I want to be close to the people in remote places. In my short novel, I described a group of people who made every effort to protect our country, but after the war, a few people who fought against the war in the remote areas in the country – I want to explain the reason why they did that and why others fought against such people. Especially in remote places.'

In the South in particular? 'Everywhere. There are still a few people living in Hue who had intentions against the government, I realize this, and there were a lot of intellectual writers who had fought the government.'

I ask him about writers' societies in Hue.

'There are so many writers, but no one else tells . . . can write the true lives like me. They don't dare.'

Has he ever been in prison – gaol – for anything that he has written? I have to draw a picture of a barred window to help the student interpretor to understand 'prison', 'gaol'.

No, he has never been in prison for things he has written.

'The influence of Buddhism on the people of Hue – Buddhism always repairs wrong actions. Other people in their families or their relatives, they have to live, they have to be human beings.' In the novel, *The Deep Area*, he wrote about the people who had fought against the US in the war, but after the war they suffered from the suspicion of their comrades, that they had secretly worked for the US. Because of this wrong suspicion, they and their families underwent numerous hardships, but many of them still lived in dignity, despite injustice. This is because, deep inside, they have Buddhist values as their foundation. Adhering to those values, they do not let other people's faults drive them into making further mistakes. Even though they suffer from suspicion and injustice, they still live a life of dignity, to be genuine human beings.

243

Happily, I have a second chat with To Nhuan Vy, this time translated by his daughter, To Dieu Lan, a professional interpretor.

I ask which types of people, what levels of society he wrote about in his novels?

' First of all, all levels of society, both the rich, the poor and the military, but in the latter two novels, I mainly focused on the intellectual people.'

How are Hue people different from people in other cities of Vietnam?

'I believe that this question has been answered by many people you have interviewed, but I would like to give my own answer. First of all, Hue is like two cultures poured into one. The Hong river (Red river in Hanoi) and the Dong Nai river. The Red river is the typical culture of Dai Viet (the North), and Dong Nai river (the South), the typical culture of Champa. So that is why there is a combination of the essences of the two civilizations.

'Let me now give you an example in music. *Tuong* is not the speciality of this area. Originally, *tuong* and court music came from China. *Ca Hue* is a combination of the cultures of Dai Viet and Champa, a combination of both cultures in Vietnam. But the *ca Hue* that you hear on the river is not authentic *ca Hue,* not the real *ca Hue.* For a time, Mr Vo Que organized performances of *ca Hue* (periodically, Tuesdays and Fridays at 7.30 at 25 Le Loi). The combination of these two cultures is the first distinguishing characteristic of Hue. For instance, the typical colour of the *ao dai,* purple, originally came from Champa culture.

'Second, the Buddhist culture is submerged in every aspect of life of the people here. You cannot see that in the rush of this very busy life in other parts of the country. Traditional values have been lost, but these values have been retained in Hue. This Buddhist culture is very intellectual and is visibly reflected in the way of thinking, in the way of life, in the way people talk and in the way people take care of plants in the garden, of bonsai – in big things and in details. It is unique. It is not noisy at all and it is not rushing at all. But people are aware of this Buddhist culture in so many corners of life in Hue.

'Third, what makes Hue different from other regions is the historical events that happened here, which entailed mixed experiences – both victories and failures, both joys and pains.

'And this has happened at least since the nineteenth century until now. An example, when the French first came to invade Vietnam, the first serious resistance happened right here, because it was then the feudal capital of Vietnam. This is a unique place. Many people, military, mandarin and average people alike, were killed during the first encounter with the French. That's why almost all families in Hue always worship the people who were killed when the French invaded Hue, the 23rd of the fifth month of the lunar calendar, 1885. Almost every house in Hue worships regularly, the people who were killed – organised by normal people, long before the birth of the Communist party. The people here have fought against the French and that is why Hue is the unique place in Vietnam where it is remembered by normal people – not the government.

'Fourth, the fight between Buddhists and the Catholics under the regime of Ngo Dinh Diem, the severe fights between the two religions, that happened right here.

'Another example, during the entire American War, in the cities, the major cities of Vietnam, the movement against the Americans was led by intellectuals and students. It was mostly supported in Ho Chi Minh City, but they first came from Hue.

' One more example, Hue is actually the most devastated area in the world because the fighting between the American Government and the Republic of Vietnam (South Vietnam) on one side, and the Northern military – the Liberation Army on the other side, the most severe fighting between the two sides, where both sides tried to seize the land and the people, that happened here. This area highlights such fighting, with both its peak victory and its deepest sufferings.

'The Tet Offensive in 1968 was on one hand a military victory that later on drove the American Government to the peace talks. But on the other hand, during this time, the most sufferings were also caused by the so-called revolutionary side, in the overall resistance against the Americans. Those are the fundamental characteristics of Hue that are found nowhere else in Vietnam. No other region can have such characteristics because of such historical incidents, and Hue had some gains and losses because of its distinctive characteristics, and both are unparalleled.

'Regarding the Tet Offensive, because it was war and in the war there were many people who had assumed cover, but they were cooperating with the other side – the South – it was impossible to distinguish whether they were affiliated people or agents and so, people were killed. As for the Viet Cong, we also had secret agents in the American forces, who provided us with the list of those who were cooperating with the American forces. If the secret agents cooperating with the South side were caught by the North side, then their neighbours thought they were civilians, and not working for the American side. But the trick was also used by our Northern agents working in the South, who, when caught by the South, claimed that they were only civilians. That is why many people think that the wrong people were killed. The leaders never ever had the policy to kill the wrong people.

'The implementers, under the harshness of bombs and attacks, might have unnecessarily imprisoned people, and might have arrested people who should not have been arrested. So later on in peace time, there was a policy to apologize. If one family – we make apology there. It is still not very clear and this policy is not always implemented, and this lack of clearness, the wrong and the right, the real secret agents, it was not done very clearly. This communication fails and that is why the hostile forces have always used this communication to exaggerate how many were killed. The other side made up stories of the number of people who were killed wrongly. If you google, you will see so many brutal figures – 1,500 at first – but the number kept being increased, year by year. And now, forty years plus later, it is 7,000 or 8,000.

'I am different from other writers because I knew the truth and I say the truth. There were many people who were killed, but they do not say it out loud and I say it – the wrong people were killed, and we have to apologize for what they did wrong. I say things that are not favoured by the government, but I say – the wrong people were killed – it happened.'

'For instance, before Hoang Phu Ngoc Tuong joined the Viet Cong and went to the mountains, he was a very famous teacher. During the Tet Offensive, he was in the mountains and did not set foot in Hue. But the other side made up brutal stories about him, saying that he convened trials in Hue during the Tet Offensive and sentenced people to death. Such made-up stories go on and on, and gradually many people come to believe. He never set foot in Hue during the Tet Offensive.'

The Tranquil River was written about the times that To Nhuan Vy lived through – and it was an overall picture of life in the rural areas, in the city and in the military.

'It was so thick, so in the later books, I focused on fewer issues. In *The Tranquil River*, I wanted to focus on many issues. You may see that in my way of telling about the Tet Offensive. I was a journalist in the Tet Offensive and I was a living witness – not unique, but one of the few during the Tet Offensive.'

Do modern writers in Vietnam have trouble writing the truth these days?

The government is more open now, more in-depth things can be written about the war, but often to this level only. For example, in the past the government only allowed good things to be written about the victory – and not things about poor fates. And recently, they allow more personal thinking. However, if things are revealed in a blunt and very true way, they don't like it here. My two recent books, *The Deep Area* and *The Cultural Strength* – here his daughter explains that by 'the deep area' he means mentally and spiritually – what is in people's hearts, 'these two books had some difficulty at first to find publishing houses. They did not dare to publish, but the books still got published. So, there was some kind of reaction from the government, but the level of democracy is now higher.'

When were they published?

'*The Deep Area* in 2012, and *The Cultural Strength* in 2013. There is a higher level of democracy. I am a kind of activist, I am one of the few people in the country of Vietnam who righteously and openly suggest some changes in orientations of the Communist Party. They may not like me – when the Chinese constructed 981 (the oil rig, Haiyang Shiyou 981, in the Paracel Islands, 2014), the Government did not allow people to demonstrate. But a few intellectuals in Central Vietnam, including me, demonstrated against the Chinese Government then. I was also one of the few who wrote to the Communist Party to change their policy, because I felt some of our policies were not right for the country. But I have always done it righteously and publicly, so when the two books got published, the government did not cause me any trouble, so the level of democracy is higher now.'

What is he writing about in the current novel?

'Many people now mention patriotism, but I think if people truly love the country, they can reconcile. Everybody can say they love the country, both peoples can say they love the country, but in reality, some love their position more. They love the doctrine more than they love the country and may not like reconciliation, really.

But if you are truly patriotic, you can act together regardless of what side you belong to. For example, many people say they love the country and they shout in the name of patriotism, but they are more loyal to the doctrine of Chinese expansion.

'And some Vietnamese people in California do not want to see one united Vietnam, they want a Republic of Vietnam, apart from North Vietnam. They don't want one united Vietnam. And I have also told many of my friends living abroad that deep down, they still do not want to have one Vietnam.

'We could learn from Poland. There used to be a fight between the Communists and the United Trade Union in Poland. However, they have got over it and they really came together for a truly unique reconciliation. It comes from true patriotism, genuine nationalism in Poland in the eighties. They taught us a lesson that no matter where, which side you came from, if you want good things for Poland, you can always sit together.'

Is it still true that the government only builds cemeteries for soldiers from the North?

Bien Hoa Cemetery used to be a military cemetery for officers of the South. About the cemetery, in the case of Bien Hoa, the government has reclaimed the parts of the cemetery that had been claimed for other uses – to allow people to come to visit. However, they can't go so far as to allow people from abroad to build big graves for the dead. The government doesn't allow such big graves by the Vietnamese Americans – much more than for the soldiers for the North. There were some very big reactions from the people from the North – "Their tombs are so splendid and ours so poor." That is why the government doesn't allow people to come back and rebuild.'

Are people from the South still barred from government jobs?

'No, they are not. Actually, many young people nowadays do not want to take government jobs. I believe that this is a good trend. In fact, many of those who only want to work for the government are not the excellent ones; the best ones really want to work on their own and don't need to depend on anyone else. The situation has improved in the last decade in Vietnam.'

To Nguan Vy's youngest daughter is studying in the States.

PART VIII

HUE'S SPIRITUAL LIFE

RELIGIONS

Divination makes spirits appear,
the brush drives away filth
– Vietnamese proverb

Spiritual roots run deep in Hue. The Viets were received with hostility by what remained of a conquered population seething with hatred – 'in fierce O District, where one could feel frightened on hearing the birds singing or tremble on seeing a fish flopping.'

Very early on, the Nguyen lords felt that only an orthodox religion could draw together the divided peoples of Thuan Hoa into a cohesive, unified society. The Viet Nguyen lords carefully and deliberately planted the seeds for a society blending 'the three religions of equal importance: Confucianism, Taoism and Buddhism *(Tam Giao Dong Nguyen).'* All three religions, they hoped, would contribute to building a new cohesive nation from a land of disparate, formerly warring peoples.

Although Confucian themselves, 'Confucianism was not considered appropriate as its emphasis on secularism was an alien construct to the local population and the Brahmanism or Hinduism of the Chams was perceived as incompatible with the theism of the northerners,' writes historian Mai Khac Ung. Over time, the Chams' Hinduism and worship of a goddess was quenched or driven further south by the arrival of the dominant Viets.

Confucianism, the official ideology – more a structure for society than a religion – describes 'first behaviours' through classical Confucian literature. And it must be remembered that it was the examinations over the Confucian classics that qualified a young man to become a mandarin, earlier in Hanoi, and later in Hue.

249

Confucianism laid down the strict Three Moral Bonds: respect for the emperor, respect for teachers, and piety for parents. The Five Constant Virtues included: kindness, decorum, uprightness, wisdom and fidelity. The Three Subjections of a Woman were to her father, to her husband and to her sons. And the Four Virtues of a Woman were: household arts, beauty, language and virtue.

Even in present-day Hue, consciously or unconsciously, I see these four virtues of a woman steadfastly adhered to. Even successful, highly educated women place great store on their appearance, on their kindness, on their manner of speaking and on their cooking.

The early Nguyen lords did not abandon Confucianism. Four miles (7 km) west of the Citadel, the sixth Nguyen lord, Nguyen Phuc Khoat, built Van Thanh temple in 1770 to worship Confucius and his disciples (Tu, Tang Tu, Tu Tu, Manh Tu).

Later, the first Nguyen emperor, Gia Long (1802-1820), built a new Van Thanh temple in Anh Ninh commune to replace the original, Van Thanh, which was renamed Khai Thanh temple and dedicated to the parents of Confucius. Its moon-shaped gate symbolizes 'the intellectual completeness of Confucian scholasticism,' explains writer Nguyen Dac Xuan.

Khai Thanh temple played a central role in the Nguyen court.

'The emperor was represented by mandarin at the Confucian Offering Day ceremonies, held on the same day at both temples. At *Tet* (lunar New Year), four festivals – *Chinh Dan, Doan Duong, Soc and Vong* – were celebrated at Van Thanh temple by students of Quoc Tu Giam, the university established by Emperor Gia Long in 1803, to teach prospective mandarin the tenets of Confucianism. Van Thanh temple's role in society was to venerate and promote learning amongst young people and to inspire them to strive for an important position in life,' writes Nguyen Dac Xuan. During the Nguyen dynasty, thirty-nine national triennial examinations were held, awarding five hundred fifty-eight candidates as doctors.

Nguyen Dac Xuan goes on to explain the differences between the three religions simplistically. 'Confucianism was applied by the Nguyen emperors and mandarins when dealing with public issues; Taoism when they were resting, enjoying flowers, gazing at the moon or reciting and writing poetry. When they were tired of life or when career and fame ceased to hold little interest, they turned to the gentle oblivion of Buddhism.'

250

Taoism venerated the worship of ancestors and the purity of the natural and spiritual worlds. Linh Huu pagoda was built in 1829 in the tenth year of Minh Mang's reign to honour and worship Laozi (Tao). 'The Shaman and Taoist hermits who worked there were appointed by – and paid a salary – by the royal court,' writes Nguyen Dac Xuan. He goes on to explain that a book written during the reign of Emperor Tu Duc (1847-1883) ranked Linh Huu pagoda as first on a list of pagodas.

Tu Duc's father, Emperor Thieu Tri, had earlier written one of his famous Twenty Poems on Hue Beauty Spots, (poem number thirteen) entitled, *The Sound of the Musical Stones at Linh Huu pagoda*. Only a few of these historic beauty spots remain: Tinh Tam lake in the Citadel (poem number three); the Huong river (poem number eleven); Ngu Binh mount (poem number twelve); and Thien Mu pagoda (poem number fourteen). Unhappily, Linh Huu pagoda was destroyed by the French in 1886 when they built a military camp and later a church on the site.

Buddhism, strongly encouraged and promoted by the Nguyen lords and emperors to rule the hearts and souls of the people, sought to engender a spirit of compassion, wisdom, mercy and forgiveness. As early as 1601, Lord Nguyen Hoang had built the first modest Thien Mu pagoda, as well as many other Buddhist pagodas throughout Thuan Hoa. 'Buddhist theosophy was effortlessly assimilated into the existing belief systems of the two migrant groups and through acculturation became the dominant religion,' writes historian Mai Khac Ung.

'During the brief Tay Son regime, many pagodas and temples used for public services were destroyed or badly damaged. Emperor Gia Long began restoration of Thien Mu pagoda and during the reign of Emperor Thieu Tri, fully restored, it was considered the first ranking beauty spot in Hue,' writes Nguyen Duc Xuan. By many people of Hue, it still is.

The newly installed Nguyen dynasty, the emperors and their families, used both public funds and solicited donations from among themselves to rebuild pagodas that had been destroyed,' writes Mai Khac Ung. The Nguyen emperors and members of their families built many Buddhist pagodas. It is said that there are more than five hundred Buddhist pagodas in Hue and throughout the villages and surrounding hills.

Buddhism held a particularly strong appeal to the women of the royal family. 'Many imperial concubines and princesses left the Forbidden Palace to become nuns in their old age,' writes Nguyen Duc Xuan. Lady My Tan, during Emperor Thanh Thai's reign, became a nun and established the present Lieu Duc pagoda. Lady Tu Cung, Khai Dinh's wife and mother of the last emperor, Bao Dai, (the dowager queen mother, served by Pham Van Thiet), did not become a nun, but she ate only vegetarian food, sequestered herself to pray to Buddha at least four days of each month and is said to have become 'a nun at home.'

Emperor Thieu Tri built Dieu De (Noble Truth) pagoda to honour his birthplace in Bach Dan Street of Xuan Doc Village, on the canal that runs beside Dong Ba market (near Thai Kim Lan's house).

Much later in the early sixties, just as the Vietnam War was starting, Dieu De became a centre of Buddhist protests against the persecution of Buddhists exercised by the Catholic Ngo Dinh Diem administration in Saigon.

Every year, Dieu De plays an important role in the commemoration of Buddha's Birthday *(Vesak)*. On the eighth day of the fourth month of the lunar year, a long procession – hundreds of monks and Buddhist worshippers – walk the several miles from Dieu De pagoda, along the Perfume river, across Eiffel's Truong Tien bridge, on along the south bank of the river to Tu Dam pagoda.

The second Nguyen emperor, Minh Mang, ordered the building of Giac Hoang pagoda, which translates as 'enlightened emperors, or enlightened royal families' – for his own and for the use of the royal family (now occupied by the enlightened Hue Monuments Conservation Center).

No doubt with pacification in mind, Emperor Minh Mang also built the Hoi temple in Thuy Bieu commune for the worship of the conquered Cham Kings! In February and in August, the Nguyen emperors dutifully sent civil mandarin to perform offering ceremonies at this temple, dedicated to the 'traditional owners of the land', the moral being 'to be grateful to the benefactors – the people who had settled the land,' writes historian and writer, Mai Khac Ung.

'The monks of the three national pagodas – Thien Mu, Dieu De and Thanh Du Yen (Ty Van) – were appointed by the court and paid a salary by the State,' writes Nguyen Dan Yuan.

More than one person in Hue had told me that Hue remains the Buddhist centre of central and southern Vietnam and that it has

252

been since the time of the Nguyen lords. And it must be said that time and again, I have been bowled over by the small kindnesses and generosity of total strangers in Hue.

Two specific instances of many, immediately come to mind. When I was searching for a particular cafe to meet someone, I was led to it by a stranger, who then engaged me in conversation, telling me about his children who lived abroad, that he had taught himself English with the help of the BBC, and then – who invited me to meet his family at his home.

Another time, I had paused beside busy Le Loi Street, waiting for a break in the traffic to cross, when an idle cyclo driver, unknown to me, watching, approached from behind, put his arm around my shoulders and said, 'Come, mama,' and led me across the street. I had to chuckle as I was not obeying the rules of the street in Vietnam – to simply walk slowly into the traffic looking straight ahead, so that drivers of bicycles, motorbikes – and anything else that might be coming – could weave round me. I was much touched by his kindness. Of course, these experiences might have occurred anywhere in Vietnam, but in Hue, they happened frequently and repeatedly.

And there was the instance of being presented with the pearl necklace at my lunchtime restaurant, and the appearance of a yellow orchid in my room after I had admired a bouquet of them on the hotel's reception desk, and the gift of a hand of small, sweet bananas one day from a friend, a notebook another day. These kindnesses and the generosity of strangers, I put down partly to their Buddhism.

'The spirituality of the Nguyen emperors and their society reflected a sophisticated and complex eclecticism that fused elements of Confucianism, Taoism and Buddhism,' writes Nguyen Dac Xuan, an expert on Hue culture – exactly what the Nguyen lords and emperors had intended.

Even as a foreigner, abiding for a short time in Hue, I found all of the spiritual values of all three religions strongly alive in the people of Hue. Very early on, several people volunteered that Hue is the most religious city in Vietnam, that in most places religion has diminished in importance, but that in Hue, religion, particularly Buddhism, is still very much alive.

One person even went so far as to say that 'in Hanoi, people go to pagodas to ask for things – prosperity, a child, help in sickness – while in Hue, people go to worship, not to ask.' Of course, in Hue as elsewhere in Vietnam, worship begins at home through ancestor worship. Naturally, there is an appropriate proverb: 'When you drink the water, remember its source.'

'Hue people, as the benefactors of the South East Asian wet rice culture, have long considered soil and water to be the sources of life. Like mother's milk. This belief is enshrined in the worship of the holy mothers: mother of water *(Thai)* and the lord of mountains and soil *(Ngan)*. The small temples to worship the holy mother in the Hue countryside symbolize soil and water, sources of the life force of plants. Princess Lieu Hahn from the northern Viets and Thien Y A Na from the Central and South – Champa – are the two sacred mothers who rank first among the holy mothers,' explains historian Mai Khac Ung. He goes on to say, 'The worshipping of ancestors symbolizes the origin of race; the worshipping of the holy mothers symbolizes the origins of life.

Ceremonies in the family are held on the anniversary of an ancestor's death. Offerings can be vegetarian or non-vegetarian, following the rule: "First for worshipping, then for serving." Offerings might be limited to incense sticks, flowers, candles, areca nuts, betal leaves or wine.'

A family altar is usually placed at the centre of the house. It will have a statue of Buddha in a central, prominent position. A higher altar behind holds photos of the deceased ancestors and any other near, deceased relatives. A small wooden temple above the ancestor altar is dedicated to a patron saint, to support the men in the family. Another small wooden temple, separate, usually attached to a wall, honours the holy mother, who protects the women in the family.

Into this genial religious mix, came Catholicism. As early as 1615, during the rule of the second lord, Nguyen Phuc Nguyen, Jean de la Crois and his son, who were Portuguese, were invited to Hue to provide technical advice on the manufacture of armaments – to fight the Trinh in Hanoi. Both father and son were Catholics and it is conjectured that a Catholic church soon followed their arrival, possibly built by the recently arrived Portuguese and Italian Jesuit priests in Hoi An.

Catholicism was an entirely foreign, conflicting religion. It prohibited polygamy and declared ancestor worship nothing more than superstition – fundamental beliefs adhered to by the local people. As a result, the Nguyen emperors became quite hostile to Catholicism, which they felt undermined their power, supported by

254

Confucianism. Nevertheless, after the French seized control of Hue in 1885, Catholicism spread fairly rapidly through evangelism and the building of new churches and cathedrals. Catholics remain a small minority in present-day Hue; Catholics represent barely twelve per cent of Vietnam's total population.

All three of the major, combined religions – Confucianism, Taoism and Buddhism – require numerous ceremonies beyond the family, sacred ceremonies that are very dear to the heart of Hue.

Most important of all was the *Nam Giao Sacrifice Ceremony,* a three-day, national ceremony requiring several thousand participants. Traditionally, prior to the ceremony, the emperor took only vegetarian food and stayed apart from his wives for seven days. Held annually in the spring from 1807 to 1907, in the interest of economy, Emperor Thanh Thai decreed that after 1907, this ceremony should be held only every three years.

The *Nam Giao* esplanade offering ceremony in Hue was celebrated 'at a time when people still worshipped the sun, considering it to be noble and sacred. People believed in an eternal relationship between the sun, the earth and humans, as humans relied on the sun and the earth for their sustenance. The *Nam Giao Ceremony* venerated the sun for protecting the country from harm, for providing favourable conditions for all life and for bringing prosperity and peace to the people. The emperor, who was perceived as the supreme being, presided over this ceremony and this demonstrated its importance in the hierarchy of religious observance,' writes Mai Kac Ung.

It was for this reason that Tu Cung, the mother of Bao Dai, had been so concerned that on marrying a Catholic, her son might convert to Catholicism, after which he would no longer be able to preside over the *Nam Giao Sacrifice Ceremony.* Worst still, if his children grew up Catholic, the *Nam Giao Sacrifice Ceremony* would end, putting the nation in peril.

A much shortened *Nam Giao* ceremony (minus the sacrifice) is still re-enacted every even year during the Hue Festival in the third lunar month, usually April, not only for the benefit of the people of Hue – it presents a fine spectacle for visiting Vietnamese and foreign visitors alike.

The second-most important ceremony in Hue is *Tet Doan Ngo* – on the fifth day of the fifth lunar month, 'which commemorates

Khuat Nguyen, the Chinese Confucian poet – the half-forgotten reason for my having been invited to a duck feast.

Another important religious ceremony held only in Hue is *Cung Dat,* honouring the god of the land, when Hue people worship the indigenous Cham people. During *Cung Dat,* 'prayers are offered to the holy saints, Buddha and other saints for the five blessings: prosperity, wealth, longevity, happiness and security. Worshipping the land to pray for peace, *Thiet Cung Ta Tho Ky An* was written to include prayers to the twenty most revered saints and spirits of the non-material world,' writes historian, Mai Kac Ung. The *Cung Dat* ceremony is held any afternoon during the second or the eighth month of the lunar calendar. If at home, offerings are placed on ceremonial tables near the garden gate. If it is a public ceremony, a popular place is chosen in the community for the ceremonial tables.

'Offerings must include: grilled fish, boiled eggs, three boiled crabs, one dish of boiled sweet potato leaves, a small bowl of fish paste, a symbolic papoose made of a young banana plant and votive paper. In addition to the cooked dishes mentioned, there must be a large bowl of uncooked rice upon which money is placed. Cooked food is offered to express gratitude to the ancient people; the uncooked rice and money are offered to request propitious conditions, such as a successful business for the coming year and protection against misfortune,' explains Mai Kac Ung.

Another annual ceremony, unique to Hue, runs from the twenty-third to the end of the fifth lunar month. This ceremony, *Cung Am Hon,* honours the dead souls who died in the fall of Hue in (July) 1885, when the French killed more than a thousand people, burnt the Citadel and destroyed much of the fabric of the city. The day also became known at National Hatred Day.

The main ceremony takes place at a temple in Le Thanh Ton Street, Thuan Loc ward. Here, dead soldiers and victims of the siege are venerated. The shrine is divided into three levels: mandarin, generals and soldiers at the top level; the general population at the middle level; the homeless and those without an ancestral worshipping place, at the lowest level.

'Hue pays respect to those who were slaughtered on this day. The ceremony is conducted by elderly men and worshipping occurs throughout the city. Hue people believe that pain is part of the human condition and through worshipping dead souls, harmony is restored. The ceremony cherishes selflessness and kind-heartedness,' writes

256

Mai Kac Ung – selflessness and kind-heartedness to the dead souls, who perhaps have no families left to venerate them.

Another ceremony dedicated to dead souls, *(Nguyen Tieu),* is celebrated on the fifteenth day of the first lunar month, at the end of *Tet,* the Vietnamese New Year.

'It is believed that the souls of those who died in the street and remain unclaimed (by family) are helpless. At the Lunar New Year, they have nowhere to celebrate and no one to depend upon. The kind Hue people demonstrate their selflessness and compassion towards the lonely, dead souls through this special ceremony,' writes Mai Kac Ung. He goes on to explain that 'repairing graves and providing alms during the worshipping day of the lonely, dead souls is perceived as a noble act.'

Of course, Hue also celebrates the national holidays and festivals of Vietnam. Most important throughout the country is the lunar New Year, *(Tet Nguyen Dan),* which translates as Feast of the First Morning of the First Day. The date of *Tet* changes every year in the Gregorian calendar, falling on the new moon of the first lunar month, usually late January or early February.

Tet is a huge family affair. Shops and restaurants are closed, sometimes for days. Relatives flock from far and wide, large numbers flying in from abroad, to join their families in their ancestral homes to celebrate this special feast. *Tet* used to last from the twenty-third of the twelfth lunar month – the date the kitchen gods set off for heaven on the back of carp to report to the Jade Emperor (Tao) on the family's behaviour throughout the year – until *Tet Nguyen Tieu* on the fifteenth day of the first lunar month of the new year.

Ho Chi Minh decided that this was far too long for a poor, developing nation and cut the *Tet* holiday (from work) to a week. However, people throughout the country start preparing for *Tet* at least a month in advance and there are numerous *Tet* parties, rather like Westerners celebrate with Christmas parties even weeks in advance. Visiting families travelling from abroad usually stay for a month, which is why hotels throughout the country fill up around *Tet*.

National holidays include: the Mid-Spring Festival *(Xuan Ky)* in the second month of the lunar calendar and the Mid-Autumn Festival *(Thu Bao)* on the fifteenth day of the eighth lunar month. The latter is considered to be a children's festival, which features dragon and lion dances in the streets and all manner of sweets and cakes.

In villages, the Mid-Autumn Festival also includes the *Ky Yen* offering (prayer for harmony and peace at the beginning of the year) and the *Thu Te* sacrifice – at the end of the year. The *Ky Yen* and *Thu Te* ceremonies are organized in communal houses, pagodas, temples and at community shrines to worship the sacred saints that protect and care for the village. These sacred saints number good genies and living saints as well as village ancestors. These village ceremonies are often marked by gatherings of flags, parasols, drums, gongs, ceremonial music, songs and sometimes processions. Three generations participate. They line up according to age to symbolize the transfer of knowledge across the generations. Elderly and middle-aged, mostly men, wear traditional costumes; younger men and women wear ordinary clothes.

The fifth day of the seventh lunar month is Wandering Souls Day *(Trung Nguyen),* the purpose of which is to express gratitude for the lives of and to pardon the dead for whatever they might have done wrong – poor wandering souls who have no families to commemorate them on family altars.

In the autumn, on the fifteenth day of the tenth lunar month, come the ceremonies to worship the new rice, *Tet Ha Nguyen.*

Apart from national holidays and festivals, many local villages around Hue hold special ceremonies and festivals of their own. In the village of Thuan An, eight miles from Hue on the South China Sea, the villagers celebrate the Fish Praying ceremony *(Le Cau Ngut).*

Upriver from Hue at Hon Chen temple – accessible only by river as it is built into a steep riverbank cliff – the death anniversary of the Cham goddess, Y A Nha, is celebrated the second and third days of the third Lunar month, usually in April. Worshippers and participants must approach by dragon boat and ceremonies take place on the steep steps leading up to the pagoda as well as inside.

Also, various craft villages hold ceremonies to commemorate and worship the originators or founding fathers of their crafts: goldsmithing in Phu Cat, blacksmithing in Hien Luong, carpentry in Bao Vinh, pottery in Phuoc Tich, sculpture in My Xuyen.

Lively festivals accompany many of these village ceremonies: the Wrestling festival after the Spring ceremony in Sinh village, the Sea-Going festival after the Fishermen's Prayer ceremony in Thai Duong village, the *Chau Van* dancing festival after the ceremony of the Holy Mothers' procession at Hon Chen and the Boat

Racing festival on National Independence Day, on the second day of September. Hue abounds in religious ceremonies and these ceremonies and festivals remain sacred and precious to the people of Hue. Of course, it must be said that there are ceremonies and festivals throughout Vietnam. But nowhere perhaps are there quite so many, nor are they held in such quite high esteem as in Hue.

The Nguyen lords and emperors have succeeded in their aim: the three religions and the ceremonies observed in their worship have blended, and served to tightly bind together the families of Hue in a traditional, mutual bond of reverence and community.

CEREMONIES FOR A PRINCESS OR TWO

You eat slowly, that is good for the stomach;
you plough deeply, that is good for the fields
   – Vietnamese proverb

In passing through Hue towards the end of 2014, Professor Buu I invited me to accompany him to a ceremony to honour the Princess Le Ngoc Han. Daughter of the weak Le king in Thang Long (Hanoi), at sixteen she had married Nguyen Hue, who defeated the northern Trinh clan and her father. Nguyen Hue then crowned himself Emperor Quang Trung in 1788.

Nguyen Hue had been one of the three Tay Son brothers, who had mounted the rebellion against the Nguyen lords and all but wiped out the entire Nguyen clan in 1776, except for the fifteen-year-old 'prince', Nguyen Anh. Quang Trung had ruled from Phu Xuan (Hue) and died here suddenly in 1792.

It seems that after her husband's sudden, early death at forty, the princess had spent six years in this very pagoda, Kim Tien, and just possibly, had composed the now famous elegiac poem while she was sequestered here in Hue.

Understandably, having been married to the Nguyen's arch enemy, Nguyen Hue (Quang Trung), this was the first time that the princess, Le Ngoc Han, had ever been commemorated in any way in Hue. Now, the generous people of Hue felt that the long dead princess, far from her family in the North, deserved some earthly commemoration.

Waiting for people to gather for the ceremony, I was introduced to half a dozen Vietnamese writers, amongst them the historian, Nguyen Dac Xuan, who had recently published a book on each of the princesses, Le Ngoc Han and Nam Phung, the Emperor Bao Dai's catholic wife, who he had met on board ship returning from France.

Monks in the front row sat holding long red and black rosaries. A crowd of perhaps fifty people were seated facing and beside the two altars. The low altar table in front held sweet meats, fruit and yellow lilies. The higher altar behind it held candles, jugs of yellow chrysanthemums, offerings on plates wrapped in cellophane, a plate of custard apples, and a blue and white teapot and tiny cups. A monk rose to speak and people applauded occasionally, presumably to register approval or agreement. Several other gentlemen gave speeches. Professor Buu I stood and read a poem. Monks rose to place burning joss sticks, then bowed before the altar; several other people came forward to place joss sticks, cameras rolling. One monk poured a cup of tea from the altar, presumably for the dead princess. All was very solemn.

There were refreshments afterwards: tea and *it den,* little 'black cakes' with sweet bean centres, served at weddings to denote harmony – and now perhaps, to suggest forgiveness of the Tay Son and the princess who had been caught as a political pawn.

On the same day as the ceremony in Kim Tien, Professor Buu I invited me to accompany him to the formal opening of An Dinh villa, following its restoration.

When I first met the queen mother's old manservant, Pham Van Thiet, a few years ago, little did I dream that several years later I would have a chance to visit the grand villa that she moved to on leaving the Forbidden Purple City 'after the revolution.' This villa was later seized by Ngo Dien Diem, then President of South Vietnam, for his brother, a Catholic bishop, necessitating the queen mother's move from this villa to the villa where she ended her days and where I had met her old manservant.

An Dinh villa had been built in 1915 by her husband, Emperor Khai Dinh, on the bank of the An Cuu river, almost directly across from the Citadel, a few hundred meters upstream from where it joins the Perfume river – outside the Forbidden Purple City, even outside the walls of the Citadel. The elaborate ceramic chip mosaics of the gate near the river imitate those of the Imperial City. Inside the gate, an impressive hexagonal pavilion stands like a sentinal in front of the two-storey yellow and white villa. Potted bonsai adorn the pedestals of the three stairways leading to a rectangular porch supported by Doric columns, beneath an open gallery. Elaborate plaster floral decorations surround the symmetrically placed, arched windows. Khai Dinh was plainly influenced, architecturally, by his trips to France. Inside, the overwhelming impression in the entrance

261

hall is of gold: gilt ceilings, heavy gilt frames around the immense paintings – scenic views of Hue. The walls, not covered by the huge paintings, have been painted in a pattern to imitate wallpaper. Off to the left is a formal salon and tea room. The dining room opposite holds a large portrait of Tu Cung, Khai Dinh's wife, the lady served by Phan Van Thiet, with a few biographical notes.

Born in 1890, her original name was Hoang Thi Cuc. She came from the My Loi commune of Hue and as a young girl, worked as a soup seller in the market. Later she found a job in the household of Emperor Dong Khanh's wife, where she met the Prince Khai Dinh and became his 'lover.' In 1913, she became pregnant and gave birth in December, 1913, to Prince Nguyen Phuoc Vinh Thuy, who upon his coronation was renamed, Emperor Bao Dai. She died in 1980.

The furnishings of the villa have been recreated with the financial support of the Germany Embassy and the advice of Le Thi Dinh, who worked in the An Dinh residence as a servant to Tu Cung and Bao Dai's family.

There is a portrait of Bao Dai with his queen, Nam Phung, and five children, two sons and three daughters. He had five other wives (according to the biography), three of whom he married while he was married to Nam Phung. His last wife, Monique Baudot, was French. Bao Dai died in 1997 and is buried in the Passy Cemetery in Paris. His eldest son, Prince Bao Long, died in 2007.

Again, there is a solemn ceremony with speeches, polite applause, followed by light refreshments – and more little black cakes – outside in the garden.

BUDDHISM AND THE GOOD DOCTOR

Practice kindness, good will follow
– Vietnamese proverb

Three different people in Hue told me that if I wanted to know about Buddhism in Hue, to see Dr Duong Dinh Chau.

Although he is a specialist, a dermatologist, he also practices as a general practitioner. He also looks after all of the Buddhist monks in Hue, medically – gratis. His house, I find, is not only a home but a hospital, a private clinic. He greets me at the door, a slim man of perhaps seventy in an open-neck white shirt and dark trousers and invites me into his sitting room.

Buddhism in Hue is quite different from Buddhism in other parts of Vietnam, apparently, particularly different from Hanoi. Although both cities practice the Greater Vehicle, Mahayana Buddhism – as opposed to the Lesser Vehicle practised in Cambodia, Thailand, Laos and Myanmar – there are still major differences.

Dr Chau starts at the beginnings of Hue.

'In 1558 after the Viets migrated south from Hanoi, finding themselves with a mixed population of conquered Chams and mountain tribes, they found it very difficult to govern. It was necessary to find a religion to calm them in order to govern them. They needed to integrate the people. Taoism and Buddhism formed roots here early. Nguyen Hoang and his son, Nguyen Phuc Nguyen were both Buddhists' – as well as being Confucian.

Dr Chau tells me that there was already a pagoda on the site of Thien Mu – before the celestial lady appeared to Nguyen Hoang in 1601. He also cleared up several misconceptions. Thien Mu was not destroyed by the French, nor in the Tet Offensive of 1968. Since the damage it suffered during the Tay Son Rebellion, it has been damaged only by storms, most notably in 1904 – not at all during the recent three successive wars.

'Hue is the capital of Buddhism in Vietnam. There are three sorts of pagodas here and four national pagodas: Dieu De, Tang O, Thanh Duyes, Giac Hoang. They were the pagodas of the mandarin,' under Nguyen rule.

'Early Buddhist pagodas in Hue were originally built differently – square-shaped, with entrances only at two of the opposite corners – for defensive purposes. There are many like that, they are Chinese, but some are private. One needed more security here. There were many exiles, many immigrants.'

I ask if young boys in Hue are sent as a part of their upbringing to stay for a time, a week or several months in a pagoda?

'No, they are sent every week, but not to stay, not in Vietnam. Each pagoda has from twenty to sixty monks' – I think he is referring to the national pagodas – but these days, young boys very rarely become monks.'

He goes on to explain that there are two methods of following Buddhism here, two ways of seeking nirvana: meditation and the pure land. 'Strict Buddhists in Hue follow a very evident and particular daily routine. They meditate two or three times per day for half an hour to an hour each time. There are four paths, four miracles: life, misery, extinction and the path – and many paths along the path.

'Things have changed in Hue in the past twenty years, yet still, people here preserve their practice of Buddhism from the point of view of virtue. Here there is a regime, very strict, only in Hue.'

Dr Chau is himself a strict Buddhist – his father and grandfather were strict Buddhists – and medically, he has looked after the hundreds of Buddhist monks in Hue for the past forty years.

'At the beginning of the current political regime that viewed Buddhism as the opiate of the people, that was quite audacious. Many monks fled their pagodas in Hue and only returned after it was realized that Buddhists live by non-violence, Buddhists live in peace.'

I ask about the guardians of the gate at Thien Mu pagoda. It had puzzled me that one of the four ferocious-looking giants has a black face – in an Asian country.

'He is the cruel one, the others are gentle.'

Another characteristic of Buddhist pagodas in Hue is that there is often only one statue of Buddha, and at most, three more statues of Buddha: past, present and future, unlike in Hanoi where there are numerous personages represented by statues. I ask about the numerous statues that occupy pagodas in Hanoi: *bodhisattvas, arhats,* the kings of hell, the nine dragon altars?

'None of them appear in Hue pagodas.'

He then explains that flower offerings are ritually placed in certain ritualistic positions in a pagoda.

When I ask about the procession from pagoda to pagoda on Buddha's Birthday *(Vesak)* on the fifteenth of the fourth month of the lunar calendar, he is unable to tell me the date on the Gregorian Calendar. Clearly, Dr Chau only operates on the lunar calendar.

When I ask at what time pagoda bells ring, he tells me that 'pagodas ring their bells at midnight to prepare the land for worship and again at half past three when monks rise to pray.'

So the poor monks have no sooner got to sleep at nine or ten at night, than they are awakened at midnight, and then again, three hours later. 'Monks here in Hue are strictly vegetarian, but the rest of the Buddhist population here abstains from meat only on four days per month: the twenty-ninth and thirtieth, and on the fourteenth and fifteenth' – presumably of the lunar month.

'Some meat stalls in the market close and some restaurants in Hue do not serve meat on those days.'

When I ask about the Cham temple, he tells me that it is Hon Chen, also known as the Temple of the Jade Cup.

Dr Chao explains to me that his wife lives in Germany with their son, who is a bachelor, that she has lived there for the past seven years and that he himself goes to visit every six months. His son in Germany is a professor specializing in ear, nose and throat. His other son – and he has two grandchildren – is a lawyer in California. So why does he himself stay in Hue?

The good doctor gives me his list of reasons for staying: 'First, I am a patriot; the second is liberal education' – Dr Chau has trained more than three hundred doctors. 'And third, I work with the French on a project to correct blindness.'

Surely, the good Dr Chao will reach nirvana.

CAO DAI – A NEW RELIGION

No use preaching to a hungry man
– Vietnamese proverb

One Sunday, two consultants from the Asia Development Bank staying in my hotel invite me along with them for a drive to the fishing village of Thuan An on the coast. I jump at the chance, hoping we might deviate a bit to take in one of the national pagodas, Thanh Duyen in Vinh Hien commune.

In a pleasantly air-conditioned four-by-four, we drive south towards the airport, then off to the left to make a long loop, across to the sea and then north up the coast road. Despite the comfortable vehicle, once off the main highway, the narrow road between paddies is so rough that I am clinging to a handle most of the way.

Unhappily, the driver tells us that Thanh Duyen pagoda is eighty-four miles (140 km) away – although my information is that it is only twenty-four miles (40 km) from Hue and would have been fairly near our southern route. The driver wins, we don't go.

The narrow, coast road travelling from south to north is no smoother and there is so much ribbon development along the sea side of the road that there is rarely a glimpse of the South China Sea. At one point, a fully rounded haystack comes bouncing towards us on the back of a motorbike! This is deep country despite the houses and pagodas along the road.

Never have I seen such a density of pagodas, one after another after another, all on the sea side of the road. We must have passed several dozen, most of them *Cao Dai* with their colourful, zany, three-dimensional pillars of dragons leaping to freedom. Why so many? Breakaway factions? That there should be so many *Cao Dai* pagodas here, near Hue, is perplexing.

Cao Dai is a newish religion founded in 1926 in the Mekong delta by a Buddhist, Ngo Van Chieu, who received a message from God to found a new inclusive religion. *Cao Dai* translates as 'the great faith for the universal redemption' and worships one 'highest lord', who created the universe.

266

Symbol of the *Cao Dai* religion is God's left eye, which appears above the altar in each of their churches or cathedrals, which are wildly exuberant in their colourful decorations. Graham Green in *The Quiet American,* described the *Cao Dai* Cathedral in Tay Ninh (near Saigon) as 'Christ and Buddha looking down from the roof of a cathedral on a Walt Disney Fantasia of the East, dragons and snakes in technicolour.'

As might be expected of an inclusive religion, seeking to bring mankind together in 'a universal family for universal peace,' *Cao Dai* incorporates the beliefs and doctrines of the world's great religions: Buddhism, Taoism, Confucianism, Christianity and Islam, stating that God has spoken through many mouthpieces throughout history. Consequently, the *Cao Dai* church numbers a wide diversity of the great and good amongst its guiding 'saints': Victor Hugo, Sun Yat Sen, Buddha, Confucius, Lao Tse, Mohammed, Moses, Jesus, Joan of Arc, Louis Pasteur and Shakespeare. The basic premise of *Cao Dai-ism* is that 'all religions are one.' If only they were – in this war-torn world we live in.

We pass several enormous cemeteries, perhaps for the wealthy, who might wish for their dearly departed to enjoy the afterlife in an agreeable burial plot beside the sea, and very agreeable for those tending the graves, too. Or perhaps not. But could such vast cemeteries possibly be necessary for what used to be merely a small seaside fishing village?

Thuan An, the fishing village on the beach that we are heading for at the north end of the loop, is only eight miles (14 km) from Hue. We pause for a bit to look at the remains of an archaeological dig – a great hole.

The Thuan An I remember visiting years ago by boat, and once on the back of a motor bike, was a scruffy, muddy, very poor fishing village with no drainage. Now, new rendered houses line the beach road and the village has grown much larger, not unlike a new estate, but with the houses built very close together. Quite a few of the houses, I would guess, are weekend villas – sprouting red flags. I wonder where the fishermen have gone or if they have become more affluent, which somehow seems doubtful.

Returning along the wide, new highway towards Hue, we meet a flood of motorbikes driving towards the beach at half past five – when you might have expected Hue people to be returning to Hue from the beach. But of course, they are right. The sea at Thuan An and the nearby beautiful Tam Giang lagoon have inspired much poetry and are much beloved by the people of Hue. So they go to contemplate the sunset, or to the beach when the sun is not so hot.

Back again at the hotel, a high school graduation party is taking place – seven hundred students, the hotel lobby full of frilly white dresses and probably the first pairs of high heels. I see one young man anxiously writing a girl's telephone number on the inside of his shirt! Tables are set all the way around the lotus pond beside the Perfume river so that the young graduates can watch the sun slip down behind the river and the mountains. Proceedings begin with gentle music and speeches over a loud speaker.

PART IX

FAREWELLS

GARDEN HOUSE OPENING

Chew carefully and the stomach is content,
work well and the rice will be thick
– Vietnamese proverb

The main Zen style gate is still not quite finished, nor open. So it is a walk along the side of the house over a loose, stony path to the half-moon terrace where tables and chairs to seat sixty-four – wine glasses and silver on white tablecloths – have been set up.

The event is a splendidly stylish house-warming – they call it an 'opening' – of the new garden house(s) built by Truong Dinh Ngo, the Swiss-Vietnamese retired banker and his wife, Nguyen Ton Nu Huyen-Camille. Having arrived early by mistake, I stand on the terrace in front of the theatre facing the Perfume river and watch as the sun dips behind a fringe of willow trees, a moment of sheer beauty and tranquillity.

The theatre building, a long, low, open-faced building with hardwood pillars, tile roofs and ceramic mosaic ridge lines – like the palaces of the Citadel – is the centre piece of this garden house complex. Flowers on stands are arriving and chairs for musicians are being arranged on the open side of the theatre. My friend, Phan Van Thao from the Hue Tourist Office arrives.

Huyen-Camille has displayed her paintings in the open-sided theatre and over the arched bridge and lily pond, in the adjacent poetry pavilion. Some are also displayed in the dining hall, quite appealing paintings of ladies in *ao dais,* a few extremely delicate still lifes of flower arrangements plus a couple of abstracts.

As Thao and I chat our way through the paintings, a group of ladies arrive by dragon boat and I am struck with envy. As more people begin to arrive, pretty waitresses in *ao dais* serve two-colour, layered juice cocktails in stem glasses, a sliver of apple holding an orchid attached to each rim, an artful stick of lemon grass to stir – an artistic masterpiece in a wine glass. Waitresses also serve spring rolls and tiny, crisp, rice-paper packets, so fragile looking that I abstain.

The temperature is still at least 33 C   (85 F). Our smiling hosts appear, Huyen-Camille in a stunning strapless and therefore Western, purple silk, floor-length gown. It had to be purple, the traditional colour of Hue, her long black hair flowing loose to her waist – the epitome of an elegant Hue lady.

Ladies arrive wearing beautiful *ao dais,* a few in Western dress. The writer, To Nguen Vy, who I had interviewed a few days earlier, comes over to shake hands, but as his English-speaking daughter is not with him, communication stops there. And Nguyen Xuan Hoa, the collector of glass paintings, approaches to say hello. As I am leaving myself in a few days, it begins to feel a bit like a farewell party.

Candles are lit as we sit down. Huyen-Camille takes the stage at the edge of the open theatre and sings a Schubert song in German. Her husband, Truong Dinh Ngo, gives a welcoming speech, saying how their building of the garden houses has been a love affair with Huyen-Camille's native Hue. Thoughtfully, his poetic speech has been handed out, both in Vietnamese and in English, so that guests have it as a souvenir.

Just as the first course is being served, a lady in a white *ao dai* arrives in a little flourish and I am told in the dim candlelight that she is a professor from Germany named Lan – Thai Kim Lan – the lady I had interviewed early on, who was such an enthusiast for *tuong.* We rush together for a welcome hug. I suspect that she has come back from Germany especially for the party as she is leaving again in a very few days. At my table, along with Phan Van Thao from the Hue Tourist Office, is an English-speaking professor of mathematics from the College of Education, Tran Vui, whose children are in Saigon and the US; his wife is in Germany. The Vietnamese do spread their families around.

The seven-course meal starts with pumpkin and mushroom soup. The second course is a small plate holding three neat, bite-sized rounds. To my delight, Tran Vui, the mathematician, identifies them as fresh fermented shrimp paste *(mam tom chua)* spring rolls, one of Hue's much lauded specialities, not served in restaurants, or at least not the restaurants I have frequented. My young waiter friend, Hoang, had offered to buy a tiny bit of *mam tom chua* for me in the market to taste, but he had been quite apprehensive, saying, 'It is very strong, you may not like it.'

The *mam ton chua* is delicious – yes, a very strong taste – but I like highly flavoured, spicy food. It reminds me very vaguely of Stilton or a ripe blue cheese. I see why people have composed poems lauding *mam ton chua* – it is very, very more-ish.

The *mam tom chua* spring rolls are followed by a tiny, round dish of our host's new strain of rice, gently flavoured with herbs. Then comes a seafood and banana flower salad on a bed of mint – delicious. All of these are accompanied by a glass of white wine.

When the Burgundy is poured, I know we are ready for the main course – two main courses as it turns out: first, roast pork in a delicious sauce, served with a triangular 'pyramid' of sticky rice wrapped in a banana leaf; then roast duck in another delicious sauce, accompanied by a neat mound of cubed potatoes and apple – a brilliant combination. Happily, the portions are fairly small, although I could easily have stopped after the pork course. For desert, it has to be one of Hue's famous sweet soups – *longon* fruit stuffed with lotus seeds in a slightly sweet syrup – the same sweet soup that I had tasted at the home of Hue chef, Hoang Thi Nhu Huy.

During dinner, a couple of *Viet kieu* (overseas Vietnamese), who have flown in from Texas especially, play gentle guitar music and Huyen-Camille sings another Schubert song.

Not only does this feel like a celebratory last supper with several of the people I have interviewed having been invited, but being served the illusive, delicious *mam tom chua* and the sweet lotus and *longon* soup, as well as the rest of the delicious dinner and wine, nirvana could not be far away.

As the dinner is ending, the director of Hue Monuments Conservation Center, the busy Dr Hai, appears at the table to say goodbye. He is off next day for a fortnight in Germany to attend a UNESCO meeting. He is hoping that the poetry panels in the cornices of the royal throne palace of the Citadel might be placed on the World Heritage list. He introduces his beautiful wife.

Two ladies from the next table introduce themselves, one living in Danang, another in Saigon. Both were classmates of Huyen-Camille and the mathematics professor – childhood friends, all natives of Hue.

Huyen-Camille and Ngo have, indeed, recreated a bit of old imperial Hue, reusing original building materials whenever possible and excellent, artistic craftsmanship on every carefully designed and decorated surface in their new garden houses – very, very Hue. And they have obeyed the deep yearning felt by Hue people, no matter how far away they have been, nor for how long, whenever possible, always to return home.

LAST SUPPERS

A gift from the heart is valuable
– Vietnamese proverb

Nguyen Ngoc Tung, until recently the manager of the Huong Giang Hotel and my translator years ago when he was on the reception desk, has now moved as manager to the five-star Imperial Hotel. He drives up to his old hotel where he had worked man and boy in a big people carrier, to fetch me.

Always with a feisty sense of humour, he drives across the river, along the road to the Citadel, then turns right . . .

'Have you been here before?' he asks.

'Yes, en route to Hue Monuments Conservation Center.'

We pass the gate to the Center . . .

'Have you been here before?' he asks again.

'Well, yes.'

He turns in at the very house where I had been 'mis-delivered' during my first days in Hue – trying to find the Hue Monuments Conservation Center, when the taxi dropped me at the wrong address. It had been his wife, Tien, who had kindly donned her helmet and driven me on her motorbike a hundred meters back along the road to the Monuments Conservation Center all those weeks ago!

We find his wife, Tien, teaching an English class of youngsters of eight and nine, children who have only been studying English for four weeks – twenty of them. She asks them to volunteer to ask me questions.

'What's your name? How do you spell it? How old are you?'

I straighten them out that it is impolite to ask Western ladies their age, okay to ask men.

'Why?'

'Because Western ladies don't like to admit how old they are. They like to pretend that they are younger.'

'What is your favourite animal?'

'What is your favourite food?'

'Do you like candy?'

'Do you like pizza?'

The class ends at eleven, lunchtime, but half of their parents are late in collecting them, so eventually, we sit down to lunch with three of the young students as well as Tung's son, a hulking young man, who is a second-year student in architecture, completely different in stature from his slim father, and his ten-year-old daughter, an absolute charmer. Lunch: tiny *banh beo* Hue pancakes, fresh spring rolls, crab soup, *ban nam* wrapped in banana leaves, and a sweet soup made, Tien explains, of green beans!

Tung's wife, Tien, has a Master's degree and teaches English at the College of Education. She and Tung met at high school. But what an incredible coincidence – my having landed lost at his house, all those weeks ago!

Back at the hotel, My Phung, my friend on reception rings to remind me that I am meeting her and Miss Hoa, the new manager of the Huong Giang Hotel, for dinner at six. The temperature has tipped 38C (100F)!

My Phung was a young girl on reception when I first stayed in Hue all those years ago. Now she is not only head of reception, she is in charge of front of house. This time when I arrived, she had met me at the airport with a bouquet and the hotel car, and the following day as a special favour, she took me in the hotel car to Thien Mu pagoda, the first place in Hue I had wanted to revisit.

The farewell dinner of too many courses is served on the third floor of the hotel in a private dining room: deep fried cheese sticks and banana flower salad, pumpkin soup, tuna fish (knives and forks) with blessedly cold, blanched vegetables, followed by spaghetti Bolognese (which really was too much), then fresh fruit (papaya, mango, watermelon) – and for me, sweet green bean soup, as I had made the mistake of mentioning during the meal how much I had liked it at Tung and Tien's house.

Miss Hoa presented me with an embroidered picture of Truong Tien bridge, the Georges Eiffel bridge – framed under glass.

'The view from your window.'

I had also made the mistake of casually mentioning during dinner how much I like Hue's green tea and sesame candy. Next morning two large packages were delivered to my room: Hue's lotus tea bags and sesame candy. The kindness and generosity of Hue people can be overwhelming.

The week before I was leaving, I had received an email from Y Nhi, the niece of Vo Thi Quynh, a kind lady I had met the previous December at the pagoda ceremony for the long-dead princess, Le Ngoc Han. It was through the kindness of this lady that her niece, Y Nhi, already working away from Hue at a new job in a hotel in Danang, had arranged for two of her recently graduated college friends in Hue, Tran Linh and Nguyen Thanh Thanh, to act as my translators. The kindness of Hue people really is astonishing to a Westerner, accustomed to cool, impersonal, casual encounters.

The niece, Y Nhi, was planning to come to Hue and would like to meet – the week after I would have left. When I replied, telling her how sorry I was not to meet, she suggested asking for the day off to come a week earlier.

We meet at my favourite lunchtime restaurant, Grain. Y Nhi has brought a present from her kind auntie: a set of postcards, photos of her own intricate collages made of seeds and dried flowers. Y Nhi's former classmate, my translator Tran Linh, joins us, and I hear for the first time that his dream, his secret ambition, is to become a singer. Y Nhi, a charming young girl, hopes to travel and perhaps work abroad. As she is working in a large, international hotel, she has a good chance of succeeding.

My last supper in Hue is with Hoang, the waiter from Golden Rice restaurant. At supper at the restaurant the night before, he had handed me a suspiciously large cardboard box, telling me not to open it until I got home. Of course, I had to open it to see how and where to pack it. It was a meticulously made, wire sculpture of a Hue cyclo, complete with rubber tires and a lace-trimmed folding awning over the passenger seat. I nearly cried. His father had been a cyclo driver.

Arriving at the Golden Rice to go out elsewhere to dinner with him, I didn't mention it, as I was not supposed to have opened it. Hoang had also invited two of the waitresses from the restaurant to join us and we walked several blocks to a street cafe where Hoang ordered baguettes – why baguettes and not the ubiquitous rice? – and frogs legs in a delicious sauce.

The second course was bites of pork and okra wrapped in a leaf, again, in a succulent sauce. The baguettes were coming in handy for soaking up these delicious sauces. The third course was mussels cooked in lime juice and lemon grass – all so, so good.

275

One needs to know where to eat street food in Vietnam – best to go with a local. Hoang had chosen well. So there we were, perched on tiny, low plastic chairs at a too-small, crowded plastic table on the street pavement – without a napkin. Although it had been Hoang's invitation, I insisted upon paying, explaining that because of the vast difference in the cost of living – and earnings – in the West, that I could afford it and in any case, wanted to thank him for all of his help. Embarrassed, he reluctantly agreed. The total for the four of us, drinking tea – they were going straight back to work – was 159,000 dong ($7.36, £5.80).

En route to the restaurant, we had walked past a hotel with the proverb on the fascia: 'All those who wander are not lost!'

Next day I was leaving, happily mid-evening.

As she lives near the airport, Thanh Thanh, one of my young translators, had invited me to her house for a last meal to meet her mother, who works for an insurance company. Miss Hoa had kindly provided a hotel car.

To get us to her house in a village near the airport, Thanh Thanh suggested that I ring her on my mobile as we were leaving the hotel, hand the mobile to the driver, and she would direct him. We passed the airport and in a very few minutes, waiting with her motorbike at the entrance to a side road, was Thanh Thanh, who led us past houses, pagodas and rice paddies to her home, a bungalow with three double doors opening onto a covered veranda, a paved courtyard in front.

Cooking was done somewhere at the back, outside. Dinner was served on the front veranda where there were long benches beside a low table. Her younger brother had just graduated from university in what seemed to be estate management. During the meal it came out that to get a good job, he probably would have to pay someone the equivalent of several thousand US dollars, which the family did not have. For Thanh Thanh, finding a job as an English teacher would be easier as English teachers are in great demand. But Thanh Thanh dreams of getting a scholarship to study abroad. Her mother is extremely pretty and still young, probably in her forties. We had to make do with smiling and Thanh Thanh translating, to explain the food.

The various dishes for supper are served simultaneously: sliced green figs with green leaves and a pasty shrimp sauce; a tender

276

beef salad with lettuce and tomatoes; a steamed river fish with fish sauce; soup; fermented (pickled) bean sprouts with pork and fish sauce. Desert was a fruit that I at first took to be *longans,* the same thin, leathery skin, but slightly larger, opaque white segments covering slim brown seeds. Thanh Than called it *bon bon* and said it had several names. Many of these dishes, I had never tried before and all were utterly delicious.

In a typical gesture of the generosity of Hue people, the hotel's driver was invited to join us.

HUE PEOPLE

Poverty fetters wisdom
– Vietnamese proverb

Living along the banks of the peaceful Perfume river, flowing past the splendid palaces of the Citadel, in an old town where bells chime from melancholy pagodas, the people of Hue have been moulded by their three religions: Confucianism, Taoism and Buddhism. It took centuries to intermingle and blend the peoples and cultures of the North and South, to form the Hue character that is 'gentle and graceful, with formal manners, respecting one's superior and making concessions for one's subordinates; expecting love from the superior and obedience from the inferior,' writes historian Mai Khac Ung.

The theism of Hue is full of supernatural forces, writes professor of Vietnamese literature, Tran Dai Vinh. 'Beneficent deities and malevolent spirits are worshipped; and nowhere else in the nation are there as many village and family temples as in Hue. This is expressed in the high percentage of the annual family income invested in ceremonies, rites and rituals.'

Hue holds tenuously to its beliefs and religions. At the full moon, even a large new hotel places a table of offerings out front, and along the street, metal burners in front of private houses send up the smoke of pretend paper money, wafting best wishes to the spirits. The Golden Rice restaurant has had its pots of rice offerings on a chair out front for two days.

Tran Dai Vinh explains that the dynastic period resulted in 'the development of a local character that is best described as reserved in manner and self-conscious in behaviour. Hue people consider themselves to be reserved in terms of expressing their political opinions and also their feelings. Being restrained and discreet, they look down rather than up.'

Having lived through much political turmoil, 'Hue people realize that secular nobility is an illusion; that the highest heads are the most exposed.' Tran Dai Vinh even goes so far as to assert that, 'Hue people neither want to reach the highest ranks in civil

278

administration nor fight for the throne. Hue people only want to be teachers, intellectuals, artists, scientists, skilled artisans or peasants. Their life is fully imbued with the concept of knowing how to be satisfied with what one has.'

However, he goes on to explain that 'the ostentatious and elitist life of royal palaces, emperors, queens and mandarin had an impact on the life of the ordinary people.' Having lived in the shadow of a royal court, 'Hue people developed the following characteristics: to be cautious in daily activities, to be well-dressed though poor, to use clean bowls and plates though their food might be meagre in quantity and quality, to show their mettle though destitute and to converse in polite discourse, irrespective of their prosaic position in the social hierarchy.'

To the foreigner, this polite reserve translates into a quiet dignity. Part of this dignified conservatism is reflected in the preservation of traditional family roles.

'The distribution of labour in Hue families is traditional,' writes Tran Dai Vinh. 'A husband and father is head of the family and considered to be the main provider. Men are not expected to share any household responsibilities and after a day at work, they are able to return home, enjoy some tea, drink wine, read or take care of the garden. A wife and mother is responsible for the care of the house and the family and is usually engaged in what is considered to be secondary economic initiatives to provide supplementary income. (Elderly) parents live with the eldest or youngest child and are taken care of by all their children.'

One day I discuss royal traditions that have endured with my friend, Buu I, and he tells me that his own name, Buu I, means Precious Idea.

'Names are often researched and have significance. I was named by my grandfather. In the royal family, names were chosen with much thought, consideration and research into earlier times.'

Buu I came from a family of ten – his mother's and his step-mother's children. 'If my elder sister had lived, she would be ninety-six. Her name came from a dream of my grandfather. The day after her birth, my grandfather dreamed of a genie who appeared to him carrying a cane. The baby was therefore given the name – Cane of the Genie, or Genie's Cane (Cong Tang Ton Nu Soan Truong). Cong Tang was the family name, Ton Nu indicated that she was a female member of the royal family and Soan Truong meant Genie's Cane.

'Names in the royal family were rather complicated – each generation had a different name,' laid down by the foresighted Emperor Minh Mang. The sound of my sister's name was not sonorous, not agreeable to the ear, but the sense was elevated because the name had been given to her by her grandfather – it was precious. My other sister was named a pleasant name and it was sonorous: Cong Tang Ton Nu Au Bang. Au meant Western and Bang meant Bird. So her name meant Airplane – Bird of the West. This was in former times and this happened particularly in Central Vietnam, particularly in the royal family, there were certain traditions. And other families followed suit in their manner of living. They imitated the royal family, often without even realizing it, subconsciously.'

According to Tran Dai Vinh, Professor of Vietnamese literature, 'The Hue dialect has preserved the vocabulary of mediaeval Viet and at the same time combined it with the contemporary lexis of Vietnam. This is a result of the southern dialect having assumed a prominent place in the imperial court during the nineteenth century, as many concubines in the Nguyen royal household were daughters of mandarin from the South. As they naturally used the southern dialect, it was perceived as elegant, not only by the royal family, but by Hue society at large.'

Tran Dai Vinh quotes a female poet as saying, 'Some people outside Hue praise the Hue accent as gentle as the breeze, as sweet as sugar cane and (say it) sounds like a birdsong.' He goes on to explain, 'Hue people, when communicating and teaching their children, are very interested in using flowery and highbrow terms through folk songs and proverbs to show and emphasize their ideas. It is this manner that makes the Hue dialect more vivid, full of images and sublimates people's souls in this old capital.'

There is a close bond between the language and the people and the climate, he believes.

'Hue people mirror their climate and terrain: severe heat in summer, floods and hurricanes in winter. Irrespective of the demands of the climate, the people are industrious in study and work and mild in temperament . . . which is not to say that they cannot become indignant when confronted by violence and tyranny.'

The people of Hue fought valiantly against the French – both in Hue and along with resistance fighters from elsewhere in the country. They rose up defiantly against the persecution of Buddhist priests under the rule of Ngo Dinh Diem in Hue and in Saigon. Many of them fought against what they considered to be the American invasion during the Vietnam War, and conversely, many of them fought for the South during that same war.

My friend, Professor Buu I, has written: 'In short, Hue is distinctive for its burning heat and continuous rains and floods, the gentle and swift waters of the Huong river. The mild girls with nice conical hats seem gentle, but love passionately, that's Hue girls. Hue people often react slowly. Actions and appearances are sometimes deceptive; their receptive senses and their inner feelings perform to two different rhythms, between which is the time for a smile, a polite "yes" and a cautious consideration. This kind of timed reaction, when being carried out, will be definitive and irrevocable. That is the reason the Hue personality is described as profound and subtle.'

Professor Buu I has also written about the strong pull that Hue exerts on its native people, who for one reason or another have had to leave. 'This kind of emotion is somewhat metaphysical, as deep as the love between children and mother, the same as an endless source of burning coal beneath the ash . . .'

Tran Dai Vinh has also written that, 'Many of them wish to come back to Hue, even if only occasionally. They come home to bow at the worshipping place, at the ancestral graves, to contemplate the tranquil Huong river and to listen to the pagoda's bell toll through the morning mist. Then they leave again. For them, Hue is no longer a place to live, but a place to love and remember from a distance.'

Although the new prosperity of Hue – the smart shop buildings and mini-hotels that have shot up several stories, the new four and five-star hotels, the newly paved roads, the riverside promenades and parks – can be impressive, many young people of Hue still feel that they have to leave to find good jobs with prospects. Real poverty still exists in Hue. Some people are paid very little.

My waiter friend told me that his first job out of high school in 2004 was as housekeeper in a small guest-house where he earned 600,000 *dong* (US$30) per month, including lunch and dinner – enough for an inexperienced young man living at home, it was thought. Finding a job in Hue is hard. He stayed in the job for four years. He had desperately wanted to go to university to study English, but said that there were only twenty out of two hundred places available for a scholarship. Buu I, who was a professor of French at the College of Foreign Languages, says that it is worse than that for admission to the English Department – one out of twenty-five!

All universities are run by the government and are no longer free, as they were some years ago. Tuition is paid per term and in Hue, costs range from 1.5 to 2 million *dong* ($69-93, £55-75) – they vary dramatically from place to place.

After four years, my young friend got a job as a waiter in a restaurant where he worked for three years, until one of his fellow restaurant workers opened her own restaurant and asked him to join her. He lives with his mother, sixty-five, who has heart trouble, for whose treatment he pays. His father, a cyclo driver, died of bone cancer four years ago. He has a sister with a young baby in Danang and a younger brother, who lives with her and works in a factory. His other sister works as a secretary in Ho Chi Minh City.

But he is young. My old cyclo driver, who I befriended eighteen years ago, having retired four or five years ago, suddenly reappeared in his cyclo, touting for trade. Years ago, he had been an English teacher, but could make far more as a cyclo driver, so he gave up teaching. He is now in his seventies, bone thin, but assures me that he is in good health. Seeing him again with the cyclo, I asked if he was short of money?

'Yes.'

Nothing more. The man is proud. To explain would be to complain, to whinge. I remember years ago always having to press money upon him, unlike other cyclo drivers, who often tried it on to see how much they could extract from a foreigner. I asked how many children he had?

'Three.'

Do they help you?

'No.'

This is shocking, as one of the strongest Confucian traditions in Vietnam is that children look after their parents and grandparents: family is supremely important. He still has a wife, but I dreaded to ask if she were healthy.

While in Hue, from time to time I gave him some money, at least enough I knew, to feed himself and his wife for several days.

Another friend told me about an old lady, who walks around with a carrying pole, selling bananas. If she doesn't give her grown-up, unemployed son money every night so that he can go out and get drunk with his friends, he hits her. Despite all, she loves her son. What can she do?

I asked Buu I how much *ca Hue* singers earn?

'Five years ago, they might earn 50,000 *dong*s ($2.30, £1.85) for singing here (in Hue) at an evening event, not even enough to buy petrol for their motorbikes. Now it might be 200,000 *dong* ($9.25, £7.40). He also tells me that waiters in restaurants earn from one to two million *dong* ($46–93, £37-74) per month – 'and two million is well paid.' And he knows. His lacquer artist son also runs a restaurant.

So in addition to the *nouveau riche* and their children, swanning around in their new cars, sitting in restaurants and bars with their iPads and smart phones, many amongst the people of Hue remain poor, very poor. Of course, the standard of living for many has improved, and improved dramatically, but for many more, *plus ça change, plus ne change pas.*

Today, Hue may be no more than a charming provincial capital, but the people of Hue go on holding their heads high, proud of their royal heritage, yet equally proud of their accomplishments in craftsmanship, in the fine arts and architecture, in music and the performing arts, in poetry and literature, in their unique cuisine, but above all, in the spiritualism of Buddhism that they have held fast to in a rapidly-changing world.

While it may no longer be the capital of the nation – that ended with the abdication in 1945 – Hue remains the cultural and intellectual soul of the country. Hue's artists and writers have long been and continue to be inspired by its poetic landscapes, by the splendour of its royal palaces and pagodas; by its temples, tombs and gardens; by its tranquil river and by the gentleness of Hue women. Hue people, despite their warmth, leavened by the kindness and generosity of Buddhism, retain a certain reserve and politesse, and the legacy of court life inherited from their still-remembered grandparents – courtiers of the last imperial dynasty to rule Vietnam. It is these things, and their distinctive accomplishments, that make Hue and the people of Hue so very special – unique.

A hundred things heard are not worth one seen
– Vietnamese proverb

VIETNAMESE DYNASTIES

Ngo	939-965
Rule by the Twelve Lords	965-968
Dinh	968-980
Early Le	980-1009
Ly	1010-1225
Tran	1225-1400
Ho	1400-1407
Post-Tran	1407-1413
Chinese Rule	1414-1427
Later Le (nominally until 1788)	1428-1527
Mac	1527-1592
Trinh Lords (North)	1545-1788
Nguyen Lords (South	1558-1777

NGUYEN LORDS

Nguyen Hoang	1558-1613
Nguyen Phuc Nguyen	1613-1635
Nguyen Phuc Lan	1635-1648
Nguyen Phuc Tan	1648-1687
Nguyen Phuc Tran	1687-1691
Nguyen Phuc Chu	1691-1725
Nguyen Phuc Chu	1725-1738
Nguyen Phuc Khoat	1738-1765
Nguyen Phuc Thuan	1765-1775

TRINH OCCUPIED PHU XUAN	1775-1778

TAY SON	1778-1802

Nguyen Hue (Quang Trung)	1787-1792
Nguyen Quang Toan	1792-1802

NGUYEN DYNASTY

Gia Long	1802-1819
Minh Mang	1820-1840
Thieu Tri	1841-1847
Tu Duc	1848-1883
Duc Duc	3 days-1883
Hiep Hoa	4 mos-1883
Kien Phuc	1883-1884
Ham Nghi	1884-1885
Dong Khanh	1885-1889
Thanh Thai	1889-1907
Duy Tan	1907-1916
Khai Dinh	1916-1925
Bao Dai	1926-1945

CRAFT CONTACTS

Mo, wood carving: Le Thanh Liem, DC: K.215 Bui Thi Xuan-Hue, 0914 094 685, 0543 884 038

Mother-of-pearl, nacre: Le Thi Le, 58 Nguyen Chi Dieu, Hue, 054 352 3247, 0906 590 066, www.mynghetruongtien.com

Lanterns: www.treviethue.com

Bamboo: Nguyen Dinh Hung, 85 Dao Tuy Tu, TP Hue, 0905 511 155, 0906 494 616, www.treviethue.com

Non la hats: Tinh Hoa Nghe Viet, tel 09 05 42 27 45

Phuoc Tich pottery: Luong Thanh Hien, 0905 342 584, 0935 009 261.

Enamel, lacquer: Tran Nam Long, 66 Chi Lang Street, Hue, 8454 354 6005, 0906 510 513, www.huefinearts.com

Wood carving: Le Van Xanh, DC: 162A Ton That Thiet, Tay Loc, Hue, 0913 495 874

Wood carving: Nguyen Vinh, Hu Thai, 40 Nguyen Sinh Cung, Hue, 0914 002 317

Paper flowers: Than Van Huy, 38 Nguyen Binh Khiem Street, Hue, 8454 651 1012, or Than Tien flower village

Bamboo furniture: Tran Loi, DC: Thuy Lap, Quang Loi, Quang Dien, Thua Thien Hue, 096 527 0699, 0126 405 4695

Kites: Nguyen Van Hoang, 13/36 Nguyen Du Street, Hue, 8454 351 8570, 0905 605 155

BIBLIOGRAPHY

Chapries, Oscar, *The Last Emperors of Vietnam: from Tu Duc to Bao Dai,* Greenwood Press, 2000

Glover, Ian and Bellwood, Peter, *Southeast Asia from Prehistory to History,* Routledge Curzon, 2004

Huu Ngoc and Borton, Lady, *Hue Cuisine,* The Gioi Publishers, Hanoi, 2012

McLeod, Mark W., *The Vietnamese Response to French Intervention, 1862-1872,* Praeger, 1991

Nguyen, Viet Ke, trans. Nguyen, Phuc Vinh Ba, *Stories of the Nguyen Dynasty's Kings,* Da Nang Publishing House, 2014

Phan Thuan An, *Hue Citadel and Palaces,* The Gioi Publishers, Hanoi, 2012

Phan Thuan An, *Royal Mausoleums in Hue – a Wonder,* Da Nang Publishing House, 2014

Ton That Binh, *Life in the Forbidden Purple City,* Da Nang Publishing House, 2011

Tourism Department of Thua Thien Hue Province, Vo Phi Hung, Editor-in-Chief, *Hue World Cultural Heritage,* Statistical Printing Factory of HCM City, 2004

Various contributors, Hue University LRC International Center, *The Unique Characteristics of Hue's Culture,* The Gioi Publishers, Hanoi, 2009

Vu Hong Lien, *Royal Hue – Heritage of the Nguyen Dynasty of Vietnam,* River Books, Bangkok, 2015

Vietnam National Museum of History & Hue Monuments Conservation Centre, *Antique Jewelry of Vietnam,* published by Vietnam National Museum of History, Hanoi, 2015

Made in United States
Troutdale, OR
11/15/2023

14613080R00159